ALPACAS, SHEEP, AND MEN

The Wool Export Economy
and Regional Society in Southern Peru

STUDIES IN ANTHROPOLOGY

Under the Consulting Editorship of E. A. Hammel,
UNIVERSITY OF CALIFORNIA, BERKELEY

ALPACAS, SHEEP, AND MEN

The Wool Export Economy
and Regional Society in Southern Peru

BENJAMIN S. ORLOVE
*Division of Environmental Studies
and Department of Anthropology
University of California, Davis
Davis, California*

ACADEMIC PRESS   New York   San Francisco   London
A Subsidiary of Harcourt Brace Jovanovich, Publishers

ACADEMIC PRESS, INC.
111 Fifth Avenue, New York, New York 10003

United Kingdom Edition published by
ACADEMIC PRESS, INC. (LONDON) LTD.
24/28 Oval Road, London NW1

Library of Congress Cataloging in Publication Data

Orlove, Benjamin S

    Alpacas, sheep, and men.

    (Studies in anthropology series)
    Bibliography: p.
    1.   Wood trade industry—Peru—Sicuani region.
2.   Sicuani region, Peru—Social conditions.
I.   Title.
HD9904.P53S56   338.1'7'631409853   77-74061
ISBN 0-12-527850-0

*To my grandmother, who taught me to walk
and to my parents, who showed me
that I could find my own path*

Contents

Preface

An anecdote that circulated in the early 1970s among the graduate students in the anthropology department at Berkeley involved two famous anthropologists who were engaged in field research in Indonesia. As they were observing a complex ritual with political and religious overtones, one turned to the other and commented, "It never fails to strike me how completely Javanese these people are." The other replied, "That's funny. I was just thinking that they seemed very human to me." In studying the inhabitants of a region in highland Peru, this book denies neither their cultural specificity nor their humanity, but it focuses on another aspect of their existence: They live in the twentieth century. Despite the apparently archaic quality of their technology, institutions, and habits, despite the fact that their lives seem more attached to pre-Columbian Andean and medieval European traditions than to a modern industrial one, they are part, as we are, of a single world-system that is at a specific point in its history. Like many other rural peoples of the Third World, they have accommodated their society to the rhythms imposed by an export economy. The dominance of wool exports in the region has transformed the relations that people have with each other, with the land, and with the national government.

This book adopts two related tasks: the analysis of the response of this region to the export economy and its consequent integration into the nation-state, and the development of a general model for examining these two processes. It begins with a review of the theories of modernization and dependency. These are the two major paradigms in social science that have informed investigation on the dynamics of the world-system. This discussion of the theories acknowledges their differences but stresses several commonalities. They adopt the nation as the principal unit of analysis and retain a strict loyalty to a single generalized process which they use as a model to examine historical change. Each theory has specific commitments to views of the internal differentiation of the nation and the relation of the state to the economy. This book proposes an alternative, the sectorial model. This model offers several analytical constructs, including the unit (e.g., peasant household, *hacienda*, artisan shop, retail firm) and the sector (e.g., peasants, *haciendas*, artisans, traders) composed of these units. It describes how resources and constraints shape the patterns of alliance and conflict between sectors.

The book applies this model to the Sicuani region in southern highland Peru, and traces the economic and political conflicts that followed the incorporation of the region into the world wool economy in the late nineteenth century. Landlord against peasant in the countryside, landlord against trader in town; the export economy directly engendered these conflicts, and they determined the metamorphosis of a closed, isolated, localized society into an open one, integrated into national politics as well as global economics.

Following the introductory theoretical chapter, Chapters 2 and 3 summarize the development of the world market for wool and set forth the component elements of the wool economy of all of southern Peru. Some aspects of the relations between the two are discussed in Chapter 4 through a consideration of price transmission mechanisms.

The next set of chapters examines the regional society in more detail. In Chapter 5, the concept of region is reviewed, formulated in terms of the sectorial model, and applied to the particular area under study. Chapters 6 through 9 examine the economic activities of different sectors and the economic forms of articulation among them. Chapter 10 discusses political articulation on the local and regional level. The wool-producing sectors are described in Chapter 6. The importance of environmental constraints on pastoral social and economic organization is stressed. An examination of variation in forms of land tenure and labor relations in two provinces demonstrates that productivity has remained at static levels despite considerable social and political change.

Chapter 7 studies the three major groups of artisans and workers in the region who use wool. They consist of urban furriers, textile mill workers, and rural weavers. The relations of local wool manufacture to export interests are discussed. Chapter 8 describes the agricultural and artisanal sectors. Environmental and economic constraints are emphasized. The relations among herders, peasants, and artisans are shown to shift with the growth of the wool export economy. One aspect of this change is the growth of the marketing sectors. Chapter 9 traces the increase in aggregate demand and changes in the organization of marketing.

Chapter 10 focuses on regional politics, in contrast to the previous four chapters, which concentrate on economic organization. The growth of the regional elite is related to the expansion of the wool export economy and the consequent increase in power of the national government. The traders in the urban center enter into relations of mutual support with government bureaucrats to form the regional elite; the peasants and herders, who also found the bureaucrats effective allies in their struggles against the *hacendados;* not only retain their productive base, but exercise a certain amount of political power.

The final chapter uses the sectorial model to link economic and political forms of articulation described in earlier chapters. It shows the weaknesses of theories of modernization and dependency for examining historical responses to export economies. In particular, the sectorial model offers more accurate and precise analysis of the nature of social conflict and the relation between the economy and the state. The conclusions review the sectorial model and the other two theories in a general as well as a specific context.

Acknowledgments

Luis Nieto, one of the leaders of the literary and artistic circles in Sicuani in the 1930s and 1940s, dedicated one of his books of poems thus: *A Sicuani, mi linda tierra, hecha de flor y canción* (1943:7). ('To Sicuani, my lovely homeland, composed of flower and song ') I would like to share Nieto's perception of Sicuani, in which the spontaneous products of the land and the people are intermingled. My special fondness for the *provincias altas* comes from the magnificence of the landscape and the kindness and generosity of the people.

It is difficult to select among the many Peruvians who made my work in their country a rich personal experience as well as an exciting intellectual one. The hospitality and warmth of Sr. Federico Medina Vera and his wife, Sra. Agripina Fuentes de Medina, and their compadre, Sr. Félix Rivas Guillén, have left me with profound feelings of gratitude. Pedro Hinde, Betty Campbell, and another friend of theirs gave very special sorts of meaning to my time in Sicuani. There are many other individuals to whom I am indebted, not only for their assistance in gaining access to archives and informants, but for many long enjoyable and deeply remembered conversations. Parish priests and school-teachers in the Sicuani region were particularly helpful. Drs. Jorge Flores Ochoa, Oscar Núñez del Prado, and Abraham Valencia of the Universidad Nacional de San Antonio Abad del Cuzco provided special help for me while I was in the field; the members of the Instituto de Estudios Peruanos, particularly Drs. José Matos Mar, Julio Cotler, Giorgio Alberti, and Heraclio Bonilla, aided me in my work, not only when I visited Lima, but also in correspondence. I am particularly grateful to Dr. Enrique Mayer and Sra. Helaine Silverman de Mayer for their generosity and support on many occasions. Drs. Humberto Rodríguez and Julio Sumar, Srta. Graciela Sánchez Cerro, and Ingo. Armando Rivera offered me much assistance in the archival portions of my research, as did Srs. Klaus Kothe, Alfredo Ricketts, and Franz Rotmann, and I am very thankful to them.

I would like to thank other graduate students and scholars in Peru for stimulating comments on my research, especially Dan and Paula Hazen, Geoffrey Bertram, Gordon Appleby, George and Karen Primov, Michael Gonzales, and Rory Miller. Both my committee and several others in the United States provided me with invaluable help in the analysis of my data; I wish to express my gratitude to Drs. May N. Díaz, John Howland Rowe, Tulio Halperín Donghi, Nelson H. H. Graburn, Pierre van den Berghe, and Anthony Leeds. Fellow students in Berkeley gave me especially incisive comments and strong support throughout the long and difficult period of the first preparation of the manuscript; it is to the members of the thesis-writing seminar and the "complex society" seminar that I am most deeply thankful. Cecelia Odelius, Dolores DuMont, and Gayle Bacon were of great help in the preparation of this manuscript. Barbara Folsom and Jon Haughton of the Reference Department of the Shields Library, University of California, Davis, were extremely kind in offering their time to assist me in locating obscure references.

I am also grateful to the colleagues and friends, particularly Miriam Wells, who helped and supported me in the final period of corrections and revisions of the manuscript. Mario Dávila, Tulio Halperín Donghi, Gary and Janet Hamilton, Nathan Laks, Pierre van den Berghe, and Karl Yambert offered many useful comments and suggestions; William and Lynne Cobb and Daniel Meyerowitz gave other kinds of help. I owe a unique gratitude to Anthony Leeds for the particular detail and care with which he commented on an earlier draft of the manuscript. Members of the staff of Academic Press gave me many useful suggestions and pieces of advice. I am very thankful to each of these people.

This work would not have been possible without the financial support which several institutions have generously granted. I am grateful to the Cornell Quechua Studies Program for providing language training in 1970, and to the Center for Latin American Studies in Berkeley for their grant-in-aid which permitted a preliminary trip to Cuzco in 1971. I am particularly thankful for the generous support of the Foreign Area Fellowship Program during my stay in Peru, from May 1972 to October 1973, and the assistance of Drs. Richard Dye and Peter Cleaves in Lima.

Briefer trips to Peru were sponsored by the Institute of Ecology of the University of California at Davis in 1974 and by the Wenner-Gren

Foundation for Anthropological Research and by a Summer Faculty
Fellowship from Davis in 1976.

haqay karu llaqtaypi pukaqhente mayupata phawamushan.
inti raphraphurunta ninayamuriktinhina takin:
asnusuwakmasilláy, ñanpata purikmasilláy,
punapi paqocha michik, chectuyoq lliklla awak,
chakrapi k'apchi mikhuk, khuchupi q'achu qhatuk,
orqopatapi apu kallpachakuk, kruskunkapi tunpunpa wañuchisqan,
waynu takispa noqahina nin,
"'qonqallawanmi' nirankichu? imacha noqaqa qonqaykiman."
wasiykichispi chaskiwarankichis, llaqtaykichista napaykuwarankichis,
rimayta asikuyta simiykichispi, qhawayta rikuyta ñawiykichiswanhina,
llakikuyta kusikuyta sonqoykichiswanhina: imanaytapas yachachiwarankichis.
runayachikamusqaykichis kapunitáq.
yuyayuyarispa yachayacharispa kallpachanakuwanchis; atipunchisña.
kay qelqasqachayta qopusaykichis, kutipuyta qallariyniypaq.

Sources Consulted

ARCHIVES

Biblioteca Nacional. Lima
Félix Denegri Luna archive. Lima
Ricketts archive. Centro de Documentación Agraria. Lima
Biblioteca Municipal. Sicuani
Banco de la Nación. Sección de Lanas. Sicuani
Concejo Provincial de Canchis. Sicuani
Archivo de la Prelatura. Sicuani
Fábrica de Tejidos Maranganí. Chectuyoc
Subprefectura de Espinar. Yauri
Archivos Notariales. Yauri
Granja Modelo Puno. Chuquibambilla
Southern Peruvian Railway. Arequipa
Zona Agraria XI. Cuzco

NEWSPAPERS

El Sol. Cuzco
El Comercio. Cuzco
La Verdad. Sicuani
El Titán. Sicuani
El Grito. Sicuani
El Fuego. Sicuani
Pampacucho. Sicuani

Peruvian Times. Lima
Esfuerzos. Acomayo
El Picaflor. Ayaviri
El Pueblo. Arequipa

PERIODICALS

Revista Pumacahua. Sicuani
Willkamayu. Sicuani
Antorcha Caneña. Yanaoca
Organo Informativo Raqchi. San Pedro
Revista del Club Social Sicuani. Sicuani
Boletín Informativo de la Prelatura. Sicuani
Cultura Educacional. Sicuani
Pensamiento Joven. Sicuani

ALPACAS, SHEEP, AND MEN
The Wool Export Economy
and Regional Society in Southern Peru

1

Introduction: Modernization, Dependency, and the Sectorial Model

The principal object of anthropological study, the rural peoples of the Third World, has been undergoing processes of transformation older than anthropology itself. Because of the increase of international trade in raw materials, many small and isolated economies have joined a single world-system. The expansion and demise of colonial empires have simplified a diverse mixture of autonomous political systems by bringing them under the jurisdiction of a single dominant institution, the independent nation-state. These two processes, the growth of export economies and the formation of national governments, can be traced to the sixteenth century and even earlier (Wallerstein 1974), but in their contemporary form they date from the early nineteenth century, before anthropology emerged from semihistorical speculation to its more systematic academic form.

The linking of disparate economies and the establishment of new governments have strongly affected Europeans and North Americans as well as the people who experience them more closely. The impact of changing petroleum prices and the war in Vietnam show the undeniable importance of these processes. The salience of these transformations has been growing, as they affect larger portions of the world's population in increasingly direct ways. Their importance has been particularly striking since World War II, with its attendant concern for assuring sources of raw materials and the emergence of many new nations.

The processes that have led to the formation of a single world-system are composed of many diverse elements. The manner in which they operate varies from setting to setting. Venezuelan petroleum workers, Egyptian cotton farmers, Brazilian coffee growers, and South African diamond miners all experience the economic and political consequences of export economies and nation-states in different ways. The coherence that underlies this apparent disunity is not simple.

This book examines a specific part of the Third World that these two processes have profoundly transformed. Peruvian national independence and wool exports, both of which began in the third decade of the nineteenth century, have shaped the Sicuani region in the southern highlands. This book uses the history of the area to evaluate three different analytical frameworks that explain these processes.

Because of their importance on a global scale, these two processes merit the attention of anthropologists. Although they are not directly germane to some major foci of the discipline, such as kinship and symbolism, they are central to many others. The interest that individual anthropologists have taken in the study of these processes depends in part on their particular specializations. Furthermore, by seeking to investigate the full diversity of human society and culture, anthropologists have developed a skill for finding remote, relatively isolated populations to study. The choice of such research problems and field sites may be taken as one response of anthropologists to the growth of export economies and nation-states.

The choice to ignore or to deny is only one of several options. Lamentation is another. Nostalgia for primitive peoples and the tragic sense of responsibility to record their ways of life have led many anthropologists to view their informants as representatives not only of particular cultures but of an entire type of untouched cultures, soon to disappear under the juggernaut of Westernization. In contrast to this concern with salvage ethnography is the adoption of a more smug tone based on the belief that the strength of indigenous cultures is proved by the ultimate test—resilience in the face of incorporation by Western economic and political institutions. Despite the efforts of the United States Army, the Bureau of Indian Affairs, mining companies, and other groups, the Navajo continue to be Navajo; even after the death of Mao, the Chinese remain fundamentally the same Chinese they were in imperial days. These choices often rest implicitly on a standard division of scholarly labor that leaves economics to the economists, politics to the political scientists, and, in some cases, change to the historians.

Anthropologists retain other empirical concerns. In this manner, anthropologists can acknowledge these two processes without directly examining them.

Other anthropologists partly rework this pattern of specialization by examining small segments of these large-scale processes. They may begin to encroach on the empirical and theoretical limits of other disciplines. Studies of patterns of adoption of a new crop, the migration of peasants to an agricultural frontier, the cooptation of a group of village elders by agencies of a national government, and the imposition of national legal codes on local means of conflict resolution all address these processes but fail to examine them directly. The growth of export economies and the expansion of nation-states involve more than local populations, last longer than periods of a few years, and connect individual phenomena in larger sets of transformations.

The scale of the analytical framework that examines these processes should correspond to the scale of the processes themselves. It should recognize both the global character of these transformations and the more local and regional character of many economic and political systems. Some anthropologists, by linking their studies to these larger concerns, have chosen this alternative. Recent trends in other social sciences have influenced their work (Poggie and Lynch 1974). To a large extent, they have been dominated by two major paradigms, modernization and dependency. The remainder of this chapter examines these approaches and uses this review to develop an alternative one. This third framework, the sectorial model, orients the description and analysis of the Sicuani region and its response to the wool export economy and the Peruvian national government. This book, then, argues that anthropologists can contribute to the understanding of these transformations through the development of an alternative model. This model provides concepts to analyze the responses of societies to the external forces, recognizing both the global character of these changes and the differences of each specific case. The historical processes of change in the Sicuani region serve to test the comparative utility of the modernization, dependency, and sectorial models.

THE MODERNIZATION PARADIGM

The modernization paradigm developed fully after World War II, but it draws on a number of earlier major figures in the social sciences, including Weber, Durkheim, Maine, and Tönnies. The paradigm provides a set of concepts to describe social, political, and economic change in a variety of settings. It adopts national societies as the primary unit of analysis. Institutions and other collective patterns of the behavior of individuals are also accorded importance. The theory postulates two types of society, traditional and modern, which are described by a number of variables and stand at opposite extremes of the continua defined by those variables. They also form consistent, coherent wholes. Modernization is the process, commonly thought to be gradual, by which societies shift from traditional to modern. It is generated internally rather than externally, and as a society moves toward the modern pole of certain continua, the other variables tend to follow.

Traditional societies, it is argued, have relatively low social, economic, and political differentiation. Social relationships are based on kinship, religious affiliation, regionalism, and ethnic identity, so that statuses tend to be ascribed. Many roles are affectively charged. Face-to-face relationships are important. Individuals are recruited to positions on particularistic grounds. Because of these characteristics, roles are multiplex: Two individuals have social ties in a number of different contexts. Characteristic forms of economic and political behavior are associated with these kinds of roles. Economic activity tends to be inflexible; since individuals are tied into a dense network of overlapping social relationships, it is difficult for them to engage in new sorts of economic activity. Entrepreneurship is of limited importance, and political authority is based on custom or what Weber termed traditional legitimacy. This static social, economic, and political order tends to acquire sacred legitimation. Traditional world views emphasize sacred power and supernatural forces rather than rational, mechanistic explanations of reality.

Modern societies contrast along all these dimensions. They have a high degree of social, economic, and political differentiation. Statuses are based on achievement rather than ascription. Roles are affectively neutral, and face-to-face relationships are unimportant, since individuals interact with one another in single rather than multiple contexts. Individuals are recruited to positions on universalistic rather than particularistic criteria. Economic activity is flexible, since individuals are free from strong personal commitments. Political authority is based on legally established norms, and bureaucracies acquire a central place in systems of administration. These features favor rapid social, economic, and political change. A secular, pragmatic world view is associated with these changes, permitting the extension of rational choice making to a large number of contexts of action.

Traditional societies, then, are characterized by static social structures and economies. Modern societies continuously undergo change. Furthermore, their institutions favor change. Routine economic behavior in traditional societies prevents the adoption of new forms of technology and the investment of capital in new enterprises. Traditional political orders lock individuals into specific roles and deny most of them access to power. Modern economies, by contrast, are dynamic because they emphasize achieved rather than ascribed statuses, universalistic rather than particularistic criteria for recruitment to new positions, and secular rather than sacred world views. Capital, labor, land, and material goods are available to all individuals, regardless of their position at birth; these resources may be allocated rationally to maximize production, and entrepreneurship flourishes. Any traditional system would have irrational blockages to resource allocation, leading to less efficient systems of production.

Certain political forms correspond to this open economy. Economic and political differentiation lead to specialization, interdependence, and solidarity, so that modern societies have low levels of conflict. All individuals have access to political decision making; no particular group or sector may impose its will upon others. Representative electoral democracy appears to be the most characteristic form, since universal adult suffrage guarantees full participation for individuals and allows the development of other participatory institutions, especially interest groups, social movements, political parties, and the less tangible but equally vital entity known as public opinion. Only such a state can act to favor the development of modern economies, by acting as a clearinghouse for necessary institutional innovations, as an agency for resolution of conflicts among group interests, and as a major entrepreneur for socially required infrastructure (Kuznets 1971). The state and the economy thus have complementary tasks in assuring the modernization of society.

As Tipps demonstrates, in his review of the modernization paradigm, theorists have disagreed on the relative emphasis to place on different elements of this scheme.

> Most conceptualizations of modernization fall into one of two categories: they are either "critical variable" theories, in the sense that they equate modernization with a single type of social change, or they are "dichotomous" theories in that modernization is defined in such a manner that it will serve to conceptualize the process whereby "traditional" societies acquire the attributes of "modernity." [1973: 203]

Common examples of critical variables chosen by different authors are industrialization, rationality, and social mobility. Dichotomous approaches view the process of modernization as the movement through a number of intermediate stages from the ideal type of traditional society to that of modern society. They develop sequences of transitional types, and they construct indicators to measure this movement.

Quite ambitious claims have been proposed for the modernization paradigm. Many of its supporters believed that it could summarize and explain the social, economic, and political transformations that followed the rise of the contemporary nation-state and the predominance of industry in the world economy. This paradigm would account for the first nations to modernize in Western Europe and North America and for more recent cases such as Japan; it would also predict the trajectory of nations still wholly or partly traditional (Parsons 1966). These claims led to strong objections. It has been argued that the paradigm is excessively rigid and ethnocentric, since it argues that all societies must follow the route laid down by a few nations in the nineteenth century. Other critics state that modernization theory only examines a limited range of processes.

Faced with this attack, the paradigm underwent some elaboration and refinement. It has been proposed that under certain conditions, tradition can serve modernity rather than limit it. One classic instance is the importance of the family firm in developing economies; a traditional social element (large, kin-based economic units) favors a modern economic feature (higher per capita income) (Benedict 1968). More generally, traditional elites may foster economic and political modernization (Eisenstadt 1973: 285–286). It has also been argued that there are many different routes from tradition to modernity (Bendix 1967: 322–323), that early and late cases of modernization are different (Levy 1972), that there are large costs to modernization, as well as benefits (Eisenstadt 1964), and that some nations may never modernize at all (Eisenstadt 1973). Other studies suggest that the different institutional spheres are not as tightly connected as the early instances of the modernization paradigm suggested. Social, economic, and political institutions may have different patterns of change, and a high degree of modernity in one does not require a high degree of modernity in the others (Bendix 1967). These revisions suggest that tradition and modernity should be considered not as simple unitary types but rather as sets of types.

These latter alterations are particularly significant, since they permit the splitting of the modernization paradigm into component subparadigms. These often correspond to the different academic disciplines that the modernization paradigm proposed to unite. Economists have elaborated the most systematized variants of the paradigm in their models of economic development. They interrelate a number of national economic variables, such as levels of investment, per capita income, rates of inflation, and distribution of the gross national product among different sectors. Rostow's *The Stages of Economic Growth* (1961) is a famous example. Other works provide different scenarios for the shift from static to dynamic economies and from low to high per capita gross national products. A great deal of the debate centers on the relative importance of the supply of money, the fiscal policy of the national government, and the institutional structure of production and distribution. The different opinions in these debates predict different consequences of the expansion of export economies.

In a similar vein, political scientists have developed models of political modernization. An early formulation proposed that political modernization consisted of the sequence of urbanization, literacy, growth of mass media, wider economic participation, and increasing participation in national elections (Lerner 1958). A more recent study, which also takes a "dichotomous" approach, lists the following characteristics of political modernization: the rise of a differentiated, centralized, and goal-oriented political structure; the expansion of the institutions of the central government into all realms of activity; universal political participation; and the replacement of traditional legitimation of rulers by accountability of officials to the populace (Eisenstadt 1973: 74). These models all examine the expansion and consolidation of the nation-state as an institution.

These different subparadigms presumably examine different aspects of the same process. Anthropologists may also proceed in a similar manner by examining small components of major processes, so that a study of the adjustment of rural migrants to a large city may be located in the larger framework of modernization. Another example of the adoption of the modernization paradigm in anthropology is the analysis of peasant society and culture. Peasants are presented as members of traditional societies. Roles tend to be particularistic and multiplex. Face-to-face relationships are of great importance, as the discussion of kinship, fictive kinship, patron–client relations, and trading partnerships shows. Bound by custom, economic activities change slowly. Peasant conservatism is part of the traditional, routinized culture. It is treated both as a cognitive orientation (the image of limited good) and as a basic value (amoral familism), but in both cases it is linked to a traditional world view. As certain elements of modern societies penetrate, they destroy this coherent peasant world. Many anthropologists have had difficulty in describing what happens to the peasants who have received strong modernizing influences, as the awkwardness of the term "post-peasant" demonstrates (Geertz 1962; Weingrod and Morin 1971; Orlove 1977c).

Despite these reformulations, several common elements in modernization theory remain. The fundamental units of analysis are nation-states. Major variables describe the aggregate behavior of individuals and the institutions. Societal change is taken to be the relatively slow and smooth shift of these variables. The source of change is generally internal; the change of one important variable (e.g., literacy, urbanization, industrialization) prompts other variables to follow. In all these cases, researchers examine different cases of societal change by comparing them to the ideal type of modernization. The epistemological status of modernization is quite ambiguous, since some writers use it as an ideal type in the Weberian sense while others argue that it is an inductive generalization (Shiner 1975).

In short, modernization theory has not fully responded to its critics. Their objections remain valid, and its continued assumptions need reexamination. Important processes do take place on levels other than the nation, social change is not necessarily slow, and the source of change is often external. The excessive simplification of history also remains problematic. It is unclear why the different attributes of modern and traditional societies should adhere as closely as the paradigm suggests. Furthermore, it seems methodologically weak, since ideal types are tools of convenience rather than unalterable depictions of reality (Runciman 1972), and the status of modernization theory as an inductive generalization is weakened by the cases that do not fit it. These difficulties all center on the fact that modernization theory looks at only one process rather than admitting diversity.

The criticisms may at least serve to indicate the lines of an alternative framework. Such a framework would examine a range of processes rather than lumping them all into a single type or set of similar types. The units would include levels both above and below the nation and would account for rapid discontinuities as well as slow, steady change. The relative importance of internal and external forces would be weighed rather than assumed in favor of the former.

DEPENDENCY THEORY

In recent years, some social scientists in Latin America have proposed an interlinked set of ideas commonly known as dependency theory. This framework has explicitly attempted to reject and replace the modernization paradigm. It grew out of the failure of certain economic development programs in Latin America, particularly those of the United Nations *Comisión Económica para América Latina,* or Economic Commission for Latin America (CEPAL or ECLA), and it adopted many elements of the Marxist analysis of capitalism and imperialism. Dependency theory is more difficult to summarize than modernization theory, since it is newer and less systematized and since it draws upon a variety of historical experiences in different nations. Therefore, generalizations about dependency theory are less secure and more open to exceptions (Kahl 1976).

Like modernization, dependency theory adopts nations as the basic unit of analysis. It accepts the contrast of two types of societies, calling one "metropolitan" and the other "satellite." These terms generally correspond to "modern" and "traditional." In particular, metropolitan and satellite nations are those economists have labelled "developed" and "underdeveloped," respectively. These types stand at opposite extremes of variables that describe a nation and the aggregate characteristics of its people; they also form consistent wholes. Dependency theory is more materialist in orientation than modernization theory, so that the major variables are economic. They include the level of capital investment, the importance of industry in the national economy, levels of technology, degree of foreign indebtedness, unemployment, and inflation.

The relationship between the two types is different in the two theories, however. The poverty and stagnation of the satellite cannot be explained by internal features, as modernization theorists would claim, but by metropolitan domination and satellite dependence. This structural relation is of fundamental importance in distinguishing dependency theory from modernization theory. The metropolis, which has a capitalist economy, exploits the satellite countries through various forms of economic and political domination, including conquest, unequal trade relations, and investments of capital. The backwardness of the satellite, sharply contrasted with the wealth of the metropolis, is not caused by the absence of metropolitan elements but by the control by the metropolis for its own benefit. The characteristics previously associated with underdevelopment are thus not inherent conditions; they are the result of the pillage and exploitation by the metropolis.

The satellite nations become dependent on the metropolis. The metropolis purchases the raw materials of the satellite, providing it with foreign reserves and capital to obtain goods that it cannot manufacture. Satellite economies become structured to produce exports, but the metropolitan nations retain most of the value produced. The dependent nation cannot fully industrialize or offer its inhabitants adequate levels of employment and income. By coming to depend on the metropolis for investments and loans to prevent national bankruptcy, the satellite countries are placed in a sort of international debt peonage. They are unable to manage their economies autonomously, and they are directly or indirectly forced to adopt policies that benefit the dominant nations rather than themselves. The inequality between the two continues to increase unless some international crisis, such as a war or a depression, temporarily weakens the metropolis. It ends only when a socialist revolution permanently frees the dependent nation of its subjugation.

Dependency theory tends to divide the people of satellite countries into two classes, the dependent national bourgeoisie who follow the interests of the capitalist classes in the metropolis and the proletarianized masses. The dependency of the satellite on the metropolis is replicated within the dependent nation, as the national bourgeoisie controls and exploits the proletariat for its own benefit as well as for that of the metropolis. At times, this relationship between classes becomes a relationship between regions. Elites in certain hinterland areas act as agents of the national bourgeoisie, orienting agriculture toward export. In this manner, the international and national relations of dominance and dependence appear within the region as well. Like the nations, interior regions are divided into two classes. The regions become decapitalized, and the internal interregional flow of capital, manufactured goods, and raw materials parallels international trade. This analysis borrows from earlier developments in Mexican social science, especially the concepts of "region of refuge" (Aguirre Beltrán 1967) and "internal colonialism" (González Casanova 1965). They examine the domination of regions and sectors of Mexico by national and regional elites. In other instances, there may be dependencies between ethnic groups; one dominant group exploits others for its own benefit (Bonilla and Girling 1973). These views all deny the claim of modernization theory that class, regional, and ethnic differentiation will tend to decline with economic growth (Bath and James 1976).

Like modernization theory, dependency theory makes very ambitious claims. It proposes to summarize the economic and political transformations of the Third World that followed the development of industrial capitalism in Europe and indicate the interrelationship of social, economic, and political structures within dependent nations. It will account for early cases of dependency such as Latin America and later ones such as Africa (Frank 1966, 1967; Amin 1970; Cockcroft *et al.* 1972). Dependency theory, then, is open to the charge that it tends to divide all societies into two types and to assume that there is only one kind of relation between them. Many early dependency theorists did not admit alternatives to the process by which autonomous societies were colonized, came to depend on the metropolis, and then achieved autonomy again through revolution. In addition, other criticisms have been made of dependency theory. It has been argued that dependency theory assumes that dominant and dependent economies are entirely capitalist, without retaining any elements of earlier modes of production (Chilcote 1974). It has tended to reify classes by neglecting the process of class formation. It assumes that economic pressures will force dominant and dependent classes to crystallize. Other authors have criticized the political program that dependency theory suggests. They argue that it stresses external domination over internal domination in all cases, and views the latter exclusively as a product of the former (Fernández and Ocampo 1974). Dependency theory focuses so strongly on class structures that it offers weak analyses of the role of the state in dependent societies (Hein and Stenzel 1973; Hamilton 1975). Unlike modernization theory, which argues that the state and the economy have complementary functions, dependency theory tends to assume that the state is a mechanism that metropolitan and dependent national bourgeoisies use to further their interests. The economic system determines the position of the state, so that the state has no autonomy as an institution.

The response of dependency theory to these criticisms shows interesting formal similarities to those of modernization theory. Some have argued that there are different routes into and out of dependency and that early and late cases of dependency may be different (Stavenhagen 1969). Several types of dependency have been recognized, including colonial, financial, and industrial dependency (Cardoso and Faletto 1969). In addition, different sectors of a society may become dependent in somewhat different fashion: Economic, political, and cultural aspects of dependency may change in somewhat separate ways (Bonilla and Girling 1973).

Despite these modifications, dependency has not fully responded to its critics. It retains certain elements of the modernization paradigm from which it emerged. It keeps the nation-state as the fundamental unit of analysis. It proposes only two types of society and a single relation between them. It assumes that the principal opposition and contradiction is always that between dominant and dependent societies (Quijano 1971, 1972). Like modernization theory, it is typological; it does not admit the range of responses of different societies to incorporation in the world-system.

Dependency theory still offers a useful corrective to certain weak-

nesses of modernization theory. It introduces an awareness of exploitation that modernization, with its functionalist outlook, often ignores. It
examines levels both above and below that of the nation. Social change
is often rapid, as dependency may be suddenly increased by conquest
or the establishment of new trade relations, or abruptly ended by
revolution. The source of change is external, since the problems of the
dependent nations are rooted in their relations with other nations.
Dependency theory also indicates the importance of social classes, regionalism, ethnicity, and other internal divisions within societies.

THE SECTORIAL MODEL

Modernization and dependency theories, then, show a
number of structural similarities. They are also opposed on several
specific issues. An alternative model of the growth of export economies
and the expansion of national governments would draw on these
theories, adopting their common strengths, utilizing the domains in
which they are complementary, and rejecting their common weaknesses. Among their strengths can be included the desire to investigate
large-scale processes, the attempts at an integrated examination of
social, economic, and political phenomena, and the interdisciplinary
character of research and analysis. Modernization and dependency
theory are complementary in that the former emphasizes gradual, con-
sensual, internally generated change while the latter stresses sudden,
conflictive, externally generated change. There are also several issues on
which they disagree but on which an alternative model might successfully side with the dependency theorists. These issues are the importance of material over ideological factors in historical change and the
predominance of divisions within a nation over its internal
homogeneity.

The weaknesses include the rigid, limited typologizing and the focus
on the nation as the primary unit of investigation. Each theory postulates two types of society with simple assumptions about the internal
structure of each and the processes through which they pass. A new
model would permit more detailed examination of specific cases and
present the growth of export economies and the expansion of nation-
states as the sum of particular cases as well as a single process. An
examination of the links between local, regional, and national societies,
on the one hand, and the world-system, on the other, would avoid
weak generalizations about the uniform nature of the processes of
transformation.

This review of modernization and dependency theory, then, offers some suggestions for an alternative model of the major processes of transformation mentioned earlier. There are several reasons why anthropology could contribute to a new model. Anthropologists have a deep familiarity with other societies, often deeper than that of other social scientists. The commitment of anthropology to the study of entire cultures makes it particularly receptive to the interdisciplinary emphasis that this alternative model would require. In addition, certain areas of anthropology offer particularly useful concepts. Recent work in the study of complex society examines the manner in which large economic and political systems constrain the activities of local groups. They allow one to examine the relations between different levels of a society (Adams 1966, 1970; Leeds 1964a, 1964b, 1969; Wolf 1956, 1966, 1967, 1969). Patron–client relations are a particularly important notion; this concept was initially developed by anthropologists and more recently adopted by political scientists (Scott 1972; Kaufman 1974). Secondly, cultural ecology studies the interactions between human populations and their environments. It assesses the importance of ecological constraints on social and economic activity. It offers a coherent, rigorous materialist analysis of systems of production. Certain studies indicate the power of linking studies of complex society with cultural ecology (Cole and Wolf 1974; Collier 1975). Cultural ecology emphasizes local constraints and studies of complex society extralocal constraints; their complementarity is particularly striking in the agrarian populations of state societies, as in the cases mentioned above (Love 1977). These recent studies indicate a new trend, particularly since they were not carried out in societies based on hunting and gathering, on pastoral nomadism, or on shifting cultivation, where the cultural ecological approach has been utilized most often and environmental constraints might appear to be strongest (Orlove 1977f).

Decision-making models offer a third component from anthropology. Such models view social behavior as the outcome of choices made by individuals who allocate resources in order to meet a series of goals. They see individuals as actively constructing their lives rather than passively accepting the roles and behaviors assigned to them. Many features of social structure and culture are viewed as constraints that limit an individual's alternatives rather than fixed rules that rigidly impose behavior. These models are compatible with studies of complex society and cultural ecology (Richerson 1977). Bennett (1969), Forman (1970), and Ortiz (1973) are recent efforts toward such a synthesis.

The eclectic methodology of anthropology may also prove useful, particularly in the early stages of generating an alternative model.

Survey and statistical data are more difficult to obtain in rural areas of the Third World than in urban areas of industrialized nations. Census data, for example, are often incomplete and unreliable. The tendency of anthropologists to use a variety of sources of data can correct for both the weakness of such data and the inherent subjective bias of participant observation. By comparing surveys, archival sources, and interviews, one may check the validity of each. A more elaborate methodology relying on fewer data sources might prove weaker simply because of the difficulties of obtaining reliable data. Quantitative and qualitative data are thus seen as complementary rather than opposed.

The alternative model proposed in this monograph is called the sectorial model. The term "model" contrasts deliberately with the terms "paradigm" and "theory," which are applicable to modernization and dependency frameworks since they are sets of interrelated causal propositions. The sectorial model advances a set of analytical categories which may be used in a wide range of empirical situations. These categories and the formal relations among them predispose the investigator to examine certain causal links. However, the sectorial model is not falsifiable, as a theory or a paradigm is.

The presentation of the data on the Sicuani region follows the outline that the sectorial model suggests, and the explanation of processes of change relies on it. The model is based on several related concepts: resource, activity, unit, and sector. They are drawn from the three areas of anthropology mentioned previously, but they also reflect the influence of the same social thinkers on whose work modernization and dependency theorists draw, particularly Marx and Weber.

The two fundamental components of the sectorial model are *material resources* and *human activity*. Resources are the elements that can be used or exchanged to attain desired ends. Several basic types of activity are included. In production activities, resources are transformed into new objects. In distribution activities, resources are exchanged and transported to reach intermediate or final consumers. In administrative and bureaucratic activities, resources are allocated to direct and constrain other activities. The principal activities, then, are economic and political in nature.

A minimum set of interdependent roles may be identified with the performance of any particular activity. This set of roles will be termed a *unit*, and the individuals who perform these roles are the members of the unit. These units are organized to permit relatively autonomous decision making in the performance of this activity. The members of a unit may change; the unit itself has a life history. Examples would include a factory or a farm in production, a trading firm or a store in distribution, and a government office or agency in administration. It is possible for an individual to engage in more than one activity and hence to participate in more than one unit.

Units control certain resources and seek certain goals connected either directly or indirectly with the performance of their activities. They face constraints, which may be defined as external conditions that impose limits on the number and range of alternative forms of activity by either increasing the costs associated with some alternatives or eliminating them entirely. Activities and constraints reciprocally influence each other. For example, a ranch may be affected by environmental constraints, such as lack of pasture, and political constraints, such as registration of animals; but its responses, such as shifts in transhumance patterns or the mobilization of patron–client relations, will affect in turn the system of environmental and political constraints.

The resources, goals, and constraints determine the organization of the roles within a unit. A shift in any of them would lead the members of the unit to alter the system of roles. The activity and organization, in turn, shape the interests of the unit. They may seek to shift the distribution of resources and the nature of economic and political constraints. A unit may attempt to increase its long-term security, expand the scope of its activities, or do both. This sequence of activity, organization, and interest is both a genetic and a historical one.

In a number of contexts, units have ties with other units. Their activities may generate these ties, those involved in the sharing of common resources, for example. Various situations lead to cooperation or conflict. Each unit may favor other units by increasing the demand for its activity or product, or by raising the aggregate level of the activity above critical thresholds for further investment in infrastructure. It may organize groups with other units to further their economic and political interests. Units may also compete for resources or markets. Such competition may also give rise to the formation of interest groups that selectively incorporate units on the basis of size, specialization, location, or other variables.

Rather than assuming the importance of the nation-state as an object of study in all contexts, as the modernization and dependency theories do, the sectorial model locates the object of study empirically. Certain boundaries and discontinuities appear in sets of interacting units. Within any boundary, significant interaction is relatively frequent; ties across a boundary are less numerous and restricted to a few channels. The boundary of the area under study may coincide with the distribution of an important resource or be imposed as a constraint by a wider system. Nations are clearly examples of such areas; others may appear at higher levels, such as international blocs or the global economy.

Within an area of study, one may identify *sectors*. These are defined as the sets of all units engaged in the same activity. When obvious discontinuities appear in the activities and units, they may be caused by the nature of the resources used by the units and the organization or scale of the units. Peasant households, wholesale trading firms, and mines are examples of sectors.

The interaction between sectors is also of importance in the sectorial model. Most such interaction contains both economic and political elements, although one often predominates. An input–output analysis of an economy is an example of a purely economic set of interactions in which one sector uses the products of others. A pluralist model of interest groups would be based on political interactions. Models of class conflict would include both sorts of interactions. The specific nature of intersectorial relations strongly affects their general form (e.g., conflict, cooperation, alliance). The type of interaction between sectors vary from case to case and depend on the nature of the principal economic activities and the wider political system. In the Sicuani region, five sorts of interaction are particularly important. Three are predominantly economic, and two involve both economics and politics. A special term, "modes of articulation," has been developed for the first three, since they form a distinct set of alternatives for a number of units and sectors. They primarily refer to the patterns by which goods are transferred between sectors, although they include a few cases in which services are exchanged for goods or other services.

1. *The joint production mode.* The members of one unit may engage in a second activity and thus have direct access to its products and services. Some herders, for instance, are part-time agriculturalists; the different timing of the labor requirements of herd animals and crops permits this dual production strategy.

2. *The barter mode.* The products or services of one sector may be exchanged directly for those of another. Cash is not used, and the exchange takes place without any intermediaries. The issue of the stability of rates of barter exchange, an important theme in the ethnographic literature on the Andes, will be discussed later.

3. *The cash mode.* The products or services of one sector are purchased by members of another. In this instance, cash is used, and the exchange usually takes place through intermediaries. In nearly all cases, this

mode involves a third unit (a distributor) in the exchange between two other units.

The two other forms of articulation involve both political and economic activity. They might take a number of forms, including the indirect exercise of influence, open hostility, and the involvement of judicial and administrative agencies.

4. *Resource competition.* Two units or sectors may compete over scarce resources, such as irrigation water or government revenue.

5. *Policy issues.* Two units or sectors may agree or disagree over more general issues, such as the authority of particular agencies in the region, or the degree of enforcement of labor laws. They may try to influence the making and implementing of policy.

This sectorial model focuses explicitly on process. Firstly, the notion of activity itself involves time. The performance of specific activities, the life histories of individual units, and the interaction of units and sectors all take place in different time spans. For instance, the expansion of one sector might lead to changes in its modes of articulation with other sectors, engendering changes in those sectors. Competition between two sectors for resources may weaken a third sector by limiting its access to those resources. Two allied sectors might initiate changes in policy that alter the system of economic constraints and change the relations among other sectors. Stated more generally, a given set of intersectorial relations has an internal dynamic generated by conflict and cooperation that channels activity and decisions in certain directions. The cumulative consequences of this interaction alter the distribution of resources and the system of constraints. In this fashion, one set of intersectorial relations could lead to a new set of such relations.

Secondly, external dynamics are also a source of change. New resources may be exogenously generated, and old ones may increase or diminish. New units may appear outside the area under study that affect those within it, or there may be new connections with previously existing units. These internal and external dynamics are interrelated, as the history of the Sicuani region repeatedly demonstrates. External changes, such as the growth of the wool export economy, influenced the relations of sectors within the region. These changes, in turn, had important consequences for the direction taken by the wool export economy.

This sectorial model also has certain implications for research methodology. By emphasizing the activities, organization, and interests of units and sectors, it suggests certain basic lines of inquiry in a relatively unknown situation. A general outline of the major activities in a particular area serves to locate units and objects of study. Comparisons with other cases offer economic and political processes to examine. The early stages of research are based on unstructured "gathering of . . . data on systems of work and other practices of local people"[1] (Vargas Llosa 1973:46); later stages are more systematic. Initial case studies of particular units will suggest items for surveys and questionnaires at a later point. The emphasis on process suggests an attempt to carry ethnography backward and history forward by a search in each period for parallels to phenomena found in others. Life history data may also prove useful in indicating the development of particular units and links between units. Statistical measures and surveys can test hypotheses generated earlier in the research.

The sectorial model draws elements from modernization and dependency theory but corrects some flaws. Like these two theories, it looks at large-scale processes and links social, economic, and political phenomena. It addresses the transformations generated by the growth of export economies and the expansion of national governments. It presupposes neither evolutionary nor revolutionary changes, however, and favors neither internal nor external dynamics. New elements from outside or a sudden shift in the internal balance of sectors may bring rapid change, but slower, steadier change from internal and external sources is also possible. In contrast to both theories, the sectorial model examines both individual decision making and structural constraints.

Most important, the sectorial model keeps certain questions open. It allows the nature of internal divisions to be established empirically, rather than assuming the sort of differentiated interdependence that modernization theory proposes or the division into two antagonistic classes that dependency theory suggests. It assumes that the state is a crucial element in processes of change because of the importance of political constraints, but it does not declare beforehand the nature of the relations between the economy and the state. Modernization theory presupposes complementary support of the two institutions, and dependency theory postulates determination of the activities of the state by the economy.

The sectorial model offers a different procedure from that of the other theories. It neither looks for immediate generalizations nor suggests that all cases can be assimilated to a single type. Instead, it proposes a

---

[1] "recoger interesantes datos relacionados con el sistema de trabajo y costumbres del personal del lugar."

set of comparable elements that can be identified in different settings. Similarities and differences in cooperation and conflict can be examined and related to patterns of resource distribution, economic and political constraints, and previous sets of intersectorial relations. The model thus goes beyond simple description to more general analysis without pre-supposing the simple typologies and processes that the theories of modernization and dependency establish.

Unlike modernization and dependency theories, the sectorial model is not falsifiable. It provides a general analytical framework rather than a set of specific predictions. The test of the sectorial model, then, lies as much in its utility as in its validity. Its greatest strength is its ability to offer precise and parsimonious explanations of the responses of specific societies to the expansion of export economies and national govern-ments. The accumulation of such studies is one of the necessary pre-conditions to further theory-building.

The sectorial model will be used to examine in detail the reactions of the inhabitants of a remote area high in the Peruvian Andes to foreign demand for their wool and the growth of the national government. The model will account for elements in these processes that the moderniza-tion and dependency theories would not predict; it will suggest more accurately the reasons for past changes and the possibilities of future ones. The history of the Sicuani region thus serves to examine the relative merits of the sectorial model and the other two theories with which it is contrasted.

Like other parts of the world, the Sicuani region responds to global forces through its own system of activities, units, and sectors. The processes of articulation, cooperation, and conflict operate there as they do elsewhere. Thus what the Sicuani region shares with all other areas is neither its uniqueness nor its inclusion in a world-system, but the confrontation of specificity and generality in its history that permits an empirical analysis of the type suggested by the sectorial model.

2

The History of the World Wool Market

The first shipments of Peruvian wool to England in the 1830s directly linked two economic systems that had been relatively isolated from each other. After that time, the processes of change in the Peruvian wool economy can be understood only in terms of its connections with the international wool trade. Because the world wool market has inherited features that stem from its medieval and early modern origins and differentiate it sharply from other international commodity markets (e.g., cotton, sugar, copper, or petroleum), a study of the contemporary Peruvian wool economy entails a brief historical review of the world wool economy. In this chapter, there will be no attempt to cover this history in all its complexity but only to touch on those aspects germane to the subject at hand. Similarly, only the most general features of the preconquest and colonial history of the Peruvian wool economy are outlined. The wool economy of southern Peru in the republican period is presented in more detail in Chapter 3.

WORLD WOOL[1]

Several different wool manufacturing centers emerged in Europe as trade began to grow again during the Middle Ages. In the

---

[1] This chapter is based on secondary sources. Rather than footnoting each sentence, I am giving references for each subsection. See Carus-Wilson (1952).

thirteenth century, artisans in Flemish towns produced a variety of
woolen goods from local wool and from wool imported from England.
Italian traders carried these fabrics to the prosperous eastern Mediterranean where they were exchanged for other products, notably dye-
stuffs and mordants crucial to the industry itself. By the fourteenth
century, the Italians had developed the cloth-finishing industry. Ben-
efiting from interrupted trade relations between England and Flanders
and severe Flemish political crises, Italian cities became the new centers
of cloth production, dependent on English and Spanish supplies. Italian
wool merchants enjoyed an additional advantage because of their position as papal collectors, since Catholic monasteries held an important
portion of the English herds.

The Growth of the English Wool Trade[2]

At the same time that English export duties made the raw material
more expensive, however, technological innovations (particularly the
spinning wheel and the fulling mill) spread through England. Edward
III settled Flemish artisans in England to teach their more advanced
techniques to his subjects. Parliamentary regulations forbidding the
wearing of foreign woolens and restricting the export of English wools
(linked to royal policies opposing the Italian merchants) also favored the
development of the English wool industry.

Unlike Flanders and Italy, England had a rural rather than an urban
wool industry, reflecting the fact that, with the exception of London,
England was more rural than the continent. The various crafts were
dispersed over the English countryside in small domestic units rather
than concentrated in shops. The artisans engaged in a mixed economy,
often working as farm laborers and petty traders at the same time.
Unlike their Flemish and Italian counterparts, they escaped the confin-
ing regulations of guild organization, in which each particular craft had
specified forms of activity and rates of pay. English artisans were also
able to market their own wares directly, rather than having to sell them
to members of a merchant guild as in the continental industries. These
factors favored adaptation to changes in demand through the use of
new designs, materials, tools, and forms of organization. Since entry
into the crafts was not restricted by rigid apprenticeship as on the
continent, the number of laborers involved in cloth manufacture could
vary with demand. Although competition among laborers drove wages

---

[2] See Blau (1946), Bowden (1962), Brearley (1963), Carus-Wilson (1952), Cole (1952),
Heaton (1965), and Hill (1860).

perhaps lower than they were in Europe, English artisans were also able to draw earnings from other activities. The cost of transportation in England, particularly by land, led to local processing of local wool output; Bowden shows that the type of wool and regional specialization in types of cloth closely corresponded (Bowden 1962: maps on pp. 29, 46).[3] Different breeds of sheep with wool of different characteristics developed in a number of regions.

The replacement of continental centers of cloth production was a slow process, and English wool continued to be exported (often by smuggling) for several centuries longer. Exports of raw wool continued to be dominant until about 1550, when textiles, chiefly heavy woolens, became the major form of wool export. Stimulated by the demand, wool prices rose rapidly. The trend toward increased wool manufacture in England favored the conversion to pasture of both agricultural land and land, such as forests and marshes, not previously put to intensive use. The famous enclosure movement greatly increased the availability of grazing land and hence the production of wool. Because former agricultural land provided better pasture than the more marginal areas to which sheep had previously been restricted, the quality of wool changed correspondingly, becoming coarser and somewhat longer in staple. English wool lost its reputation for fineness and shortness to Spanish wool. For the first time, England became an importer of raw wool, from Spain.

However, these longer wools permitted the growth of the "new draperies." The earlier cloths were woolens[4] and quite heavy; they were

---

[3] One hundred years intervene between the two maps referred to, but the varieties of sheep in the different counties had not changed much during that period.

[4] Bowden's definitions of woolens and worsteds seems the most useful. He says that woolens are also known as "cloth," and that worsteds may be divided into "worsted proper" and "stuffs."

> These differences lay mainly in the character of the yarn that was used, and this in turn depended partly upon the character of the wool and partly upon the processes through which the wool was passed prior to spinning.
> Cloth relied mainly for its strength on the felting property of wool; and it was made from short-staple fibres which, being more curly than long ones, were more easily matted together. The cohesiveness of the wool was accentuated by a process known as carding in which the fibres were converted into a maze by being worked between two boards covered with wire spikes. Worsted, on the other hand, largely neglected the strength given by felting, and relied to a great extent on the strength of the warp and weft. This was particularly so in the case of full worsted: a material made entirely from long-staple wool, which was combed instead of carded. Combining straightened the wool fibres and laid them in a similar parallel direction. In addition, it extracted from the long fibres any short ones which might be present, by causing them (by reason of their greater curl) to twist round the teeth of the comb.

sold in northern Europe and increasingly in the American colonies. They were made from carded wool and tended to use the short staple fiber. The new draperies were worsteds and much lighter; they were made from combed wools, which required a longer staple. Shipped to the Mediterranean and Africa, they became dominant among woolen export fabrics by the beginning of the eighteenth century and accounted for much of the rise in textile production. Production of woolens continued to expand, but not as rapidly as before.

The English Wool Industry in the Eighteenth and Nineteenth Centuries[5]

The eighteenth century in England saw continued growth of the wool textile industry, along with gradual increases in capital investment and the growth of the internal market. The various stages in the preparation of wool, weaving, and finishing continued to be done in small domestic workshops, although there was an increasing concentration of wealth and economic control in the hands of merchant capitalists through the putting-out system. These individuals provided artisans with wool and often rented them their looms and other tools, introducing some of the elements of modern industrial relations without directly establishing the workshop or factory form of organization. Technological innovations, first developed for cotton textile production, spread rather slowly to wool, not until the 1850s in some cases. Textile factories began developing quickly in the 1820s. Many of the cloth merchants became manufacturers, setting up their various operatives under a single roof. England's early lead in industrialization gave the wool industry an added advantage with increased mechanization; British woolen and worsted production boomed, serving a rapidly expanding domestic market and a somewhat less dynamic foreign one.

However, the textile industry remained frozen in what Hobsbawm called an

> extremely decentralized and disintegrated business structure . . . the product of its emergence from the unplanned activities of small men. It emerged as, and it has

---

The difference in the treatment of cloth and worsted fabrics continued after weaving. With one or two exceptions all woolen cloths were fulled: a process in which the material was soaped and beaten in a damp state so as to make it warmer, opaque and more durable. During this operation fibres of warp and weft interlocked still more thoroughly until the woven pattern of the cloth often ceased to be visible. Worsted proper was not fulled.[1962: 41–43]

[5] See Bowden (1962), Brearley (1963), Carus-Wilson (1952), Cole (1952), Hill (1967), Hobsbawm (1968), Mantoux (1965), Ponting (1961), and Thompson (1963).

largely remained, a complex of highly specialized firms of medium size, often highly localized—merchants of various kinds, spinners, weavers, dyers, finishers, bleachers, printers and so on, often specialized even within their branches, linked with each other by a complex web of individual business transactions in "the market." Such a form of business structure has the advantage of flexibility and lends itself readily to rapid initial expansion, but at later stages of industrial development, when the technical and economic advantages of planning and integration are far greater, develop considerable rigidities and inefficiencies. [Hobsbawm 1968: 64–65][6]

These inefficiencies did not catch up with English wool manufacturing until the late nineteenth and early twentieth centuries. The structure described above permitted increased production; capital investment in machinery provided increased capacity. As demand continued to increase, the scarce resource became wool itself.

The Shift to Southern Hemisphere Wool[7]

In England, the fine Merino wools of Spain supplemented locally raised wools through the end of the eighteenth century. Expanding textile production required larger supplies; assuring adequate sources of wool was a frequent problem in the late eighteenth and early nineteenth centuries. Changing Spanish commercial policy (aided by the invasions of the Napoleonic Wars) led to the spread of the Merino to other countries of Europe, to the newly independent American republics (principally Argentina and Uruguay), and to England's relatively underpopulated but rapidly expanding colonies, Australia and New Zealand, and later South Africa. These areas produced the wool that British industry needed. Land was virtually free in these areas of the Southern Hemisphere. Native populations were eliminated, contained, or driven back beyond well-defined frontiers. An extensive form of pastoralism developed that more than compensated for the relative scarcity of labor in these areas. This factor also favored capital investments and led to higher productivity there than in the older wool-producing areas. Different areas entered production at different periods. For instance, the spread of sheepherding through Australia took several decades, and Patagonia became a wool-producing area later than the rest of Argentina.

These new areas were favored by reduced shipping costs brought about by improvements in sailing ships and later the introduction of

---

[6] The quotation refers directly to the cotton textile industry, but Hobsbawm (1968) also states that similar structure prevailed in other industries; other sources show that they did in the case of wool.

[7] See Blau (1946), Clapham (1907), Hobsbawm (1968), Landes (1965), Munz (1950), Ponting (1961), Sigsworth (1958), and Smith and Haile (1929).

steamships. Continental sources of wool began to be cut off at the same time by governments intent on developing their own textile industries. Several European countries wanted to resist the expansion of British woolen textile exports. However, cheaper labor and more expensive fuel on the continent retarded the growth of a mechanized textile industry until the 1860s for France, the 1870s for Germany, and even later for other nations.

Colonial wools replaced European wools between 1830 and 1860, Australian wools entering the market first and continuing as the largest single supply to the present. The "Plate" wools, produced in Argentina and Uruguay, also began to appear in this period and picked up slightly later with improved breeding and management. The marketing system changed with the new areas of supply. Wool auctions began in 1835, replacing the older system of private arrangements between selling brokers (representatives of the growers or their financiers) and buying brokers (representatives of the manufacturers). The first auctions were held in London, and others began later in the manufacturing towns of Bradford and Liverpool.

The English domination of the wool auctions was reinforced by the importance of English capital investment to wool brokerage houses and, to a lesser degree, to producers. The leading role of the British merchant marine in international shipping was also significant. London became the trading center through which European nations and, to some extent, the United States acquired the wool they needed to augment national supplies.[8] Neither the colonies nor the European traders liked this system, which (they felt) gave the British wool traders unduly high profits through the monopoly of international trade, the control of the formation of stocks, and the manipulation of short-term price fluctuations.

International exhibitions in Australia in 1879 and 1880 attracted the already interested continental buyers of wool. The appearance in Australian and New Zealand ports of French, German, and Belgian shipping lines in the 1880s and of Japanese and North American ones soon afterwards ended the English domination of the trade. The rather minor wool auctions held in Australia since 1843 grew rapidly. Representatives of associations of growers, brokers, and buyers gathered to organize and schedule these auctions. By 1900, half the Australian clip was sold there; by 1960 this figure exceeded 95%.

Because of the availability of land, technical improvements, and capi-

---

[8] For a description of different patterns for selling South African wool, see Clapham (1907: 98).

tal investment, the clips from the new wool-producing areas in the nineteenth century increased the world supply of wool faster than industrialization and population growth increased the demand. Sheep raisers, whose products had been in great demand, found themselves with chronic problems of overproduction from the end of the nineteenth century onward. This oversupply led to sharp price fluctuations. These difficulties were augmented by the interruption of shipping during World Wars I and II. The British government controlled the marketing and distribution of Dominion wools during both World Wars, but returned the sales to private hands soon afterward. Decontrolling accentuated the variation in wool prices, and favored the development of a diversified export structure.

Unlike other international commodities markets the wool market never successfully developed a future market despite the difficulties with price fluctuations. A different system has evolved: Brokers received wool on consignment and sold it at auction. In effect, each lot was sold as a unique item. Each dealer and broker had his mark, and his wool was sold by its reputation. Peru is one of the few areas where this system of marks is still retained. Other countries have developed standardization in sorting and packing. In part, this lack of a futures market is a result of the enormous range in grades of wool, 1500 in the case of Australia, reflecting differences in breed, pasture, herding techniques, part of animal shorn, and so on. This variety is also the heritage of early English wool production, with a number of different breeds adapted to variations in local conditions, and is maintained by the structure of textile manufacturing summarized above. Such variety has made standardization difficult. There are relatively low annual fluctuations in global production. It is easier to take a mine or a cotton field temporarily out of production than a herd of sheep.

There is also a relatively rapid movement of the wool clip, and stocks are correspondingly low. Since growers and purchasing firms tend to build up short-term debts that must be repaid, they do not have independent funds that would permit them to retain their clips. The system of auctions also encourages immediate sale. Thus supply is relatively inelastic with respect to demand, and prices fluctuate more sharply than those of most other world commodities. Potential holders of wool futures would therefore run higher risks than holders of other commodities because the danger of gluts is greater.

Because of the nature of the wool trade, wool-producing nations have not developed a commodity cartel corresponding to OPEC among the petroleum-producing nations. The elasticity of demand for wool is high, the barriers to entry for producers are low, and there is relatively low market concentration (Bergsten 1974; Krasner 1974); the formation of a producer cartel is discouraged by these characteristics, none of which apply to petroleum. Furthermore, both the United States and the Soviet Union are relatively self-sufficient in wool supplies, so they are not subject to pressure from producer cartels. Finally, the importance of the British Dominions in wool production makes such a cartel even less likely. The experiences of World Wars I and II have created a tradition of cooperation rather than conflict in handling disequilibria in the world wool trade.

Unlike sheep wool, alpaca was marketed by private deals between brokers rather than by auction until the 1930s. The demand was restricted to a small number of manufacturers who specialized in it, and the number of firms that supplied this market—the largely British-based import–export houses in a few Peruvian cities—was likewise small. The competition was hence less extensive than for sheep wool. Sigsworth refers to the collusive agreements among the three major Yorkshire manufacturers of alpaca textiles and their successful efforts to prevent the establishment of sales of alpaca wool by auction. His description appears to have applied through the 1930s:

> the alpaca trade was quite distinct from the [sheep] wool trade in the nature of the material, the conditions of supply, organization of the market and, above all, in the nature in the demand for the commodity, which was characterized by a high degree of imperfect competition . . . from the early 1850s to 1883. [Sigsworth 1958: 238]

During times of severe crisis, the wool-exporting firms also entered into collusive agreements among themselves. They quickly rallied forces to oppose the attempt of the national government in 1930 to grant a monopoly of alpaca wool exports to a single foreign firm (La Verdad 15.2.30, 16.4.30, 8.5.30). Low foreign demand led them at several points to seek to reduce competition by maintaining price levels and by deciding to take fixed percentages of the export market.

England has continued to be the major distribution center for Peruvian sheep and alpaca wools. Local auctions in Peru that would change this pattern have been discouraged not only by the small scale of the operation but also by the lack of effective organization among the producers and traders, who have been unable to obtain government support for such an undertaking. Other countries have made inroads into the British domination of the Peruvian wool trade, but have not ended it. In the early twentieth century, North American mining companies bought up sheep haciendas in the central sierra and exported their wool to the United States. The appearance of non-British shipping lines led to some wool exports to Europe, the United States, and Japan;

but Peru has not diversified the markets for its wool as much as other Southern Hemisphere producers.

The next section of this chapter briefly sketches the history of Peruvian wool production before the export period. The following chapter will show the articulation of these two economies by the British-based export houses and the consequences for the internal organization of the southern sierra wool economy.

PERUVIAN WOOL[9]

The documented history of Peruvian wool production is scanty in comparison to what exists for Europe; this section mentions only broad and generally well-accepted aspects. The next chapter examines the recent history of the wool economy of southern Peru in more detail.

At the time of the Spanish conquest, the Andean area was the only part of the New World that had domesticated mammals for the production of meat and wool.[10] The period of domestication is now the subject of investigation. The difficulty in distinguishing the bones of wild and domesticated members of a single species has limited the progress of this work. Some sources suggest that llamas and alpacas were domesticated between 1500 and 1000 B.C. Since the Early Horizon (1400–400 B.C.), a large variety of weaving techniques were used, adapted to the variations in fiber.

During the Inca Empire, there were large numbers of llamas and alpacas, the latter confined primarily to the Lake Titicaca area. The herds of the royalty and the nobility and those assigned to the state religion were larger than those held by the commoners. Some individuals and groups were full-time herding specialists. The animals supplied wool, meat, hides, dung, and sinew. Cameloid textiles had great importance in the Inca economy. They also played an important role in the state religion. Llama sacrifice was a key element in several major imperial ceremonies. Techniques of breeding these animals were being developed.

The Spanish introduced sheep in the sixteenth century, chiefly the

[9] See Aparicio Vega (1965, 1971), Lanning (1967), Lewin (1967), Macera (1966, 1968), Mörner (in press), Murra (1965), Rowe (1946), Sigsworth (1958), Silva Santisteban (1964), and South African Wool Board (1970).

[10] The dog and the turkey were also domesticated in Mesoamerica, and the duck, the dog, and the guinea pig in the Andes. The llama and the alpaca were the only wool-bearing animals that were domesticated in the New World.

Merino and Churra breeds. The Indian depopulation during the 150 years following the conquest was accompanied by the abandonment of agricultural land and increase of grazing lands; sheep replaced men in many areas. There is very little available information about the social characteristics of the people who raised sheep and alpacas during the colonial period. It appears that many haciendas were predominantly agricultural. Macera lists the value of the Jesuit estates in Peru in 1767. Less than 3% of the total value was held in the form of *estancias* (ranches) and *pastos* (pastures); this figure includes cattle and horses as well as sheep, alpacas, and llamas (Macera 1966, cuadro 1). In a later work, he documents this agricultural emphasis of the Jesuits for the case of their haciendas in the Cuzco diocese (Macera 1968: 3–70). Aparicio Vega's brief study of the diocese of Cuzco in 1786 contains a description of the different *partidos,* which roughly correspond to the present-day provinces. Haciendas are mentioned only for the predominantly agricultural *partidos* in Urubamba and Paucartambo. This general characteristic of the diocese in 1786 is confirmed for the *partido* of Calca. Mörner shows that the haciendas concentrated on wheat and maize production, and that less than 40% of the sheep in the *partido,* where there were 2.7 sheep per capita, were owned by *hacendados.* The only conclusions that can be drawn from these studies are that wool-producing animals were not held in the larger, more capitalized production units of the period and that there were possibly a number of smaller herds in the Indian communities and hamlets. There is no information on the particular techniques of herding, breeding, or shearing.

There was active production of rough cloth called *bayeta* and of other kinds of cloth and hats in workshops *(obrajes, chorrillos).* The *obrajes,* which introduced European looms, were run with *mita* labor (a sort of forced-labor draft of peasants) under harsh conditions. A large part of their production was destined for the Spanish mines; the *obrajes* of Cuzco produced cloth garments and sacks for the mines of Potosí in what is now Bolivia. The widespread uprisings of the 1780s, during which the workshops were an object of attack, marked the start of their decline. They continued to decline into the early nineteenth century, as competition from British textiles and falling mine production reduced their markets and internal civil disorder disrupted the trade routes.

At the time of independence, Peru had large numbers of wool-bearing animals—alpacas, llamas, and sheep, the last having degenerated somewhat because of a lack of continued selective breeding. The herds appear to have been owned by peasant families rather than by wealthy *hacendados.* A sizable portion of the population was long accustomed to herding and knew a variety of weaving techniques.

As the next chapter shows, independence provided this rather archaic Peruvian wool economy with British markets, and exports grew quickly. British commercial firms monopolized the export of the wool. These new relations led to repercussions throughout the Peruvian wool economy.

3

The Wool Economy in
Southern Peru

The wool economy in the southern highlands directly involves more individuals than the other Peruvian export economies, in both production and marketing; and a number of different kinds of wool are raised. Although the bulk of the wool is exported, a number of local consumers use a certain portion of it. This chapter considers several aspects of this rather complex economy: the uses to which wool is put, and the organization of production and distribution. Appendix 1 describes more technical aspects of wool production, such as the physical properties of wool and the physiology and behavior of the wool-bearing animals.

THE USES OF WOOL

The varied wool output is used for a number of different purposes. Although relative figures are difficult to establish, most wool is clearly exported. Craft uses and barter consume a smaller portion of the total clip. Consumption by domestic industry reflects the institutional structure developed during an earlier period of heavier exports. Through mechanisms described later in this chapter, the Arequipa import–export firms were able to continue buying, bulking, and reselling the major portion of the output of southern Peru during the growth

MAP 1. The provinces of southern Peru.

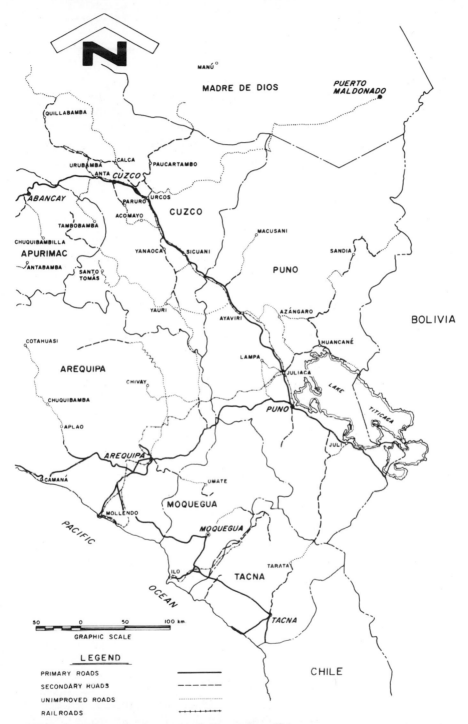

MAP 2. The transportation networks in southern Peru.

Legend:

- PRIMARY ROADS
- SECONDARY ROADS
- UNIMPROVED ROADS
- RAILROADS

GRAPHIC SCALE: 50 0 50 100 km.

LEGEND

Labels on map:

MANÚ

MADRE DE DIOS

PUERTO MALDONADO

QUILLABAMBA

URUBAMBA CALCA
ANTA CUZCO PAUCARTAMBO
ABANCAY PARURO URCOS
ACOMAYO CUZCO
TAMBOBAMBA
CHUQUIBAMBILLA
APURIMAC YANAOCA SICUANI
ANTABAMBA SANTO TOMÁS
MACUSANI
SANDIA
PUNO
YAURI
AZÁNGARO
AYAVIRI
BOLIVIA
COTAHUASI
HUANCANÉ
AREQUIPA LAMPA
CHIVAY JULIACA
LAKE
CHUQUIBAMBA PUNO TITICACA
APLAO
JULI
AREQUIPA
CAMANÁ UMATE
MOLLENDO MOQUEGUA
PACIFIC
MOQUEGUA
TARATA
ILO TACNA
OCEAN
TACNA
CHILE

35

of woolen textile factories in Lima and Arequipa, even during the complete cessation of sheep wool exports from 1971 to 1973. This shift in final destination has not affected the wool production and marketing systems in southern Peru developed under foreign markets; this continuity of the institutional structure justifies retaining the term *export economy* for the southern Peru wool economy as a whole, even though there has been a decline in the proportion of the total clip exported. A more detailed examination of each of the different uses of wool follows.

Export

A large portion of the wool sold for cash by the producers finds its way overseas. Britain was the principal foreign market for all Peruvian wools until World War II (Ross 1912). Britain's general domination of the world wool market and its early lead in the development of a textile industry described in Chapter 2 were reinforced by its position as a leader in the foreign trade of the west coast of South America. Throughout the nineteenth century, the major sources of foreign credit, the trading companies involved in the import–export business, and shipping lines were primarily in British hands.

The coarseness and large amounts of kemp of southern Peruvian sheep wools restrict them to certain uses, principally hosiery, tweeds, and felt. Alpaca wool had a more varied history. Since the wool is so fine, it can be spun into a thin yarn, making a very lightweight fabric. It was used for tropical suiting and summer jackets in settings ranging from the Belgian Congo to New Orleans (see Conrad 1963: 18; Williams 1947: 100). In the 1940s it was a common outstanding fiber on pile fabrics.

Lining was one of the oldest uses of alpaca wool because of the advantages of its low felting quality. The sharp rise in alpaca wool prices in 1950–1951 was caused by its use as lining for aviator jackets during the Korean War. With the advent of synthetic fibers in large quantities, the softness and luster of alpaca wool replaced its fineness as its most marketable quality. It has become a luxury fiber, used in fashion items such as women's coats, golf sweaters, and the like (Dorado 1973: 135–144).

Peruvian exporters sold their wool through a number of arrangements. At times, dealers would buy their wool and resell it to manufacturers. It has been more common to work through brokerage houses or commission agents through which brokers place Peruvian exporters in contact with foreign manufacturers and receive their commissions. The wool auctions in London, dating from the early nineteenth century (Lipson 1953: 8), retained their importance for Peruvian wools long after auctions had sprung up in other producing nations. Around 1940 they began to be replaced by direct sale. In both cases, London and Liverpool brokers sold to European manufacturers as well as to British ones, exercising a virtual monopoly over alpaca wool. A noted French fashion designer seems to have spoken with sincerity when he remarked in 1971 that he believed that alpacas were raised in England (Barrionueva 1973: 64). However, other nations have been purchasing some Peruvian wool directly since the 1930s and 1940s.

Domestic Industry

Textiles are one of the earliest industrial sectors to develop, both among European nations and the United States—which underwent industrialization in the nineteenth century—and those underdeveloped countries which have experienced it more recently. In the latter case, textiles have the advantage of using locally available raw material to make a well-established consumer good without unduly high initial capital investment; they are classic instances of import-substitution industries. This was the case in Peru, where both cotton and wool textile manufacturing began in the late nineteenth century. The woolen textile mills have tended to be family firms, a number run by descendants of southern European immigrants and old elite families. The mills are vertically integrated, buying raw wool and scouring, carding, spinning, dyeing, and weaving it into textiles which the mills finish and, in several cases, market. Men's and women's suitings, blankets, shawls, and yarns for hand knitting are the main products.

Such vertical integration causes certain inefficiencies because of the small size of the factories, the relatively short runs common in the trade, the poor coordination between different operations in the same factory, and difficulties in obtaining spare parts for the antiquated imported machinery. The market for the goods, however, seems large and steady, despite a history of relatively low import duties on foreign textiles and the competition of synthetic fibers. On occasion, Peruvian woolens have been exported to neighboring countries, often smuggled into Bolivia.

A few plants have recently diverged from the pattern of vertical integration. They manufacture tops, wool that has been scoured and combed but not yet spun into yarn. Sheep wool tops are sold to domestic textile mills and yarn spinning plants; alpaca wool tops are generally exported.

Some textile mills are supplied in part with wool from haciendas belonging to their owners. A few of them send purchasing agents to the weekly markets and annual fairs in the wool-producing regions. Several

Peruvian textile mills have attempted to establish regular wool purchases but failed for a number of reasons. The established wool-buying firms benefit from a detailed knowledge of the market and from long-term contacts with suppliers. Since these firms handle a larger amount of wool than most factories, economies of scale offer them a second advantage. They can present a prospective buyer with a wider range of colors and grades of wool than he could purchase himself. Most important, the wool-buying firms continue to enjoy relatively good access to credit. The woolen mills that established purchasing divisions soon found that they had to pay their wool suppliers in cash, straining their already limited capital resources. The textile mills must obtain wool on credit, since their capital is insufficient to permit them to buy it directly and meet their other short-term liquidity needs. By accepting sixty and ninety day letters of credit and commercial drafts from the textile mills, the Arequipa firms continue to their wool suppliers.

In other words, the institutional structure of wool marketing did not change when the final market shifted. The Arequipa firms that originally supplied products to foreign buyers switched to domestic ones without any basic transformations. For this reason, the southern Peruvian wool economy has remained little changed, as further discussion will demonstrate more amply. A section of Chapter 10 examines the impact of the reforms of the military government that took power in 1968.

Craft Uses: Artisans and Household Producers

Household producers can be distinguished from artisans, not by the particular techniques used or ownership of tools, but by the scale of operations and the market. Only those whose products are used primarily by people outside their families will be called artisans. The use of wool in homes and by artisans is extensive in the southern highlands; in many areas, virtually all the adults know how to spin and weave. Common products are a rough cloth known as *bayeta,* wide-brimmed felt hats, sacks, rope, blankets, carrying cloths, and ponchos, in order of decreasing commercialization. Some families purchase wool if their herds provide an insufficient amount. The textile-producing families market their products directly, although there are some middlemen dealing in *bayeta* and a few small craft cooperatives in Cuzco, Puno, and Arequipa.

Artisans use the grades of wool that command the lowest market prices: "pulled" sheep wool (sheared from skins of dead animals), kempy wool, llama wool, and colored alpaca wool. In certain cases, the equivalent return for labor time is higher for these cheaper wools than for more expensive ones. The price of sacks made of predominantly white wool is only slightly higher than the price of those made of dark wool, but the wool itself is considerably more expensive.

Another traditional craft is rug making. The skins of infant alpacas with their fleece are tanned and sewn into rugs with geometric patterns (Barker 1927: 108, figure 74). This craft has expanded with the increasing number of tourists coming to the highlands from the coast and abroad. Similar techniques are used to make slippers, hats, and toy animals. Larger workshops employing 10 to 40 workers have been established in Cuzco and Lima. A few of them market their items directly, but most sell through middlemen to large stores offering other souvenirs and trinkets. Some individuals work as professional weavers, either fulltime or during the slow periods of the agricultural year. Urban families and prosperous peasants commission rugs, blankets, and ponchos. They provide the weaver with spun, dyed wool, give him food and lodging during his work, and pay some cash when it is completed.

The collapse of the artisan class during the early stages of industrialization is frequently mentioned in the scenarios of economic development and change prepared by social scientists influenced by the theories of modernization and dependency. It is important to note that this event does not always take place, and southern Peru is one such exception. Though traveling weavers are becoming rarer and furriers owe their success to a particular set of circumstances, namely, the desire of tourists for relatively inexpensive handmade objects that they seem to identify with a tradition simultaneously pre-Columbian and preindustrial, the other crafts are successful. As the cash income of peasants and herders slowly increases, they buy traditional items such as *bayeta* in greater quantity as well as shifting to manufactured items. The market in highland towns and cities for *bayeta* is also considerable, as an examination of clotheslines reveals. Cash prices for *bayeta* have more than tripled between 1968 and 1973.

Barter

Herders from the puna engage in long trips to agricultural zones. Using llamas as pack animals, they bring wool (in fleeces and as craft items), hides, and meat to these lower zones, where they barter them for agricultural produce. This system is sufficiently well described elsewhere and does not need repetition here (Centeno Zela 1953; Concha Contreras 1971; Flores 1968; Custred 1974, Mayer 1971, 1974). The

FIGURE 1. Herders from the puna engage in long trips to agricultural zones. Using llamas as pack animals, they bring wool, hides, meat, and potatoes to these lower areas, where they exchange them for agricultural products. Some herders, such as this one in the province of Chumbivilcas, travel alone; others are accompanied by relatives. [Photograph by Glynn Custred.]

rates of exchange between items in this barter are not fixed by immutable tradition, as some sources suggest. Changes occur both seasonally and permanently. For instance, cooking pots to be bartered are exchanged for twice their capacity in potatoes, as anthropologists never tire of asking and peasants never escape replying; at the time of the potato harvest, however, the pot vendor demands a substantial *yapa*, or overweight; several months after the harvest, he must content himself with pots only three-quarters full. The potato harvest lasts only a month or two, but pots are produced during the entire dry season, when the weather does not interfere with firing them; the laws of supply and demand operate in a classic fashion. The evidence of long-term trends is similarly unambiguous. Eight *varas* (ells) of *bayeta* are now exchanged for the same amount of maize that ten *varas* brought several years ago, and similar shifts have been documented for meat. These fluctuations correspond to the cash prices of these goods. The use of

FIGURE 2. The use of barter does not indicate the isolation of the peasant from the monetarized national economy. In this photograph, taken in a market in San Pablo, province of Canchis, one onion vendor is in the act of bartering her goods for *habas*, or broad beans, while another peasant woman in the background is replacing her money purse in her carrying cloth after having purchased some onions with cash. The vendor in the foreground is paying a market tax in cash.

barter does not indicate the isolation of the peasant from the monetarized national economy but rather his articulation with it and his adaptation to the scarcity of cash.

THE PRODUCTION AND DISTRIBUTION OF WOOL

The institutional structure of the wool economy in southern Peru is quite complex. To a greater extent than in other export commodities, production is divided among a large number of units, often quite small, and the commercial network channeling the product from its producer to the final buyer is elaborate. There is also considerable regional variation in the organization of wool production and distribution. This chapter begins to examine this diversity by considering the

FIGURE 3. A hacienda in the province of Melgar, department of Puno. It is better capitalized than most haciendas in the Sicuani region, but less so than many other haciendas in the department of Puno. This *caseíro* (see p. 89), in addition to the residences of the employees, the hacienda offices, and warehouses, includes a chapel with a bell tower, a circular bull ring, and stables with metal roofs. Before the agrarian reform, this hacienda was owned by the Mejía family of Sicuani (see pp. 99–102).

units that operate within it, leaving the relationships among them and the social and economic processes in which they take part for later discussion.

The historical situation favors this approach, since the organization of the units of production and the market system have changed relatively little in the past hundred years. The most recent changes, the agrarian reform and the entrance of the government into wool marketing, are summarized in Chapter 10. Several preliminary points are in order. The positions described here are held not only by individuals but also by groups. Individuals and groups may occupy more than one position in the system; the herder who becomes a local wool buyer and the wool-exporting house that buys shares of a hacienda are examples. Furthermore, many of the individuals and groups engage in economic activities not directly related to wool: One wool export firm also ships coffee abroad, many herders cultivate fields of potatoes, and so forth.

Production: Hacendados, *Peons*, Comuneros

At first glance, the landholding system in the southern sierra appears to be a classic case of the *latifundia–minifundia* pattern described for many other agrarian economies; the haciendas would correspond to the large estates and the peasant and herder holdings to the small plots and herds. Such a view is useful to emphasize the great disparities in the distribution of wealth and land. It is important, however, to recognize the inequality and heterogeneity among *latifundistas* and *minifundistas*.

The highland haciendas have a labor force composed of two sorts of workers: permanent peons who perform the routine herding and temporary day laborers hired for work peaks at shearing, slaughter, and marking times. In some cases, specific sorts of labor are required from the peons; in others, they merely have to deliver a certain amount of wool and meat each year and ensure that the size of the hacienda herds does not decrease. The peon families remain on the hacienda for many years, frequently for generations. A peon receives some cash, but his principal return is the right to graze his own herds, called *waqcho,* on hacienda land. In many cases, fewer than half the animals on an hacienda belong to the owner.

When haciendas are sold, the peons and their *waqchos* remain. This has often been taken as a sign of feudalism, equating the peons with serfs on medieval manors. A better interpretation in many cases would regard the peons as tenant farmers whose rent is paid in goods or labor rather than cash. The fact that the peons remain for generations does not indicate that they are bonded to the land but rather that the *hacendado* is unable to dislodge them (Martinez-Alier 1973).

Day laborers are drawn from the population of *comuneros,* or community peasants and herders. In a number of instances, groups of peasant families have received official recognition from the government as *comunidades indigenas* (Indian communities) or *comunidades campesinas* (peasant communities) according to provisions of the 1920 national constitution. The land held by such communities cannot be sold to individuals outside them, although it can be owned as individual property, as the property of small, localized kin groups, or as communal grazing land. In all these cases, the land can be rented out by the owner. These official communities bear a complex relation to earlier peasant communities. In some instances, old communities achieved official recognition; in a number of cases, older communities split into smaller units as groups of families claimed and received title to sections of pasture land, often the best. These older communities held land in some sort of collectively inalienable tenure. Other features associated with

highland communities appear to have existed in varying degrees, notably a civil–religious hierarchy associated with local political posts and
patron saint celebrations and collective work projects for the construction and maintenance of irrigation systems and roads. The memories of
older informants and the written sources provide little information for
periods earlier than the late nineteenth century; it seems futile to attempt anything more than sketchy reconstruction. The term *comunero* is
thus to be taken cautiously.

Whatever the nature of the access to land, *comunero* households and
peon households operate as independent production units. The labor
resources of the household are sufficient for routine herding chores;
additional labor is obtained at times of greater need through reciprocal
labor exchanges and employment of other herders for cash wages. The
inequalities of wealth assure that richer herders can locate labor when
they need it.

These inequalities are worthy of brief additional scrutiny. The
poorest families own neither land nor animals. They attach themselves
to herd owners, receiving little more than food and lodging in return for
their labor. In some instances, they receive a part of the annual increase
of the herd. After a decade or two they can establish themselves as
independent herders by purchasing or renting land. The utter destitu-
tion of the poorest peasants is also evidenced by child sale. In years of
drought and famine, some peasant families are entirely without food.
Some give their children to *compadres,* who treat them much like
domestic servants; others sell their children for cash or barter them for
agricultural produce.

The obverse of this poverty is the wealth found among certain *comuneros.* Some individuals acquire large herds of animals and a permanent labor supply through occasional violence and the manipulation of
various social relations, including kinship ties, reciprocal forms of labor
exchange, and community membership. Sometimes rich *comuneros*
become *hacendados,* much as the poorest *hacendados* can be absorbed
into the peasant and herder sectors (Orlove 1974).

This section describes the relatively undercapitalized production
units. Without fences, it is difficult for one herder to separate his ewes
from rams belonging to others, and the improvement of breeds is
virtually impossible. Veterinary medicine would be similarly wasted,
since the possibility of reinfection is always present. Both *hacendados*
and peasants would be unwilling to start sowing grasses for fodder or
hay, since animals other than their own might eat it.

The shift to a more capital-intensive wool production, then, requires
a number of simultaneous changes. Fences can be used to introduce the

paddock system, but as long as *waqcho* and hacienda herds are not segregated, there is relatively little advantage to this innovation. Some *hacendados* have attempted to keep hacienda and *waqcho* animals in different paddocks and castrate *waqcho* rams, lending improved hacienda stock for stud; this scheme met with resistance from peons, who saw a close relation in the attempts to fence land and reduce *waqcho* herds. Complete replacement of peons and their *waqchos* with permanent wage laborers has been impossible in nearly all cases. Even on the experimental alpaca ranch run jointly by the *Ministerio de Agricultura* and Peru's oldest and most prestigious university, the *Universidad Nacional Mayor de San Marcos,* the herders own *waqcho*. *Hacendados* who have put up fences and introduced more capital-intensive production techniques have had strong political connections. The extensive use of fences in the province of Melgar in the department of Puno, for instance, dates from the 1940s, when the local *hacendados* had established ties with senators, other officials, and government banks which provided them with credit on very generous terms. The American mining corporations in the central highlands were also able to build fences because of their wealth and political power. These areas developed highly productive methods of raising wool. Later chapters discuss the lack of such political connections among the *hacendados* of the Sicuani region and the consequent lower levels of capital investment and productivity.

Distribution: Middlemen and the Arequipa Export Firms

Many of the general frameworks suggested by anthropologists to describe peasant marketing share the notion of hierarchy: There is a single marketing system composed of a fixed number of levels of markets through which rural produce moves upward to urban and foreign markets and manufactured items flow downward. Central place theory in geography is one source for this idea (Marshall 1969); another is the "studies of complex society" which posit the finite number of clearly demarcated levels as a more satisfactory replacement of the folk–urban continuum and see increasing numbers of levels as a sign of a society's position in well-defined trajectories of sociocultural evolution (Steward 1951, 1955, 1956; Wolf 1967). A certain confusion often remains between marketplaces and market phenomena (as defined by economists) in general.

The literature on wool marketing in Peru uses a hierarchical framework (Sotillo Humire 1962). Such a view correctly emphasizes two aspects of wool marketing: the centralization and the importance of vertical rather than horizontal movements of goods. The wool is funneled upward from producers through various sets of intermediaries to Arequipa, where the export houses are located. There are, however, a number of alternative channels it can pass through; the system is neither unitary nor divided into the same sets of levels throughout.

The even, unindented coastline of southern Peru offers no site any particular advantage for port facilities. Smaller boats known as lighters brought goods from ships lying at anchor some distance offshore. Since the coast is extremely dry and barren, provisioning settlements there with water is difficult and expensive. The location of ports changed several times, and the settlements around them were quite small. Arequipa enjoys a better climate, sufficient water, and nearby irrigated fields to supply it with food. It is well located to act as a distribution center, linking sierra areas in the Lake Titicaca basin in Peru and Bolivia and the intermontane valleys with other places, particularly Lima and foreign countries. Some foodstuffs, such as rice and sugar, and manufactured items are shipped to the sierra, while other produce, like maize and potatoes and export items (wool, minerals, coffee, cinchona bark, annatto, and coca) move to the coast. The climate favors wool merchants in still another way; the Rio Chili provides water to wash the wool, while the low humidity and sunny weather allow it to dry easily. The coast, though rainless, is often fogbound.

Arequipa has dominated the international trade of southern Peru since Peruvian independence as it did throughout the colonial period. The construction of the Southern Peruvian Railway, reaching Puno in 1876, Sicuani in 1897, and Cuzco in 1907, assured it the southern sierra market. The railroad linked new areas in what had been isolated eastern portions of the Andes with Arequipa. The end of the nineteenth century and the beginning of the twentieth also witnessed a decline in the importance of the smaller ports on the south coast, such as Pisco and Chala. The immediate hinterlands of these ports were tied more directly to the growing commercial center of Arequipa (Centro de Colaboración 1951).

The Arequipa wool export houses are the descendants of the import–export merchant firms established there after independence and throughout the nineteenth century, as they were elsewhere in Latin America. Until this century, these firms were European, primarily British; they imported manufactured goods from the home country and exported raw materials. In smaller cities like Arequipa, they were often agencies of larger firms. They also acted as representatives of banks, manufacturing firms, and shipping lines. The earliest firms were British consignment agents, but many of these went into bankruptcy; the stabler firms reappearing after 1850 were often branches or agencies of larger firms. A firm started by a Spanish immigrant family in 1878 broke the British monopoly,[1] and other non-British and Peruvian firms entered the wool trade. The direct links with Britain proved valuable, but so did connections with the Arequipa elite. Matrimony followed economic ties. The British consul in Arequipa has frequently been chosen from these Anglo-Peruvian wool families. These export firms are powerful in national politics and have played an important role in the many Arequipa-based military *coups d'état* (Flores Galindo 1976).

The Arequipa firms buy wool that has undergone at most a simple classification. They sort cameloid and sheep wool into about two dozen grades each (cameloid wool by species, color, and, to a lesser extent, fineness; sheep wool by fineness, length, and amount of kemp), scour it, and bale it. They also perform the extensive paperwork necessary for export. Finally, they establish and maintain contacts with buyers and brokers abroad, purchasing agents of domestic textile mills, sources of credit, and suppliers of wool in the highlands. There are only small economies of scale in the processing of wool, particularly in the sorting. The principal advantage of handling large volumes of wool is being able to offer the full range of grades.

Middlemen in the highlands switch from one Arequipa firm to another if they are offered higher prices for their wool. This factor leads to a competitive market situation; the firms bid against one another to ensure supplies. Although annual wool production varies little, the wool supply is in fact somewhat price elastic, since producers hold stocks. Herders switch wool from artisanal and domestic uses and barter exchange to marketing cash. During periods of rising prices, new firms enter the wool trade, and competition becomes particularly severe. With falling prices, smaller firms are often caught short, forced to sell wool acquired at high prices for lower ones, and many have gone bankrupt.

A common pattern is the formation of new wool export firms by the

---

[1] This new competition is reported by an agent of Anthony Gibbs & Sons, in a letter dated 22 May 1878 found by William Albert in the archives of that company. Earlier reports mention other non-British traders. Tristan, describing Arequipa in the mid-1830s, mentions one French import–export firm and two French shopkeepers (Tristan 1971: 256–258). Hill, who visited the city a little over 20 years later, states "the commerce of the city is considerable, and is chiefly carried on by foreign merchants, the greater part of whom are English" (Hill 1860: 94) and mentioned German merchants there (p. 112). It is likely however, that the English merchants were the only ones to engage in the wool trade.

employees and managers of old ones. The contacts with sierra middlemen, overseas buyers, and sources of credit seem to be the critical
advantages offered by people in this position. Third-generation firms
are not unknown, and there is at least one instance of a fourth-
generation firm.

The poor transportation system (only short stretches of the principal
highways are paved, and many areas are accessible only on foot or
horseback) and the geographical dispersion of the fragmented units of
production require a large number of middlemen to gather the wool and
transport it to the buyers. The timing of production adds further difficulties. Shearing takes place during the rainy season, when the roads
wash out and landslides sometimes block the railroad.

Some buyers make trips through the puna, buying wool directly from
the herders who produce it. Weekly markets and annual fairs are held in
a number of locations in the area, where petty traders buy skins and
fleeces, a few at a time, and larger merchants both buy in small quan-

FIGURE 4. Important middlemen in the wool trade often bring several truckloads of
sacks of wool to railroad stations on a single day. They hire workers to unload the wool
from the trucks. The wool in this photograph was purchased by a Sicuani trader in the
province of Melgar and was being shipped to Arequipa from the railroad station in
Ayaviri.

tities and purchase most of the wool that the traveling buyers and smaller merchants have acquired.

The middlemen who operate with the largest volume are found in the biggest towns, such as Juliaca, Sicuani, Ayaviri, and Ilave. They buy wool from the larger traders. Most of the hacienda wool enters the marketing chain at this point (although the output of the largest haciendas is sold directly to the Arequipa houses); such sales, though less numerous than transactions with the peasants, give the merchant large volumes of high-grade wool. These major urban wholesalers sell to the Arequipa houses. They make rudimentary distinctions between different classes of wool, separating it into *lana de finca* (estate wool) and *lana corriente* (ordinary wool). The former is presumed to come from haciendas and be somewhat longer and finer because of the admixture of Merino and Corriedale blood and the greater care of the animals. Alpaca wool is graded into three shades: white, tan (known in Spanish as *LF* from the English *light fawn*), and darker shades, and occasionally the lower-quality wool is separated out.

Wool enters the market through other individuals as well. Some shopkeepers in the towns accept wool rather than cash for payment. In many cases, a herder will take his relatives' and neighbors' wool to market to sell with his own, receiving a better price per unit weight; the individuals who engage in this practice shade imperceptibly into the traveling buyers. In recent years, *hacendados* have been purchasing the wool from the *waqcho* herds belonging to their peons. They claim that they can offer their peons better prices for wool than the middlemen by entering the marketing chain higher up, by including the wool in a larger unit, and by passing it off as *lana de finca*. Although they are in a position to give their peons substantially higher prices than the middlemen, they do not always do so.

In other ways, the marketing system is relatively simple. It is very rare for middlemen to extend credit to producers with the clip as security, although this practice is common in other wool-producing countries. Loans between middlemen are short term, usually only a week or two.

In the following chapter, the different sorts of relations between producers and middlemen are examined in greater detail. The relationship of the units described in this chapter is presented there. Chapter 4 also discusses the mechanisms by which prices are established.

4

Credit, Stocks, and Price Transmission Mechanisms

The wool-producing *hacendados* and peasant herders in the southern sierra are distant from the foreign purchasers of their wool in terms of market stimuli as well as spatial location. Since wool passes through several sets of middlemen before being exported, herd owners make decisions about production based not on export prices (of which they are often altogether unaware) but on local prices.

This feature is unique to the wool export economy in Peru, since it differs from procedures with other products. In the case of copper and iron, mines ship ore directly overseas.[1] The marketing mechanism in sugar exports involves one or two sets of intermediaries who introduce relatively little noise into the transmission of information about prices.[2] The separation between exporters and producers is so great in the case of wool that it has been claimed that producers, especially the more isolated peasant herders, are involved in an economy variously labeled traditional, subsistence, and nonmarket. This chapter demonstrates that all producers are articulated with a marketing system strongly

[1] The mines often ship the ore in the form of concentrates, but this first form of elaboration and processing is performed by the mining company itself.

[2] The specific relations and organization of marketing have changed in the case of sugar. The large haciendas used to maintain their own port facilities; now a government agency handles sugar export (Klaren 1970: 92–114; Yépes del Castillo 1972: 155–6).

dominated by foreign buyers. This fact is important for an understanding of the activities of producers and middlemen.

The specific organization of the marketing system varies from place to place and has changed through history. Therefore a description of the marketing system as a whole would be lengthy, tedious, and unenlightening. Instead this chapter proposes a general model of the activity of marketing units. These units will be referred to as *middlemen*, although a small percentage of them are actually firms with more than one member. This model shows the parameters along which sales and purchases vary and the sets of constraints that shape their decision making. The general organizational principles of the marketing system are related to this model. The particular channels by which information about prices is passed through different middlemen to the buyers are termed *price transmission mechanisms.*

THE ACTIVITY OF WOOL MARKETING

Chapter 3 contains a description of the middlemen in the wool trade, emphasizing their large numbers, the high degree of competition among them, and their organization into several different hierarchical levels. This large and complex marketing system can be understood through an examination of the operations of individual marketers. The middlemen all engage in the same activity, and similar sets of constraints shape the particular choices they make. This consistency leads to certain general organizational patterns which in turn form the price transmission mechanisms.

The activity of all middlemen consists of buying and selling wool.[3] Each particular transaction may be described in terms of four parameters: timing, partner, volume, and price. The purchase or sale takes place at a particular moment between the middleman and another individual. A certain quantity of wool is exchanged for a specific price per unit weight. Transactions frequently involve several different grades and colors of wool. Since such mixed lots are often not divided up when they are sold, they will be considered as single transactions, with a multiple volume and price structure for the different sorts of wool.

At the most general level, an individual middleman has two goals: survival and expansion (Adams 1970: 39–44). It is frequently impossible to distinguish between the two, since they are frequently blended in the highly competitive marketing system. Many firms that fail to expand decline and go out of business. Rates of entry and bankruptcy are high.

---

[3] The middlemen also engage in other economic activities; see Chapter 8.

There is, however, a difference in general strategy. Some middlemen try to expand their operations rapidly, and others aim for slower growth or a steady level of activity. To a certain extent, the fluctuations and uncertainties external market conditions impose this choice. When wool prices fall, middlemen attempt to survive, and when they rise, they try to expand. In other words, short- and long-term strategies of income maximization may be opposed.

There are five principal constraints under which middlemen operate.[4] Although they may be separated analytically, in concrete situations they interact in complex ways, reinforcing each other at different times.

1. *Profit.* A trader seeks to make as high a return as possible in both the short and long run. He attempts to maintain his buying prices low and his selling prices high, as do traders in other products.

2. *Volume.* Traders also wish to maintain high levels of volume of wool they handle. Faced with a choice between two equally profitable sales, one with a small volume at a large unit profit and another with a large volume at a small unit profit, they would tend to choose the latter. By handling large volumes of wool, a middleman can come to dominate a local market and exercise a certain degree of monopolistic power.

3. *Turnover.* Volume and turnover are closely related. The majority of wool traders operate with relatively fixed amounts of capital, whether they use their own money, receive credit from a buyer, or both. If wool is held for a long time, the middleman suffers a loss by foregoing transactions he could have made by selling the wool and using the income to purchase more.[5] He is faced with a similar problem when he makes loans to his suppliers; their delays in returning with wool reduce his earnings by creating opportunity costs in the form of foregone transactions and interest. (For this reason, wool prices are lower in remote areas. Buyers are unwilling to pay higher prices because of the length of time required to transport the wool, particularly during the rainy season.) High rates of inflation also favor rapid turnover by discouraging the retention of capital.

4. *Suppliers.* A middleman has to balance two somewhat opposed

---

[4] No wool middleman told me that there were five and only five parameters to each decision. Their conversations were framed in terms of these parameters, however, and they would assent to their importance. I am not attempting to establish a precise description of the cognitive processes of the middlemen, simply because I believe that these processes differ from individual to individual and include a high tolerance for uncertainty and ambiguity (Davis 1973).

[5] This argument held equally well during the times when wool was exchanged for goods, such as salt, sugar, *aguardiente*, and metal utensils.

principles in his relations with producers and other middlemen who supply him with wool. He may keep permanent trading relations with suppliers linked exclusively to him in order to maintain a steady supply of wool. The total supply of wool is inelastic, particularly in times of rising prices when the stocks retained by producers have already entered the market. Flexibility as well as stability is also advantageous. A middleman may end trading relations with a supplier who repeatedly brings low-grade wool or insists on excessively high prices. It is also useful to be able to establish contacts with new suppliers.

The balance between these two elements varies in different situations. A small-scale buyer might wish to establish new relationships, but a large-scale one would maintain the ones he already has against predation from other buyers.

5. *Buyers.* The same principles operate with regard to buyers. Permanent personal relations with a buyer help assure a middleman against being left with stocks he cannot sell. By establishing links with new buyers, however, he might receive better prices or more generous terms of credit.

An individual middleman acts as buyer with respect to one individual, as supplier to another. In general, a middleman finds it advantageous to maintain stable ties with suppliers and flexible ones with buyers, as will be shown in the following section.

These constraints interact in a complex way. A middleman needs ties with his buyers in order to receive credit so that he can give loans to his suppliers, thus tying them to him and ensuring a higher volume of wool handled. The effect of the constraints on decision making is shown in the parameters of the marketing activity. Middlemen pick strategies in accordance with their assessment of the situation and their particular goals. Profit and turnover may be opposed; a middleman has to decide between the advantages of holding stocks in a time of rising prices and more rapid turnover. Each sale or purchase implies foregoing another; giving more credit to one supplier means giving less to another. However, certain structural principles emerge from this immense number of decisions, as the following section shows.

VERTICAL LINKAGES AND THEIR CONSEQUENCES

Certain structural features of wool marketing emerge from the large number of decisions made by the middlemen operating under the constraints described in the preceding section. This section discusses only the most general ones that shape the price transmission mechanisms.

The most striking is the importance of direct vertical ties in marketing, corresponding to the difficulty of geographic mobility. A middleman tends to establish personal ties with several suppliers and one purchaser. These ties often last for many years. They are reinforced by the granting of credit and loans. Correspondingly there are virtually no horizontal links between middlemen operating on the same level, with the exception of occasional price-fixing and market-splitting agreements among the export houses in Arequipa.[6] The high degree of competition among them is consonant with this.

The lack of cooperation among middlemen operating on the same

[6] It is important to distinguish links related directly to marketing activities and other sorts of collective actions. The Sicuani wool merchants pressed for paved streets in town, smaller traders opposed market taxes that would keep peasants away from marketplaces, and so forth, but these actions (discussed in greater detail in Chapter 10) are different from price-fixing and market-splitting agreements.

FIGURE 5. This open-air marketplace in the district of Coata, province and department of Puno, is representative of district capital marketplaces in southern highland Peru. Many traders arrive by truck. There are large numbers of vendors and customers.

level in the marketing system is evident in the local marketplaces. It is commonly assumed that the open-air marketplaces operate as price-regulating mechanisms. There are a number of individuals purchasing wool, and the herders and middlemen who bring wool can potentially choose among them. Since both buyers and sellers operate on a small scale, there is a situation of perfect competition, and the law of supply and demand should operate to produce equilibrium. In most cases, an anthropologist making inquiry will find that the people in the marketplace agree verbally on the prices offered for different shades and colors of wool. However, the majority of the peasants and small middlemen go to their established buyers. The maintenance of personal relations produces significant variations in price between sellers, despite their apparent uniformity. There are three principal ways in which these come about. Wool, especially in the form of whole skins and fleeces, can be sold and bargained over as a unit, rather than being weighed.[7] The second manner is bargaining over weight rather than over volume. If the buyer and seller agree that the price for white alpaca wool of good quality is S/40 per pound,[8] they must still agree on the weight. Hand-held spring balances are used for smaller weights and steelyards and small platform scales for larger ones; there are techniques to distort them in both cases. The purchaser may state that the wool is moist or dirty, so that the weight that appears on the scale includes a certain amount of water or earth. The weight can be discounted by as much as 10 to 15% to compensate for these impurities. Third, there can be disagreement over the quality of the wool. In the case of white sheep wool, for instance, the seller may claim that it is from sheep with some Merino or Corriedale ancestry; the buyer may respond that the amount of colored wool mixed in is too great to be acceptable.

This "play" takes place throughout the wool marketing system; it is not restricted to the small-scale traders and herders. The largest *hacendado* in the Sicuani area had long disagreements with the company that purchased his wool, illustrating the latter two mechanisms (Ricketts, Vol. 40, p. 357; Vol. 373, 30.3.22, 26.4.22). Only well into the twentieth century were techniques to establish full standardization of weight and

----

[7] On several occasions I attempted to weigh fleeces and hides after the sale had been completed. I met with great resistance from both buyer and seller; it took a good deal of explaining to make them accept this action.

[8] The exchange rate for the Peruvian *sol* was S/43.38 to US $1 from 1968 until the series of devaluations which began in 1975. Unless otherwise stated, this exchange rate applies throughout this monograph.

quality agreed upon for the international trade in alpaca wool. Some Arequipa firms still lodge complaints against their overseas purchasers.

By establishing permanent relations with a purchaser, a seller is less likely to be subject to haggling of this nature. He will get a better price for his wool, even though he might be selling it under circumstances that have the appearance of classic perfect competition.

PRICE TRANSMISSION MECHANISMS

Information about prices tends to be passed directly from purchaser to seller, rather than through less personal channels. An individual with wool to sell is unlikely to know the prices other sellers are receiving in other areas; even if he does know them, he is frequently unable to insist on obtaining them. Three related factors are responsible for this phenomenon, all associated with the structural features described in the previous section.

The first is the permanence of the personal relations between buyers and sellers. Many agents of Arequipa export houses give cash advances to smaller wool merchants and to the traveling buyers in the punas. Some of the smaller merchants also give advances to their suppliers in the form of cash and goods. These debts make the contacts more permanent. Even when a supplier is not tied in this way to the buyer, the relations are longlasting. There are ties not only between middlemen and buyers but also between producers and middlemen. *Hacendados* tend to sell year after year to the same agent of an Arequipa firm. Many herders form stable ties with the small-scale traders to whom they sell.

The second factor is the poorly developed price communication system. On occasion, publications have appeared stating market prices for wool, but these are infrequent, irregular, and do not account for short-term fluctuations or the considerable price variation in the sierra. They often reach the potential wool seller several weeks late. At best, they serve to inform some *hacendados* and large-scale wool wholesalers of general trends and, on rare occasions, of specific prices.

Less formal mechanisms also fail to communicate full information on prices. Wool prices are a common topic of conversation, but information travels slowly outside an area larger than a province. Stories tend to be exaggerated, and information spread by word of mouth is most inaccurate when prices are changing rapidly. Even within small areas, information about price rises may be kept a secret. One buyer may give his suppliers an increase of 5 to 10% without the others knowing for several weeks.

The third factor is the relative monopoly of buyers in certain areas. On the lower levels of the wool marketing system, it is common for an individual to have a monopoly on purchasing in a given area.[9] One individual may be the only traveling buyer in a certain section of the puna. A herder may take the clip of several others along with his own to town, returning with a sad tale of the low prices offered there. A village may have only one shopkeeper who buys wool; this is the case of Santa Bárbara in the province of Canchis. In the case of the Layo market in Canas, individuals known as *alcanzadores* station themselves at points several hundred meters outside town; they buy wool and other goods from the peasants as they come in on different routes. In this manner, they divide the market into several monopolistic or semimonopolistic zones. In some cases, individual Arequipa houses control certain areas; thus most of the wool from the province of Cailloma is purchased by Ricketts, and wool from the sierra of Tacna by Sarfaty. The agents of these firms dominate the local markets. In recent years, especially, it has become common for *hacendados* to buy their peons' wool. Often with some justification, they claim that they can mix *waqcho* wool with hacienda wool and sell the whole lot as superior hacienda wool, obtaining further additional benefits from the larger size of the lot. However, the *hacendados* are unlikely to pass much of this benefit on to the herders.

These blocks in the price transmission mechanisms offer particular advantage to individuals on higher levels at times of rising prices. The Arequipa firms maintain a large number of buyers who receive cash advances. They are paid a fixed amount per unit weight rather than working on a percentage commission basis. The firms can delay increasing the amount they pay their buyers for wool, while receiving higher prices overseas. On the lower levels, a buyer is likely to find out about price increases well before his suppliers. *Hacendados* are also in a better position than herders, since they spend more time in the towns where they are likely to hear of the prices other *hacendados* have received. They also enter the marketing system at a higher level where they may receive more accurate information about price trends. In times of falling prices, individuals at higher levels of the marketing system are able to avoid costly losses; the smaller buyers may be caught with stocks they can dispose of only at a loss.

Prices do not always rise and fall uniformly, but the entire wool price structure may change. Fluctuations in the prices of different colors and qualities somewhat independent of each other allow buyers at higher

---

[9] This practice is technically known as monopsony.

levels yet another advantage. The agents of the Arequipa firms and some of the larger independent middlemen classify alpaca wool according to color (white, LF, or shade)[10] and can buy selectively as the prices of these three shift in ways of which their suppliers are unaware. Their flexibility is limited because they usually cannot buy only one part of a total lot, but they can refuse lots with too much of an undesirable color or offer premiums for those with large amounts of attractive colors. The Arequipa firms carry this selection much further. As in the case of *hacendados* purchasing peon wool, economies of scale and access to information converge.

Producers have one large advantage over buyers, however; they can hold their stocks. Buyers make profits on large volume and rapid turnover and run high risks when they keep their capital tied up in large stocks. This is true on all levels, from the agents of the Arequipa firms to the men trading *aguardiente* for wool in the remote punas. Many middlemen go out of business.

The need for ready cash is not as pressing for the producers. Both herders and *hacendados* may hold wool for several years. Rather than conscious speculation, this action seems to reflect a concept of a minimum acceptable price, particularly among the peasants. Herders are more likely to bring wool to market when they have some indication that acceptable prices are being offered; *hacendados* are more often sought out by buyers.

Despite this ability of producers to hold stocks, middlemen still retain much of the profits because of their other advantages. Consequently, the rates of return on capital investment are often higher in marketing than in wool production. Thus wool export firms have tended to plow profits back into trade rather than enter production by purchasing *haciendas*,[11] and many herders have become petty wool merchants rather than expanding production.[12]

The price transmission mechanisms not only offer advantages to

---

[10] *Shade* is the term used by British wool merchants to refer to all colors other than white and LF.

[11] Hacienda purchases by the Arequipa firms (during the 1920s in particular) took place when competition with other firms limited the possibility of increasing the share of the market and when there were few alternatives (such as light industry) for investment. They tended to purchase sheep rather than alpaca haciendas, even though alpaca wool is more valuable, because sheep haciendas could absorb larger amounts of capital in the form of improved stock, medicine, and the like. Sheep haciendas were also better located with respect to transportation routes. The Arequipa firms controlled less than one-third of the total wool production.

[12] See Orlove 1977b for contrary cases. However, many more herders entered trade than became *comuneros ricos*.

middlemen but also affect the decisions of producers. In the 1920s, Arequipa firms offered higher prices for the wool of Merino sheep. *Hacendados* purchased sheep of this breed even though they recognized that it did not face the rigors of the sierra climate well.[13]

The higher prices offered for white alpaca wool has led to selective breeding for this color. Although the inheritance of wool color in the alpaca is complex and poorly understood, selective breeding of lighter animals has led to an increase in the percentage of lighter shades in the herd. In the early 1950s, the proportion of white wool in the round lots[14] accurately reflecting the proportion of the total clip; but by the early 1970s it was about 50%. The percentage is even higher on some haciendas, but the herders have also clearly been engaged in such breeding. This breeding has been carried out even though it directly opposes traditional color preferences. One criterion by which traditional alpaca weaving is judged is the uniformity of color in each band or portion of solid color. The intense breeding of white alpacas has led to a decrease in the proportion of black, brown, and dark gray wool. Informants noted that they had increasing difficulty in obtaining enough of these colors to get acceptably uniform yarn for their weaving.

Two factors have encouraged this selective breeding. The demand for alpaca meat is increasing, among both traditional consumers and new ones. It is now sold openly in Arequipa and clandestinely in the form of jerked meat in Lima. The market for infant alpaca skins among furriers, described in Chapter 7, encourages the slaughter of animals within three months of birth. The darker skins are in demand as well as the white; the price differential between white and dark wool is less for elaborated products than for unworked wool and skins, because of both consumer preferences and the fixed value added. Although the young are born toward the beginning of the rainy season when pasture is most abundant, they are not weaned until well into the dry season. Since milk production falls when the mothers have less pasture, culling the dark animals permits the young white ones, which are more delicate and prone to disease (Fernández Baca 1971: 9), to get more milk than they would otherwise as the mothers of the dark ones cease lactating.

This process has hastened the increase of the proportion of white alpaca wool in Peru. The price differentials that stimulate selective

[13] Recopilación de datos formulada por el Ing° Jorge Gallegos sobre el desarrollo y evolución de la Granja Modelo Puno en su XXV aniversario. 19.5.46. Chuquibambilla archive.

[14] Round lots consisted of 12% white, 18% LF, and 70% shades. The German and American buyers began splitting up round lots.

breeding have not been present to such an extent in Bolivia. Bolivia has had many more governments than Peru, and many revolutions there have been followed by changes in economic policy. For this reason, Bolivian export duties on wool fluctuate much more sharply than Peruvian. When the duties are lowered, wool stocks crowd the market, receiving good prices independent of color. Producers' stocks are called into the market, and considerable quantities of wool are smuggled into Bolivia from Peru for export. When the duties are raised, producers retain stocks, again virtually independent of the color. The influence of differential prices for white, LF, and shades is hence dampened sharply, and there has been little selection for white animals.

THE INTERNATIONAL CONNECTION

The nature of the commercial relations between the Arequipa export houses and the overseas markets for their wool has tended towards more direct price transmission mechanisms. As goods and information move more rapidly, the number of intermediaries declines, the monopolistic power of the purchasers lessens, and the holding of stocks becomes less important. A similar process has taken place in the relations between the Arequipa firms and their suppliers.

In the late nineteenth and early twentieth centuries, each Arequipa firm was tied to one British merchant house which marketed the wool directly or through brokerage firms. The ties between the two tended to be relatively permanent, reinforced by granting of loans, whether the Arequipa firm was a direct branch of the British firm or, more commonly, its agent. The practice of shipping wool to England on consignment continued through the 1950s. It led to a certain degree of speculative buying of Peruvian wool on the part of both Arequipa and British firms. The latter sent information about current prices in England to Peru, along with suggested purchasing prices. This shipping of consignments was paralleled by ties between Arequipa firms and their large-scale suppliers in the sierra. The Arequipa firms also suggested a list of prices for the different grades and colors of wool.

The consignment system of shipping wool to Britain outlasted the relative monopoly that country enjoyed over southern Peruvian wool. The latter began to break down in the 1930s and 1940s as European and North American buyers made direct bids to the Arequipa firms. Germany in particular purchased wool in quantity for army uniforms. London's role as a distribution center for Peruvian wool was declining.

These shifts in international wool marketing were followed by larger ones. The crash that came after the economic boom of the Korean War led to a major change in commercial policy that altered the price transmission mechanisms. A number of firms had gone out of business, and the risky policy of consignment and speculative buying ended.[15] The more cautious technique of *venta a firma* was followed; Arequipa firms would purchase wool only to fill contracts already made with buyers by their brokers. This practice was replicated on the next lower level, where Arequipa firms also sent orders to their agents in the sierra. They maintained much smaller stocks since they could no longer be sure of disposing of larger ones. The increasing use of synthetic fibers in the two decades after the Korean War made the market for alpaca wool even more volatile than before. By raising the risks of speculation in this fashion, it further encouraged the more prudent *venta a firma* arrangement.

This shift was of considerable importance to the southern sierra. Changes among the wool producers affected the other sectors. In the Sicuani area, they led to a series of political changes that are described in Chapter 10. To understand them, it is first necessary to examine the region itself.

---

[15] The final collapse occurred around 1960; the last Arequipa firm stopped shipping round lots in 1966. For this reason, information about shifts in price structure is passed on more directly from overseas to Arequipa.

5

The Sicuani Region:
A Capsule Description

The wool export economy described in Chapters 3 and 4 has greatly transformed southern Peru. It is useful to investigate the mechanisms by which the growth of wool exports has led to changes in other parts of the economy and in power structures at the regional level. Interactions between sectors often occur at the regional level rather than the national or local one.

The following chapters analyze the different sectors, discuss the economic relations among them, and then examine the political processes which articulate them. General information about the region as a whole, however, serves as a basis for understanding any part of it. To talk about a region at all, it is necessary to explain briefly what is meant by the term "region" in the context of this book and the sectorial model.

AN APPROACH TO THE CONCEPT OF REGION

The concept of *region* is fundamental to several disciplines, particularly geography and economics. Studies have traced the development of this concept in both fields (Meyer 1963; Grigg 1965; Abler *et al.* 1971; Olsen 1976; Smith 1976c, 1976d). Two general sorts of criteria have been used to define regions (Smith 1976c: 6): patterns of trait

distribution and systems of nodal relations. In the first, a single trait or
a few traits may be used to mark off a region, or statistical techniques
such as factor analysis may be used to examine a larger number of traits
to establish variables whose distribution defines regions. In the second,
patterns of exchange and flows of goods, services, and information are
used to define nested, hierarchical sets of local and regional subsystems
within a larger system. Central-place theory in economic geography,
which has provided the dominant model for these latter definitions, has
inspired a number of elegant studies of marketing systems (Skinner
1964, 1965; Smith 1976a, 1976b).

The sectorial model favors the latter type of definition of region. The
interactions of units engaged in their characteristic activities are likely
to show spatial patterning. The emphasis in the model on material
resources suggests that environmental constraints strongly affect this
patterning. Constraints imposed by wider economic and political systems may also impose boundaries on regions. Unlike the studies influenced by a central-place theory, which tend to focus on a single activity
such as marketing, the sectorial model suggests that regions should be
defined by the spatial patterning of a variety of types of economic and
political interactions among units and sectors. Different activities may
have different spatial boundaries, so that it may not be possible to
define regions precisely in all settings. Hence the importance of the
region as a bounded unit and a level of organization may vary in
different societies; regional ties are only one of several sorts of subnational but supralocal ties (Geertz 1963a).

In this study, three criteria are taken to define regions:

1. *Internal organization*. Groups and individuals engage in activities
that establish long-lasting ties cutting across local boundaries but remaining within those of a larger territorial area. In Adams' use of the
term, actors operate at a regional level of articulation (Adams 1970:
53–70). Regional institutions, a powerful regional elite, and a central
town are frequently associated with important regional activities, and
may be taken to indicate strong internal organization (Beck 1976).

2. *Boundedness*. The supralocal ties between actors do not form an
unbounded network, but rather correspond to certain territorial limits.
The ties are based on location within a delimited geographical area.
They do not rest solely on spatial proximity, and they do not form only
actor-centered networks. This territorial aspect distinguishes regions
from other supralocal, subnational groups such as those based on class,
ethnicity, religion, and language, though these latter groups may also
be territorial.

3. *External links*. The regional level is not a maximal level of organization. Regions form parts of supraregional systems, the most frequent example of which is the nation. The higher-level institutions are able to exercise control over the regional ones. In many cases, individuals act as representatives of the region to link it with the wider society; brokers in Wolf's sense of the term (Wolf 1956: 1077–8) are one important type.

In this discussion, these three criteria are considered necessary and sufficient to mark an area off as a region. Although they are considerably more stringent than those used by geographers and economists (Grigg 1965; Meyer 1963), these criteria are continuous rather than discrete variables. For instance, internal organization is rarely altogether missing, but it varies greatly in importance. Furthermore, different activities and institutions may define regions differently along these variables. Hence an area can process varying degrees of "regionness." In practice, the application of these criteria is not often problematic (Brownrigg 1974; Reiter 1972).

This chapter and those that follow show that the Sicuani area is a region by this definition. Constrained by the mountainous topography of the Andes and the hierarchical organization of the Peruvian state, several sorts of activities within the area meet all three criteria. Of great importance are economic relations, particularly marketing institutions and the accompanying regional specialization of production and the interregional movement of goods. Political institutions and organizations also significantly affect the relation of the area to the Peruvian state and mold the links of regional elites to national and local administrative entities and sources of power.

The boundaries that mark off these economic and political activities tend to coincide, since they are in part imposed by geography. The Sicuani region is surrounded by natural barriers: the narrow river gorges of the Ríos Apurimac, Vilcanota, and Mara to the north, the Nevados de Condoroma and the Cordillera de Chilca to the south, the barren high puna to the west, and the Cordillera de Vilcanota and the Cordillera de Carabaya to the east. These correspond to the provinces of Canas, Canchis, Espinar, and Chumbivilcas. The Sicuani region is thus defined as these four provinces; adjacent areas of other provinces, particularly Quispicanchis, Acomayo, Melgar, and Cailloma, share some activities with the Sicuani region but do not form part of it.

This chapter examines the second and third criteria, boundedness and external links, through a presentation of background information on the region, and the next five chapters evaluate the internal organization criterion in detail. A number of geographical factors in the area act as constraints on human activity and thus partly determine the character of the Sicuani area as a region. Additional geographical information is included in subsequent chapters where necessary.

PRODUCTION AND DISTRIBUTION: THE MARKETING REGION

The great variations in altitude, rainfall, and soil types within relatively short distances have favored the specialization of production in southern Peru. The Sicuani area is close to four different major production zones (Baker and Little 1976; Bowman 1961; Custred 1973; Gade 1975; Troll 1958). As shown by a review of these zones, this location favored the emergence of Sicuani as a marketing center and the growth of the Sicuani area as a marketing region.

Production Zones

INTERMONTANE VALLEYS

The lands in this zone are called *quebradas* in Spanish and *qheshwa* in Quechua. Here they are simply called "valleys." They lie along a series of rivers which form part of the Ucayali-Marañón drainage. The low altitude (below 3600 meters), relatively mild climate, generally fertile soil, and abundant water favor agriculture; maize, broad beans, wheat, *tarwi* (*Lupinus mutabilis*), fruits, and other crops are grown. Of particular importance are the river valleys and dry lake basins in the provinces of Cuzco, Anta, Calca, Urubamba, Quispicanchis, Paruro, and Acomayo to the north and west of Sicuani. In these areas, altitudes are lower, and the severity of frosts is correspondingly decreased. Rainfall is more abundant than elsewhere.

Cultivation is generally restricted to the rainy season from November to March, but double cropping is possible in some places. The inhabitants of these valleys do not generally consume all the agricultural products they raise.

PUNAS

This zone consists of rolling grasslands suitable for grazing. The dominant herd animals are cattle, sheep, llamas, and alpacas. The punas are higher than the valleys, usually lying above 3600 meters. Agriculture is possible in lower and more sheltered areas during the rainy season, with a long fallow period. Except for barley, the crops are all Andean domesticates. For this reason, most of them bear unfamiliar

FIGURE 6. The puna is characterized by rolling grasslands, with many marshes and lakes. *Ichu,* the common bunch grass, is visible in the foreground. The dark area in the background is a *laymi* which has been prepared for planting with potatoes (see pp. 116–119).

names. Four of them are tubers (potato, *añu* [*Tropaeolum tuberosum*], *oca* [*Oxalis crenata*], *olluco* [*Ullucus tuberosa*]) and two are grains (*quinua* [*Chenopodium quinoa*], *cañihua* [*Chenopodium pallidicaule*]). There are extensive puna areas to the south and east of Sicuani in the Lake Titicaca basin or altiplano and in the provinces of Canas, Canchis, Espinar, and Chumbivilcas, collectively known as the *provincias altas*. The agricultural output of the puna in most cases is not sufficient for the needs of its inhabitants.

These two zones will be called the sierra. The Sicuani area contains both of them. The Río Vilcanota valley in Canchis and portions of the valley of the Río Apurimac and its tributaries in Canas and Chumbivilcas constitute valleys, and the uplands of the *provincias altas* form the puna. The Sicuani area lies between two larger extensions of these two zones. The altiplano is further removed from lower agricultural lands.

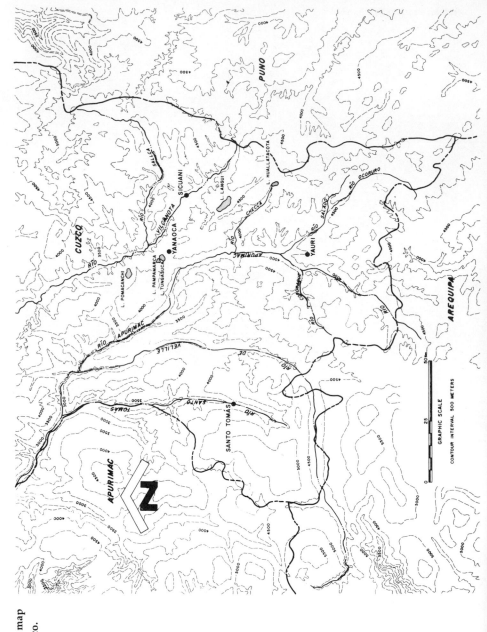

MAP 3 Contour map of southern Cuzco.

MAP 4 District capitals in southern Cuzco.

The rivers that drain to the east of it enter the Madre de Dios-Madeira drainage, passing through narrow canyons where there are few areas with topographic and climatic conditions favorable to agriculture. Though not completely lacking in nearby puna, the valleys to the north and west of the Sicuani area do not have as much of them.

MONTAÑA

Wooded slopes and the lower sections of river valleys that drop from the sierra into the tropical rain forest form this zone. The 2500-meter contour may be taken as a convenient, though somewhat arbitrary, demarcation of its upper limit. The climate is moist and warm. Although highland peoples have settled in the montaña since preconquest times, colonization in this century since the elimination of malaria has been particularly intense. A variety of tropical crops are grown, including manioc, sweet potatoes, coffee, tea, cacao, coca, fruit, and sugar cane. These montaña areas are isolated from each other. Travelers must return to the sierra to pass between them. As in the sierra, production is influenced by the timing of the rains.

THE COAST

The southern Peruvian coast forms part of the driest desert in the world. Rivers descend to the ocean from the sierra, permitting irrigation and intensive agriculture in the narrow but fertile valley oases. Agricultural products include cotton, sugar, grapes, rice, maize, sweet potatoes, and other fruits and vegetables. Manufacturing is also concentrated on the coast. Lima has been the major center, although a number of factories have been opened recently in Arequipa. Except for a few towns on Lake Titicaca, the ports that serve southern Peru for foreign trade are all located on the coast.

Markets

The markets for each zone's products are also located in different parts of southern Peru. To a certain extent, each zone supplies the other three with products to compensate them for their deficits.

The agricultural produce of the valleys is consumed in the puna and montaña. Some potatoes are also shipped to the coast. The coastal areas make up for much of their agricultural food deficit with foreign imports, especially wheat, but they ship some fruit and peppers to the sierra. In the early part of the century, the south coast and montaña supplied the southern sierra with sugar.[1] Coca has been an important trade item of the montaña since early times; it was shipped to the sierra. It was joined in the early twentieth century by fruits and some vegetables. Tea and coffee are shipped to Lima or exported, but small amounts are consumed in the sierra. Sicuani's location favored it as the center of interzonal trade. Most sierra towns are either much closer to the coast or much closer to the montaña; Sicuani has relatively good access to both. It lies near the boundary of large extensions of puna and valley land zones of agricultural deficit and surplus respectively.

---

[1] Competition from the more heavily capitalized north coast sugar haciendas virtually eliminated sierra sugar production and made heavy inroads in south coast production in the 1920s.

Much of the puna wool is exported via Arequipa, as described in Chapters 2 and 3. Artisans also use a smaller portion to produce cloth, hats, and other goods that are sold in the valleys. Some animals, especially cattle, are shipped live to the coast (and to a lesser extent to the valleys) where they are slaughtered. The meat is used for human consumption. The hides are tanned locally or exported to other countries. Sheep, llamas, and alpacas are more often slaughtered in the puna. After drying by exposure to sun and frost, the meat is sold in the valleys and montaña.

The consumers in the sierra are scattered among small villages and isolated households. The degree of urbanization is low; in the entire southern part of the country, only 10.03% of the population lives in towns of over 50,000 (Schaedel 1967: 127–128, 130–133). Barter of the products of different zones between partners with longstanding relations has overcome this dispersion. The introduction of railroad and motor vehicle transportation facilitated the rise of distribution through a system of marketplaces utilizing both barter and cash modes of articulation. Traditional barter also continued with the new means of transportation. In the sierra, a series of marketplaces developed for retailing imported goods and bulking local products to be shipped out.

The transportation routes have been adapted to a difficult topography. The southern sierra is the widest part of the Peruvian Andes. In northern sierra there is easy access between the montaña and the coast, but around Sicuani, the passes are fewer and much higher. Trade moves along routes that cross these higher and broader mountains. Ever since the Inca period, roads have been built on the flat land along the Río Vilcanota. These roads connect the valleys of the Cuzco area and the montaña around La Convención and Paucartambo with areas to the south and east, including the altiplano, Arequipa, and Bolivia. Different branches link the roads with Arequipa and the coast. One leaves the Río Vilcanota valley at Combapata and goes through Yanaoca and Yauri. Another continues to the altiplano through the pass beyond the headwaters of the river. This Vilcanota valley road continues to be of importance to the present, with the use of regular coach service in the late nineteenth century, railroad transport in the early twentieth century, improved road service in the 1920s, and heavy motor traffic in the 1940s and 1950s.

Animal trains also constituted a major means of transport of goods, both along the Río Vilcanota route and on the network of pack trails in other areas. Although mules, donkeys, and llamas were used at lower altitudes, only llamas could serve in higher portions of the puna. Some caravan routes followed the roads mentioned above; other main routes

FIGURE 7. Pack trails are important in the Sicuani region. This trail in the district of Livitaca, province of Chumbivilcas, is located in the rugged terrain close to the Río Apurimac.

FIGURE 8. The town of Sicuani is located on the Río Vilcanota. The flat lands of the valley floor contrast sharply with the adjacent slopes. The large roofed *mercado modelo* (see p. 152) is in the lower left; the large enclosed area near the right side of the valley is part of the boys' secondary school.

crisscrossed the different ranges and valleys. Geological formations present a series of natural barriers. North of the Sicuani area lie the deep canyons of the Apurimac and its tributaries, and to the east are located the high glacier-capped cordilleras. These features make northeast–southwest travel difficult, but on the whole, the animal trains could pass through the entire southern sierra.

The late nineteenth and early twentieth century saw shifts in aggregate levels and spatial patterning of marketing and transportation that were greatly influenced by the increasing foreign demand for Peruvian wool. The railroad also rerouted traffic, and coastal goods such as *aguardiente*, which had made their way laboriously by animal train, now came by railroad. Lower transportation costs and increasing commercial activity led to increases in demand. Until the arrival of the railroad, the Sicuani area was relatively isolated from external commercial stimuli. The end of the nineteenth century marked its full incorporation into the Peruvian wool export economy. This event occurred decades earlier in areas closer to the coastal ports (Centro de Colaboración 1951). The more amorphous networks of animal train routes were replaced by a flow of goods along the new and more sharply defined routes, with large marketing centers bulking local goods and distributing imported ones. The new spatial patterns of movement led to emergence of new marketplaces.

A traveler to Sicuani in 1902 described it:

> SICUANI, the capital of the province of Canchis, is also the great port of the department of Cuzco, by which is meant a *terrestrial port*. I give it this name because it is the channel which first gathers and then distributes throughout the department the products which foreign countries and neighboring towns send to it. [Fuentes 1905: 5; emphasis in the original][2]

In other words, Sicuani was the center of commercial activity, the key node in a distribution network transporting goods from different zones. It had already established marketing links between the extensive puna of the *provincias altas* and the altiplano, and it was well located to supply the puna with montaña products and the valleys with coastal products.

Other products that later became important continued to rely on the same distribution system. The sale of valley agricultural products to the puna had taken place through Sicuani as the center (see Chapter 9); when montaña fruit became a major trade item (Orlove 1975), large loads would arrive in Sicuani for redistribution. Increased consumption of manufactured goods had a similar pattern. Wholesale merchants in Sicuani received large shipments of flour, cloth, metal goods, and other factory items from Arequipa. They sold one part directly to consumers and another part to retailers. The Sunday market in Sicuani was the only important market in the region for the first three decades of the century. The growth of other marketplaces did not weaken Sicuani's position as *terrestrial port*. Retailing grew in other towns as it became a wholesale center.

The new means of transportation led to a decline in the importance of the animal trains.[3] An increasing amount of exchange took place

---

[2] SICUANI, capital de la provincia de Canchis, es á la vez el gran puerto del departamento del Cuzco, *puerto terrestre* se entiende; y lo llamamos así porque es la garganta que incauze, primero, y despues distribuye, en las entradas del departamento, los productos que le envían el extranjero y los pueblos vecinos. (Fuentes 1905: 5; emphasis in the original.)

[3] Animal trains, especially llama caravans, continue to be used in many parts of the southern sierra, and there are areas where they still form the major means of transportation of bulk goods, but they are not as important as they were a hundred years ago

FIGURE 9. Wholesale traders in Sicuani purchase grain, tubers, and broad beans from peasants and retail traders and ship these products to food deficient areas. This photograph illustrates wool, burlap, and plastic sacks. The large building with the metal roof is part of the railroad station. [Photograph by Mark Curchack.]

through a marketing system consisting of marketplaces, fairs, and stores rather than through traditional barter partnerships. The marketing system fulfills the three criteria that define an area as a region. The distribution system with its hierarchy of markets is an instance of internal organization. Internal communication is facilitated by flat punas in Canas, Espinar, and Chumbivilcas, a chain of lakes and flat ground in Canas and Acomayo, and rivers in flat-bottomed and easily accessible valleys, particularly the Ríos Vilcanota, Salcca, Pitumarca, Apurimac, Hercca, Velille, Coporaque, and Ocoruro.

The interregional trade carried out by wholesalers and some independent petty traders constitutes the links with a wider system. For instance, the representative in Sicuani of the Arequipa-based flour-milling company, Nicolini, sells to buyers from Canas, Canchis, Espinar, and Chumbivilcas. The weekly marketplaces which are supplied from Sicuani are Checacupe, Combapata, Pitumarca, San Pablo, Santa Bárbara, and Tinta in Canchis; Checca, El Descanso, Huinchiri, Langui, Layo, Pampamarca, Quehue, Tungasuca, and Yanaoca in Canas; Accocunca, Apachaco, Condoroma, Huayhuahuasi, Ocoruro, Pumahuasi, Tocroyoc, Urinsaya, Virginiyoc, and Yauri in Espinar; Colquemarca, Esquina, Livitaca, Santo Tomás, and Velille in Chumbivilcas.[4] Storekeepers in these four provinces and in parts of Quispicanchis and Acomayo also purchase their supplies in Sicuani or in other towns supplied by Sicuani. Parts of Puno, especially the province of Melgar, were also part of this system until Ayaviri emerged as an independent marketing center. In the early decades of the twentieth century, some Sicuani wholesalers maintained branches there, but they established themselves as independent. Yauri is now engaged in a similar process of separation. It has begun to link Espinar and Chumbivilcas directly with Arequipa. The increased trade associated with the opening of new mines in these provinces may complete this process. Nevertheless, trade continues to define the Sicuani area as a region, since it fills the criteria of internal organization, boundedness, and external links.

AUTHORITY AND INFLUENCE: THE ADMINISTRATIVE AND POLITICAL REGION

Political activity also defines the Sicuani area as a region. As will be elaborated in Chapter 10, the partial independence of Sicuani from the department of Cuzco is based on the interrelations of the sectors of *hacendados,* wholesale traders, and bureaucrats. These ties in turn depend on the relations of this elite to peasants, herders, artisans, and other traders on the one hand, and to national elites on the other.

Topographic and geographical features play a role in shaping the direction of political links, though not as strongly as they do in the case of trade. As the successor of a colonial intendancy, the department of Cuzco was a large and unwieldy unit at the time of independence and for the first half of the nineteenth century. Certain areas, particularly what are now the provinces of Cuzco, Anta, Urubamba, Calca, and Paucartambo, were closely linked to the capital city of Cuzco. The local *hacendados* lived in Cuzco or maintained residences there. Ecclesiastic holdings were concentrated in these provinces. The western provinces of Cotabambas, Antabamba, Aymaraes, and Abancay (recently split from Anta) were formed into the department of Apurimac in 1873, with the addition of the province of Andahuaylas from the department of

[4] Roads penetrated northern Chumbivilcas relatively late, and parts of the province, especially around Capacmarca, maintain direct ties with Cuzco on pack trails.

Ayacucho. The montaña and selva to the northeast became the new department of Madre de Dios in 1912. These two losses left the department of Cuzco with less than half of its original area.

In the colonial period, the Sicuani region corresponded to the two *partidos* of Tinta and Chumbivilcas. The former divided into the provinces of Canas and Canchis soon after independence; Espinar was separated from Canas in 1917. In these four provinces of the Sicuani region there is a separatist movement, its goal being the formation of a new department to be named Vilcanota or Tupac Amaru. This movement originated among the regional elite and their feelings of neglect on the part of Cuzco. The transportation and trade routes described above lead the Sicuani region to identify not with Cuzco but with Arequipa, along with the departments of Puno, Moquegua, and, to a lesser extent, Tacna (Orlove 1976).

Local political activities and settlements of disputes tend to center in the town of Sicuani. Sicuani was also a center under regimes that permitted independent political organizations and elections. The clientele of lawyers and notary publics are also drawn from the Sicuani region. Local officials and political leaders establish relationships with the national government. Regional elites control resources in the region; for example, the haciendas in the Sicuani region are owned by individuals from the region, and the Sicuani *hacendados* own haciendas only in the region and immediately adjacent areas, such as the district of Nuñoa in the province of Melgar.

Offices and agencies in the town of Sicuani administer the region. Several institutions also include Acomayo and Quispicanchis in their jurisdiction. These administrative regions meet the criterion of boundedness, since bureaucrats draw precise lines on maps. For instance, the office of the state bank, the *Banco de la Nación*, in Cuzco supervises the offices in Sicuani and Quillabamba, in the province of La Convención. The office in Sicuani administers the offices in its four provinces. The *Comandancia* of the *Guardia Civil* in Cuzco is divided into three *sectores* based in the towns of Cuzco, Urubamba, and Sicuani. The Sicuani *sector* is divided into four *lineas* which correspond to the provinces of Canas, Canchis, Espinar, and Chumbivilcas. In other cases, other areas are included. The post office and the state salt monopoly (*Empresa de la Sal*) are also divided into administrative regions; the one centered in Sicuani includes Acomayo as well as Canas, Canchis, Espinar, and Chumbivilcas. In some cases, the additional areas are more loosely attached to Sicuani than the four *provincias altas* are. The *Banco de Fomento Agropecuario*, for instance, has five *sectores*: two in Canchis and one each in Canas, Espinar, and Chumbivilcas. Acomayo and the southern portion of Paruro form the lower-priority unit of *inspección*, also attached to the Sicuani office.

At times, Sicuani has nearly as much importance as a departmental capital. The fifth region of the *Ministerio de Educación* in Cuzco, for instance, administers the departments of Cuzco, Madre de Dios, and Apurimac. The four zonal offices are located in the three departmental capitals and in Sicuani; the Sicuani zone is made up of the four *provincias altas*. Similar patterns occur in the *Ministerio de Agricultura* and in the Catholic Church; the Sicuani diocese, linked to the archdiocese of Cuzco, contains the same four provinces. The three criteria that define a region—internal organization, boundedness, and external links—are fulfilled on both political and economic grounds.

The Sicuani area—Canas, Canchis, Espinar, and Chumbivilcas—form a region according to the criteria presented in this chapter. Many processes take place within the region as a unit. The following chapters will examine these processes, first looking at the economy sector by sector and then showing the regional political system in which the sectors take part. These chapters will emphasize the internal organization of the region, but the external ties of the region keep appearing as major influences and forces. The international wool economy and the Peruvian nation are particularly important in this regard.

6

The Pastoral Sectors: Herds, Herders, and Herd Owners

This chapter presents an analysis of the organization of wool production in the Sicuani area. A discussion of the plants, animals, and inanimate features that form the nonhuman components of pastoral ecosystems shows that although the transhumance of herds and the annual cycle of herd management are strongly influenced by environmental constraints, the requirements of the herds can be met by several different forms of social organization. Certain factors, especially pasture and labor, become critically scarce under certain conditions but not under others. For this reason, any organization of pastoral production must be relatively flexible in some ways, though it can be rigid in others.

This characteristic of the activity of a herding unit—constrained to narrow limits in certain dimensions and wider ones in others—serves as the basis for an examination of the relations of herding units with each other and with other sectors of the regional society. Stated somewhat differently, there are ways in which pressure can be put on a herding unit by other units and other sectors, and there are ways in which the herding units can be relatively independent. Several different examples of the local organization of herding document this point. These cases and a general ecosystemic analysis demonstrate that changes in particular herding units do not affect the aggregate output of the herding sector significantly; the size, composition, and output of a unit may vary, but the overall production of the herding sector varies relatively little.

THE PUNA ECOSYSTEM

Wool production in the Sicuani area is marked by variations in organization that are often bewildering. The arrangements by which individual herd owners obtain access to pasture and recruit workers to their teams differ over short distances. Small, localized lineages with corporate rights to pasture give way to land tenure by communities in one direction and to individual ownership in another, both with scattered households and bilateral inheritance. On some haciendas, the same peon families have remained for generations; on others, there are high rates of turnover. *Comuneros* graze their animals on hacienda land through stealth, through collusion with peons, or through both short- and long-term rental of land. The ties between hacienda and community, between herd owner and herder, between pasture owner and grazer, vary in shifting but interlocking ways.

What remains largely unchanging is the harsh puna grassland environment and the physiology and behavior of the herd animals. Following Anderson (1973: 185), this chapter treats man and habitat not as separate entities, but as part of a single system in which human populations, animal populations, plant communities, and abiotic factors all form a set of interacting variables.

Some anthropological research has been done on the cultural ecology of pastoral populations (Lewis 1961; Pastner 1971; Rubel 1969; Sweet 1965). Such studies usually have two foci: the pasture requirements of the herds (often associated with dramatic patterns of transhumance) and the labor requirements of the herds (concentrating on daily activities such as grazing and milking). The discussion of the patterns of availability of pasture is often sketchy and the treatment of labor overemphasizes the routine management of the herds at the expense of the larger tasks that occur periodically. The studies underscore the consonance between pastoral social organization and the requirements of the herds, but the specific analysis is weakened by skimpy treatment of nonhuman ecosystem components. Leeds (1965) provides an exception.

An examination of the different dimensions of the severe environment in which wool production takes place is a necessary preliminary step to an investigation of the conditions that permit herding. Summarizing early work on environmental limitations on living organisms, Odum states:

> The presence and success of an organism depend upon the completeness of a complex of conditions. Absence or failure of an organism can be controlled by the qualitative or quantitative deficiency or excess with respect to any one of several factors which may approach the limits of tolerance for that organism. [1959: 89].

These limiting factors do not operate independently. An organism's range or tolerance for one factor often decreases as another factor approaches maximum or minimum tolerable limits. Hence all relevant factors in the puna must be considered: altitude, rainfall, temperature, soil moisture, and soil nutrients such as nitrogen (Baker and Little 1976).

The prevailing trade winds bring moist air from the tropical rain forest of the Amazon toward the Andes; they deposit rain as the air passes over the high mountains. In the Sicuani region, annual rainfall drops from 750 millimeters close to the tropical forest to about 400 millimeters further to the southwest, but there is considerable local variation. Rainfall is highly seasonal. Over 75% of the rain occurs during the rainy season, from November to March, and the months of June, July, and August rarely have any rain at all. The rainfall also varies greatly from year to year. In years of drought, less than 50% of the average annual amount will occur, but as much as 150% of normal may fall during wet years. It appears that these patterns of seasonality and irregularity are more accentuated in the drier areas to the southwest.

As in other high-altitude regions, the diurnal variation in temperature is great, at times exceeding 30°C. During the dry season, the shorter day length and lack of cloud cover permit greater heat loss from radiation, and the nightly frosts are correspondingly longer, more frequent, and more severe. In most places in the sierra, frosts can occur at any time of year; the risk increases with greater altitude.

Soil moisture varies greatly in different localities. The most porous soils tend to occur in the western part of the Sicuani region, where volcanic ash settling in large lakes during the Quaternary period produced extremely porous, tuffaceous soils. Greater glaciation to the north and east, corresponding to heavier precipitation in previous geological epochs, left less porous soils. The more extensive cloud cover in areas near the tropical forest also reduces surface evaporation somewhat. The greater atmospheric pressure at lower altitudes retards evaporation.

Small, localized areas, under one hectare in size, retain considerable surface moisture throughout the year. These areas, know as *bofedales* in Spanish and *oqho* in Quechua, occur where a porous aquiferous stratum lies directly above one that is less so. If the interface is exposed by

FIGURE 10. Localized areas known as *bofedales* or *oqho* have considerable surface moisture throughout the year. During the dry season, their vegetation gives them a much darker
color than the surrounding areas. They are often located at elevations above 4200 meters.

erosion or tectonic movements, water seeps out from the upper stratum.
These areas are more common closer to the tropical forest because of
seepage from the extensive snowfields and the greater porosity of glacial moraines. These two factors also lead to more frequent *bofedales* at
higher altitudes, above 4200 meters. In some cases, the area of *bofedales*
may be increased by the construction of small irrigation canals.

Finally, soil types vary locally, though the soils in general are low in
nitrogen. The alluvial fill that corresponds to the more glaciated land-
forms closer to the tropical rain forest appears to be relatively rich in
nitrogen and trace minerals. The old lake beds characteristic of areas
further to the southwest are poorer in these elements.

The vegetation is adapted to this rather harsh set of circumstances.
The dominant form is the bunch grass known locally as *ichu*. Scientific
classification divides it among several genera, *Stipa*, *Festuca*, and
Calamagrostis, each with a number of species, but the pattern of growth
is similar: dense, deeply rooted clumps 5 to 20 centimeters in diameter
and 15 to 60 centimeters high, composed of many single blades. The
plants propagate themselves by both tillering and seeding, but the

FIGURE 11. *Ichu* grass occurs in clumps. Dew and frost collect on the bunch grass and drip down to the base of the clump to provide additional moisture to the small plants located there.

former method is more important; fewer than 1% of the seeds are fertile. If allowed to grow undisturbed, the clumps take on the shape of a ring, as the outermost shoots grow up each year. When the ring is between one and two meters in diameter it begins to break up into smaller clumps.

Smaller grasses and forbs grow around the base of each clump. These plants, at most a few centimeters high, find the microclimate adjacent to bunch grass favorable. The taller *ichu* offers some protection from the wind, and increases the available moisture. Dew and frost collect on the bunch grass, dripping down to its base in the early morning. Snow accumulates more heavily around the bunch of grasses; as it melts, it keeps the bases of the *ichu* clumps moister than adjoining areas.

Although the *ichu* dominates the puna, other plants are also important. The forbs, or low plants associated with the *ichu* clumps, have already been described. Another set of low plants is called *ch'inki* in Quechua. They are adapted to growing in moist areas subject to frequent brief inundation. They occur in shallow depressions throughout the puna in the rainy season and in the *bofedales* during the whole year. Finally, a series of cushion grasses occurs in the *bofedales* of the eastern part of the area, favored by the relatively low diurnal temperature variation and the relatively high humidity. The branches or culms of the plant are crowded next to one another, so that only the tips of the most recent leaves are exposed to the surface. At a distance, a clump of cushion grass looks like a moss-covered rock.

These factors influence the spatial and temporal distribution of plants in the puna. There are cushion plants and some *ch'inki* in the *bofedales* throughout the year. The *ichu* clumps and associated small plants grow during the rainy season; they dry up soon after the rain stops. A number of features favor the northeastern part of the area over the southwestern, and its pasture is more abundant and of higher quality.

The pattern of movement of the herd animals corresponds to the availability of pasture. The herds are moved to lower areas (3600–4100 meters) early in the rainy season, coinciding with the appearance of the new low grasses and plants in moist areas and around *ichu* clumps.[1] These small plants form the bulk of the animals' diet, but it is supplemented by other sources. The previous years' growth of bunch grass, moistened by the rains, and the new shoots late in the rainy season, are also edible. As the rains continue, water flows again in stream beds and collects in small depressions, favoring the growth of *ch'inki*.

These plants all begin to dry up after the rains end. The animals spend the dry season at higher altitudes, between 4100 and 5200 meters, where pasture can be found in the *bofedales*. This pattern of movement allows the animals and the herders to escape the hailstorms and heavy snows in the high country during the rainy season. The exposure to the hard, dry, rocky surfaces in the upper zones also lowers the frequency of certain hoof diseases and parasites (Chuquibambilla 1939: 11; Moro and Guerrero 1971: 54–56). The altitudes are within the optimal range for the animals, although the incidence of respiratory tract infection among sheep increases when the animals are taken above 4400 meters.

---

[1] The specific patterns of movement vary in different localities. There are a few instances where herds move to higher ground during the rainy season, using marshy land along streams for dry season pasture.

This transhumance coincides with the reproductive cycle of the llamas and alpacas. The young are born in the early part of the rainy season, when pasture for the lactating mothers is plentiful and the risk of exposing the neonates to frost is low. Mating takes place soon after the young are born, since the gestation period is over 11 months. The herd behavior affects the reproductive cycle of the alpaca. For most of the year, male alpacas exhibit no sexual interest in females of their herd. The stimulus to rut comes only in the early months of the rainy season. The presence of new females, however, arouses males at any time of year, resulting in copulation and impregnation, but this pattern occurs only under experimental conditions.

The situation is different with sheep. The place where the animals were first domesticated may be an important variable in affecting their sexual traits. Alpacas and llamas appear to have been domesticated in the tropical Andes, while sheep were domesticated in temperate latitudes where there is considerable variation in day length during the year. Estrus in ewes is triggered in certain months by changes in the number of hours of daylight. Males initiate intercourse only with estral ewes. Since the gestation period varies little from its average of 150 days, the birth of the new lambs occurs in a relatively short period of the year, which coincides with the greater availability of pasture. In the tropics, day length is nearly constant, and estrus among ewes does not exhibit regular annual periodicity. Lambing occurs throughout the year, independent of the availability of pasture. This problem is common to all sheep in the tropics, including breeds developed there, as research among native Rhodesian sheep shows (Symington and Oliver 1966).

There are relatively low labor requirements for the daily management of the herds and the semiannual transhumance. Unlike certain other domesticated animals such as goats, both sheep and cameloids have a strong flocking tendency. This quality makes them easy to drive. Each animal will tend to imitate the animals around him so that the herd moves as a unit (Aranguren Paz 1972).

There are differences in the nature of this flocking tendency. Sheep herding behavior is allelomimetic. By contrast, the cameloids have a clear dominance hierarchy; a few adult males are the leaders of each herd. Since the other animals follow their actions, the herd acts coherently. Sheep can be exasperating animals with which to work, because herds sometimes move as if at random. Alpacas and llamas are easier to handle, since a herder can control the whole flock by controlling a few individuals. A trained herder can manage up to 400 sheep or 1000 llamas or alpacas. Additional herders can help maintain the flock by eliminating some losses from predation and straying.[2]

The herding tendency that facilitates daily management of the animals makes other sorts of care difficult. Shearing takes place early in the rainy season, so that the wool can grow back during the warmest months of the year. The entire herd is examined prior to the *saca* or annual slaughter at the beginning of the dry season. There are other occasions not tied as closely to the calendar when the herd is gathered and confined: Each year the new young are earmarked, and the females are checked for pregnancy.

These operations must be performed rapidly. A herd becomes restless if it is confined for several days. It is not possible to solve this problem by dividing the herd into sections and working them one at a time while the others graze. The animals notice the absence of their herdmates and become more difficult to control. Furthermore, there is very little systematic storage of fodder, because of the low nutritional value of the *ichu*, and the animals cannot go without food for long without becoming hungry. Any operation that must be performed on the herd should be done in a day or two. For this reason, it requires a relatively large number of individuals to work at one moment.

To recapitulate: Both the distribution of pasture and the physiology of herd animals strongly encourage transhumance. A herd must have access to both the temporary pastures in the rainy season and the *bofedales* in the dry season, as well as the freedom to move between the two. The labor requirements are similarly skewed. One person can care for most herds during the greater part of the year, but there are occasions when a larger number of workers must be present. Some of these occasions are limited to certain periods of the year, and the entire animal population of an area must be handled then.

THE ORGANIZATION OF PRODUCTIVE UNITS

Within this context of the puna environment, there are several different ways in which herders are organized, representing distinct solutions to the problems of access to pasture and labor. Much of the literature on social organization in the Andes has focused on communities and haciendas as units (Orlove and Custred 1974). This section emphasizes the herd owners. Following the sectorial model, it

[2] This pastoral economy is in contrast with other productive systems. Geertz shows that the marginal productivity of labor in terrace wet-rice cultivation remains virtually constant even in high levels of labor input (1963b: 28–37).

examines the sets of roles associated with the performance of pastoral activities. Neither haciendas nor communities are individual production units, but collections of such units. The number of units in a community is thus the number of autonomous households within it, and a hacienda with ten peon families has eleven units: the hacienda and the peon families. Each peon family participates in two units. Brief descriptions of the organization of production in the two provinces are given, and underlying patterns of articulation with other productive units and the regional society are shown.

Canchis

The province of Canchis in the southeastern part of Cuzco Department contains two distinct ecological zones: the *quebrada*, a narrow strip of flat, densely populated agricultural land along the Río Vilcanota (3400–3700 meters), and the *alturas*, the rugged uplands lying between this river valley and the chains of snowcapped peaks to the northeast (3700–6000 meters). This latter section has historically been dedicated to animal herding, an activity that continues to predominate. Its area is about 4750 km², with a population of about 4000 in 1972.

The *alturas* in turn can be divided into two sections. The lower one, within 8 kilometers of the river valley, has some areas whose sheltered locations permit the raising of crops, particularly potatoes, barley, *quinua*, and *cañihua*. In contrast to the *quebrada*, where herds are rare, the lower section of the *alturas* has large herds of sheep, as well as llamas, alpacas, and a small number of cattle. Agriculture is impossible in the upper section of the *alturas*. The geological and climatological factors described in the previous section converge to give it numerous extensive *bofedales*, as well as abundant pasture during the rainy season.

Until the early twentieth century, the lands of the lower section of the *alturas* formed part of larger communities centered in the Río Vilcanota valley. Individuals living in the lower section had access to the agricultural lands in the *quebrada*, and the valley dwellers brought animals to the pasture there; both groups cooperated on community irrigation projects. During the 1920s and 1930s, these communities split up into smaller groups and received official recognition from the national government as *comunidades indígenas*. In the cases for which firm documentation exists, it appears that the upper sections separated earlier, as their pasturelands became relatively more valuable with increases in meat and wool prices. Chapter 10 contains further information on this topic.

   The lands of the upper section first appear in the historical records soon after independence as church haciendas, rented out on long-term leases to local individuals. They passed into private ownership, apparently by the 1870s. In some cases, the descendants of the original *arrendatarios* or lessees retained ownership. Early in the twentieth century, the haciendas further encroached on remaining Indian lands in the upper section, and by 1930 they had title to all the lands in it.

   Settlement patterns, kinship, and economic organization differ in the two sections. Individuals in the lower section live in scattered households. All animals are owned by individuals and inheritance of animals, as of other material goods, is equal. All offspring receive equal shares of their parents' goods, often upon marriage in a form of anticipatory inheritance. The youngest son, or *chanaqo*, may receive a slightly larger share. Herders also sell animals to one another and on occasion purchase them at annual fairs and weekly *tabladas* or markets.

   Rights to pastureland are associated with community membership. Most communities show a relatively high degree of endogamy. Local residents receive community membership, which is ratified by participation in communal work groups, by payment of contributions or *cuotas* to community projects, and by sponsorship of fiestas in the community chapels. Some grasslands, mostly rather infertile rocky slopes, are used by members of several communities. There are numerous *bofedales* in this section, since the glacial action which deepened the Río Vilcanota valley exposed many aquiferous strata. In some cases, local groups of households within the community have exclusive rights to *bofedales*, usually small ones.

   The labor resources of the household are sufficient for routine daily herding. Two forms of reciprocal labor exchange are used to organize larger work teams. In *ayni*, an individual organizes a work team by calling others to help him. He repays each one with an equal amount of time spent at the same kind of work. The workers are also provided with meals, coca, and, in most cases, home-brewed barley or maize beer known as *chicha*. *Ayni* exchanges can occur between individuals of different degrees of wealth, since a rich person can have *ayni* exchanges with a number of other, poorer ones, each of whom has no other partners. However, *ayni* is usually predicated on a relatively egalitarian distribution of wealth. *Mink'a* is similar in that one individual organizes a work team by calling others to help him. However, the repayment is in goods rather than labor. The organizer may provide a feast with a large amount of liquor, as well as *chicha*, or he may give wool or other products as payment. *Ayni* exchanges thus involve pairs of days of work, whereas *mink'a* exchanges are completed in a single day. Although the helpers in a *mink'a* work team may call on its organizer to assist them when they organize *mink'a* teams of their own, in other cases, they may not. *Mink'a* exchanges tend to occur more frequently in situations where there is an unequal distribution of wealth than *ayni* exchanges. Work teams tend to be formed either by *ayni* exchange or by *mink'a*; the two forms are rarely mixed (Flores 1975, 1977).

In still other cases, herd owners make up the labor deficit by hiring herders on a monthly or yearly basis. They usually provide these workers with a small salary and a certain percentage of the increase in the flock. At shearing time, workers are also hired on a daily basis from within the community or nearby communities.

In the upper section of the *alturas*, haciendas have legal title to all the lands. Most haciendas maintain a *caserío*, or central complex of dwellings, storehouses, and corrals, where the foremen live. The owners and administrator stay at the *caserío* when they visit the hacienda. The herders or peons on these haciendas have a dispersed settlement pattern. Each household has two residences: a *cabaña* or principal house near the *bofedales* and an *astana* or temporary shelter in the rainy season pasture.[3] The largest part of the hacienda herds are kept in corrals adjacent to these. In addition to small sums of cash, the herders receive the right to graze their own *waqcho* animals on hacienda land in exchange for their labor. They are held responsible for preventing the loss of these animals. Hacienda animals are herded separately from *waqchos* and kept in different corrals at night. Both the *waqchos* and hacienda animals are grazed on all the pasture in the hacienda; it is not the case that each group is restricted to certain portions of it. However, hacienda herders sometimes choose to ignore *comunero* animals that enter hacienda lands. A peon may make arrangements with a *comunero* to claim that an animal belonging to the *comunero* is actually his. It is usual in such cases for the peon and the *comunero* to divide equally the increase of the latter's herd and the wool and meat produced by it.

The peon families have to care for two herds, and household members perform the routine tasks for both. In a number of cases, married children, usually sons, remain with the parents in patrilocal residence. It is difficult to build a new *cabaña*, although rooms may be added to existing ones. In some cases, the foreman or owner organizes the peons and other members of their households into larger work teams. The *comuneros* from the lower section of the *alturas* tend to go to the Río

---

[3] This pattern is the reverse of the usual one, in which the permanent house is located in the zone of the rainy season pastures.

FIGURE 12. An *astana,* or temporary shelter, can be quite small. The one shown here is constructed of stone and *ichu* grass. It contains a small stone corral.

Vilcanota valley for temporary wage labor rather than to the haciendas in the *alturas*. In other cases, the peons themselves arrange for the larger work groups and transport the wool and meat to previously designated locations in the *quebrada*. They use *ayni* and *mink'a* exchanges among themselves to care for hacienda and *waqcho* animals.

It is often difficult for the *hacendados* to organize the larger work groups. On some haciendas, the animals are sheared only every other year, which reduces the total yield (see Appendix 1). The annual slaughter of hacienda animals is often postponed because of labor scarcity; on occasion the meat rots when it has not been fully dried by the beginning of the rainy season.

Most peon families have resided in their *cabañas* for several generations. When haciendas are sold, the peons are implicitly included in the transfer. The peons' rent is paid in labor or in goods rather than in cash. Although peon families remain for generations, they are not bound to the land. Instead, the *hacendado* is unable to dislodge them, though he would prefer to replace them with other peons who would receive higher cash wages but own fewer animals. In particular, the ties among peons, based on kinship, common residence, and participation in work groups, make it difficult for the *hacendado* to exert strong pressure on any one of them (e.g., in expelling incompetent herders) without encountering resistance in the form of "slow-downs" or theft. Discontented herders collaborate more frequently with *abigeos* or rustlers; they receive money, other goods, and support from the rustlers. This activity is a form of what Hobsbawm calls social banditry; it serves to limit the power of the *hacendados* (Hobsbawm 1959; Orlove 1973).

Espinar

Like Canchis, the province of Espinar contains two ecological zones although they are not as sharply differentiated. Some agriculture is carried out in the rather flat lower zone, which ranges in altitude from 3900 to 4200 meters. The upper zone, from 4200 to 5200 meters, has a more rugged topography; it contains only grasslands (for a more detailed description of the ecology and history of the province, see Orlove 1974b, 1977c). The area of the province is 4418 km²; the population in 1972 was 41,523, of which 33,621, or 80.97%, was rural.

At the time of independence, most of the land was held by large Indian communities. A few church haciendas and lands retained by descendants of *curacas*[4] served as nuclei from which haciendas began to expand in the late nineteenth and early twentieth centuries. Violent peasant rebellions in 1921 (Piel 1970) and 1931 (Orlove 1974c) greatly slowed the process of hacienda expansion, and because of them, many *hacendados* left the province for years. During the decade between 1921 and 1931, the process of community fragmentation began, much as it did in Canchis. The units known as *ranchos* also formed during this period.

Like the *alturas* of Canchis, Espinar contains both haciendas and communities composed of sets of relatively autonomous production units, but they are interspersed rather than separated as in Canchis. They differ in both internal organization and external relations, although they face similar environmental constraints. The communities are unnucleated. The population is dispersed in units called *ranchos*, small settlements of three to seven households. Land, even pasture, is most frequently owned by individuals, but the lands of each rancho are contiguous, with one section in each zone. Equal inheritance of animals and land is the ideal; it is practiced in the case of animals. Upon marriage, a person chooses between the *rancho* of birth and that of the spouse, and the spouse who moves (usually the wife) renounces the right to inherit *rancho* lands for a cash settlement. The *ranchos*, then,

[4] These individuals were intermediate officials under the Inca Empire and retained a certain degree of power in some cases under the Spanish Empire (Rowe 1957).

approximate small, localized patrilineages. Spouses are selected from other *ranchos* within the community, but no regular pattern of wife exchange between different *ranchos* appears to exist. Informants consistently repeated that individuals tended to marry out of crowded *ranchos* and into relatively empty ones and that migration out of the area was more common from crowded *ranchos*. For these reasons, they said, *rancho* fragmentation never occurs. Recent census material corroborates this claim; the rate of annual increase of the rural population has averaged only 0.38% in the past 30 years (Orlove 1974b).

As in Canchis, the labor resources of an individual household are sufficient for the routine herding tasks. The larger work groups are usually formed by *ayni* partnerships within a single *rancho* or between affinally linked *ranchos*. The somewhat unegalitarian distribution of wealth also encourages the use of *mink'a* exchanges and wage labor.

Part of the land on some *ranchos* is held collectively, either by all the members of the *rancho* or by a smaller group within it, usually a group of brothers. Two systems apply to jointly held pasture land. In some cases, all members have access to the pasture at all times. Under the other system, called *watawata*, each member in turn has sole access to the land for a year. In a number of instances, members of a *rancho* share the pastureland they own as individuals with each other. They also merge their herds and rotate the daily herding duties.

As described in the previous section, Espinar is considerably drier than Canchis, and *bofedales* are scarcer. There are several techniques to alleviate the pressure on the limited dry season pasture. Of particular importance are the *qochawiña* and the *moya*. The former are shallow, man-made depressions that collect moisture and so have fresh pasture longer than other parts of the lower zone (Orlove 1977c). The latter are areas closed off by adobe fences where pasture is allowed to grow during the rainy season for use during the dry season. These measures only partly compensate for the lack of dry season pasture. Many *comuneros* rent land from the *hacendados*; they pay a monthly fee for each animal they graze on hacienda land, and the animals are allowed to graze anywhere within the hacienda.

The settlement pattern on the haciendas is similar to that found in Canchis, with a *caserío*, *cabañas*, and *astanas*, but the labor system is different. Peons receive somewhat larger salaries, but their *waqcho* herds are smaller. Unlike the peons in Canchis, the hacienda peons in Espinar are not permanent; in most cases they remain on the hacienda for 2 to 10 years, long enough to save their wages for the purchase of land and animals. Then they return to their *ranchos* of origin where they have retained membership rights. The peons tend to be drawn from the poorer stratum of *comuneros* and own relatively few animals. *Comuneros* compose the larger work groups on the haciendas. Sometimes they receive cash payments, but *hacendados* often use *mink'a* exchange to set up work teams. The details of this manipulation of reciprocal forms of labor exchange by *hacendados* are described in detail elsewhere (Orlove 1977b). Participation in hacienda work groups is often a necessary precondition to renting hacienda pasture in the dry season.

WIDER ARTICULATION AND PRODUCTION BOTTLENECKS

Though different in many respects, these two configurations of the organization of production share certain common features. The activities of the production units are strongly contained by the environment. In both cases, individuals can increase the size of their herds. In Canchis, *comuneros* and peons, as well as *hacendados*, can acquire more animals by purchasing them; they have rights to pasture within relatively large extensions of land. The markets for land and animals are more highly developed in Espinar, and herders can easily purchase both. In many cases, they begin by buying up the animals of the other members of their *ranchos*. (It is one of the ironies of *indigenista* policies that the legislation protecting peasant communities from the encroachment of haciendas has facilitated the concentration of landholding and wealth within them.) In order to meet the labor requirements of the larger herds, workers may be hired at very low wages on a yearly basis. In both provinces, when herd size exceeds certain limits, the owners encounter the same problem that the *hacendados* do: a shortage of labor, expecially for the larger work groups. The workers in effect insist on payment in land rights, whether in the form of *waqcho* grazing rights (as in Canchis) or the right to rent hacienda pasture (as in Espinar). Expansion of herds thus necessitates an expansion of landholding rather than the introduction of a more labor-intensive or capital-intensive form of stock raising. The *hacendados* in Canchis have tended to expand externally by taking over community lands; those in Espinar relied more on internal expansion by reducing *waqcho* herds. Both encountered political resistance from the herders when they tried to press expansion too far.

Within these constraints, there are several ways of altering the volume of production of wool. (Marketing strategies may raise its cash value somewhat.) Animals that are particularly strong, have good wool, or possess other valued qualities can be used for breeding, while less desired animals can be slaughtered or castrated. In addition, one species can replace another in some areas. In certain specific ecological conditions, alpacas, llamas, sheep, and cattle can all be raised well; sheep and cattle begin to suffer respiratory tract infections above 4400 and 4200 meters respectively, and alpaca wool production declines below 4100 meters. The choice of animal does not greatly alter herding practices, however, leaving the carrying capacity of the puna little changed.

Other methods do bring a change in productivity. On large haciendas, sheep production can be raised by maintaining separate herds for rams, pregnant ewes, "empty" ewes, male lambs, and female lambs. This practice permits the breeding of new lambs to be controlled and timed to coincide with the beginning of the rainy season. Productivity can also be raised by introducing certain technical improvements, such as medicine for the animals, better shearing scissors, and so forth.

The major difficulty in developing a more productive herding economy is that a number of changes need to be introduced simultaneously. Although purebred stud rams (*reproductores*) are available, herds of improved animals must be segregated from the unimproved to avoid backcrossing that would dilute the better qualities of the new animals. Improved veterinary techniques, such as the use of animal dips and the application of external medicine for skin parasites, similarly require isolation of the improved animals to avoid reinfection. Artificially sowing improved grasses has increased the carrying capacity of the puna in other parts of the sierra; this practice also requires limiting access to the improved grasses. These changes all require fencing as a necessary preliminary step.

Building fences, however, is not only a technical change; it is also a social and political one. In all the different forms of organizing production, animals of different owners are grazed together; recruiting workers to the large herding units requires granting such access. The need to form these large labor groups limits hacienda expansion. There has been considerable resistance from both peons and *comuneros* to the fencing of haciendas. *Hacendados* who attempt or plan it have great difficulty in recruiting labor. Fencing introduces a further problem, since it may end traditional right-of-way across hacienda lands between dry-season and rainy-season pastures. Creating fenced pathways across haciendas increases costs; in addition, the roads turn into impassable sloughs after rains. Since the introduction of fencing is so difficult, *hacendados* have attempted more limited measures, such as castrating the *waqcho* males and breeding the *waqcho* females with improved rams. This measure has also met with great resistance. Peons view it as part of an attempt to reduce the size of their herds. They are willing to receive free medical treatment for their *waqchos*, but *hacendados* find this additional expense too great, while the risk of contamination from other animals still remains. Hence, the only recourse open to an individual who wishes to increase total production is to take over more land; he must allow both his own animals and those of his workers to graze on it. This rearrangement of land ownership does not change the aggregate output of the herding sector.

To recapitulate this analysis: The individual herding units are self-sufficient in most cases for the daily management of their herds. There are exchanges of labor for the formation of larger work groups and, on many occasions, transfers of animals and pasture rights. The links between herd owners and the market shape their decisions about the composition of their herds by breed and species of animal raised. Marketing decisions affect production decisions relatively little, since herding techniques are similar for different species[5] and wool can be stored for long periods of time.

With a low level of technology and capital investment, the aggregate production of the herding sector changes relatively little, although it is distributed among different herd owners.[6] Two features remain problematic at this point: the inability of the *hacendados* to gain access to the political support and the capital that would allow them to fence the puna and introduce technological changes that would increase total wool production, and the ability of the communities to gain support in their efforts to retain their lands. *Hacendados* in other areas, such as Puno in the southern sierra and Junín in the central sierra, were able to overcome peon and *comunero* resistance and increase productivity. In some cases, it appears that landowners are not interested in such changes; the insatiable rapaciousness of *hacendados* and their desire to devour community lands has been a basic tenet of much Andean ethnography and historiography, but it cannot be assumed. In other areas, the *hacendados* are encouraged to take this type of action, especially where the pasture is rich (as in Canchis) or access to markets is particularly easy (as in Espinar). These questions direct attention to the articulation of the pastoral sector and other sectors in the regional society. The full treatment of this subject appears in Chapter 10, after a consideration of the other sectors in Chapters 7, 8, and 9.

[5] The requirements of cattle are somewhat different; the cows need milking during the rainy season, there is no shearing, and so forth. However, they are few in number and restricted to lower altitudes.

[6] Martinez-Alier (1973) proposes investigating agrarian history from the point of view of the *hacendado* as well as that of the peon. I would suggest including a third point of view: that of the herd animals. For a discussion of a fourth point of view, that of the grasslands, and an explanation of the lack of environmental degradation in the punas, see Orlove 1977e.

7

Local Uses of Wool in the Sicuani Region

Arequipa wool firms purchase the bulk of the wool output of the Sicuani region. They export most of it, although some is sent to textile factories in Lima and Arequipa. A certain portion of the wool remains in the area where it is made into several sorts of consumer goods. A textile mill, the *Fábrica de Tejidos Marangani*, produces woven goods. In a number of shops located in Sicuani, artisans known as *peleteros*, or furriers, make rugs, hats, slippers, and toys from the pelts of infant alpacas. The rough homespun cloth known as *bayeta* is woven for market sale in considerable volume. The second and third activities correspond to the sectors of urban and rural artisans, described in more detail in the next chapter. The textile mill is one of the few units in the Sicuani region that does not fit neatly into any sector.

This chapter discusses these three activities and the factors that influence their impact on the wool economy as a whole. An increase in local consumption of wool brings a decrease in exports. Local uses divert wool from export, reducing the volume of wool exported and altering the proportions of different grades. The competition is not as direct as might first appear. The local users require grades of wool of very low quality by international standards, the least profitable in which to deal and the most difficult of which to dispose. For instance, *bayeta* makers use pulled wools (sheared from the skins of slaughtered animals), difficult to card and spin by machine, since they are not of uniform length and contain large amounts of kemp. The furriers are not in competition with exporters but rather offer them indirect support. The furriers provide a market for infant alpaca skins and encourage the selection of certain animals to survive to a reproductive age. Exporters get the best prices for white alpaca wool, while the furriers need a full range of colors. Natural mortality among the somewhat more delicate white animals comes close to supplying the furriers' needs for that color; the intentional slaughter concentrates on animals with colored wool.

The textile factory uses medium- and low-grade sheep wool for its production. The finer wools, suitable for making worsted yarns and cloth, leave the area. Much of the cloth is sold to peasants and replaces household production. The availability of inexpensive manufactured woolen products allows the herders who specialize in cameloid herding to sell their alpaca wool and purchase goods made of sheep wool. A larger proportion of alpaca wool can thereby enter the export market.

To a certain extent, these alternate uses provide a potential cushion to price fluctuations in the export sector. Local wool prices follow export prices, as described in Chapter 4. A reduction in aggregate wool production would be a partial solution to the problem of falling prices, but it would be difficult to bring into effect. Aside from the retention of stocks of wool, slaughter would be the only efficient means (it is much easier to take a field or mine temporarily out of production than a sheep, and there is so little capital invested in wool production that it would be difficult to reduce annual output by withdrawing it). Furthermore, individual herders would have little incentive to slaughter their animals, since they would benefit from other herders' slaughtering much more than from their own. These alternative uses, then, might constitute a price-support mechanism, balancing the effects of a reduction in export prices by providing other markets in which to sell the wool.

The factors affecting this potential price-support effect are relatively complex. A fall in wool prices stimulates demand among the local artisans and in the factory by reducing their costs of production and hence enabling them to sell their products more cheaply. However, the costs of production are reduced only to the extent that the price of wool forms part of them. (The cost of wool accounts for only 55 to 70% of the cost of making an alpaca-skin rug but 75 to 90% of the cost of making a yard of *bayeta;* a reduction in wool costs reduces the costs of producing *bayeta* more sharply than those of producing rugs.) The ability of the different users of wool to expand and increase production also varies. To increase production may require capital investment and greater amounts of labor as well as larger amounts of wool. The organization of production affects the response of producers with regard to the entry of new productive units and the expansion of already existing units.

Finally, a fall in wool prices affects the demand for locally produced items as well as their potential supply. Because there is a decline in the amount of cash in the area generated by wool sales, the incomes and the purchasing power of the wool producers and middlemen fall, so that demand for agricultural products and artisan goods also falls. There is less commercial activity in general. Railroad statistics document this decline well; second and third class passengers travel less frequently and go shorter distances when they do, and the volume of traffic in goods such as low-grade sugar consumed by the peasants also falls off (The Peruvian Corporation, Ltd. 1957/58: 1,4; 1958/69: 1,4–9; 1959/60: 10; 1961/62: 1–2; 1962/63: 7; 1964/65: 10–17.) Hence total demand for these locally made wool products falls when wool prices fall, not only among the potential customers directly involved in wool production and marketing but in all economic sectors. These arguments require a more detailed presentation. Each of the alternate uses of wool will be described at greater length.

THE TEXTILE FACTORY

The *Fábrica de Tejidos Marangani* was founded in 1899 by Enrique Mejía. He was born in Arequipa and married the only daughter of one of the wealthiest *hacendado* families in the Sicuani region. The location he chose for his factory was advantageous not only in that it already belonged to his wife but also because it was located directly on the Southern Peruvian Railway in the village of Chectuyoc in the district of Marangani a few miles south of Sicuani in the Río Vilcanota valley near the village. At this site, raw materials could be brought in and finished products shipped out. It was near the prospective markets: the rural population of the Río Vilcanota valley and adjacent highlands and the densely populated *altiplano* in Puno and Bolivia. The Río Vilcanota provided a steady flow of water to run the looms and wash the wool. The adjacent communities provided a source of labor. Mejía also had the model of an earlier woolen mill to follow. *Fábrica de Tejidos Lucre* had been founded near Cuzco in 1861. It was functioning smoothly and profitably. Both the work force and the consumers were composed almost exclusively of sierra peasants.

It is difficult to determine where the initial capital came from; a good portion, if not all of it, was put up by private individuals in Cuzco and Arequipa who purchased shares. Within 20 years, members of the

Mejía family bought out the other stockholders. The factory remained a family firm until 1967.

It was fully integrated vertically. Raw wool was washed and graded in the factory. After passing through the carding and spinning sections of the plant, it was woven into cloth and blankets. The final finishing was also done in the plant. Most cloth was dyed after weaving, although the parts to be made black were dyed in the wool. The distribution of the finished products was also in Mejía hands. They owned a chain of 15 stores throughout Peru that were the exclusive distributors of the products. These stores, located primarily in the highlands, mostly carried lines of products aimed at peasants. The heavy woolens, shawls, and blankets replaced household products, often by imitating traditional patterns. Much of the woolen cloth went into making full skirts, or *polleras,* which were a standard feature of peasant women's dress. Woolen shirtings replaced *bayeta.* This market was (and continues to be) extremely loyal and stable, reducing the need for advertising and textile-designing departments. The owners have tended to follow a "high markup, low turnover sales policy" (Chaplin 1967: ix) common to many Peruvian textile plants, but the market appears to be capable of some expansion.

The factory was also integrated with the other Mejía enterprises. A portion of the wool came from the Mejía haciendas; local *hacendados* and Sicuani wool traders supplied the rest. Workers obtained food at the Mejía store, including meat and cheese from the Mejía haciendas and bread from the Mejía ovens. The prices of the goods were deducted from their wages. When the factory shifted from water to electric-powered looms in the 1920s, it was with power from the Mejía hydroelectric plant. Factory workers were sent to Mejía-owned fields at planting and harvest times.

This pattern has changed somewhat in recent years. The factory began marketing its products through independent retailers in the late 1950s. The Arequipa firms began to replace local sources of wool. They supply graded and scoured wool unlike the unclassified, greasy local wool. When the factory purchased wool directly, it had to buy a great deal of wool to get all the grades it wanted. It had to pay for wool in cash or by check. The Arequipa firms are willing to accept 30-day and 90-day letters of credit, in effect making short-term, low-interest loans to the factory, thus removing some of the strain on its limited capital. The factory now buys nearly 60% of its wool from Arequipa firms.

When Mejía's son died in 1967, no relatives were available to take it over. His widow sold it to a group of Spanish and Swiss investors who brought in new capital and expanded the weaving section. Since then, production has risen steadily. The larger volume has increased the reliance of the factory on the Arequipa firms, since the wool-washing facilities have not been expanded. The European investors also introduced a program of machinery maintenance and factory-wide planning. (Previously, each engineer attempted to cut costs in the branch of which he was in charge, which led to overall inefficiencies. The yarn that was least expensive for the head of the spinning section to produce was also the most likely to break.)

This expansion is in sharp contrast to the situation of the textile factories in Cuzco. Their production has either not increased or actually declined, and there has been little new investment. The position of the workers in the factory seems to be the crucial variable in explaining the difference.

The 320 workers in the Chectuyoc factory come from the communities adjacent to the factory; nearly all of them can walk to work. They continue to own and farm land in the irrigated portions of the Río Vilcanota valley. They form a stable labor force; a large proportion have worked for more than 10 years, and annual turnover is low. Workers are encouraged to remain because seniority confers certain advantages, particularly working on the more desirable machines. A number of workers have relatives who also work in the factory.

Since the workers own land and grow food, they are not completely dependent on their salaries. For this reason, organizing them into a strong union was more difficult than it was among the wholly urban textile-mill workers in the city of Cuzco. The latter have strong unions; they have led general strikes on several different occasions in 1931, 1946, 1955, and the early 1960s (La Verdad 25.3.31, 14.2.46; Neira 1964: 16). At times these unions have sent representatives to Marangani to organize unions there but met with little success. The isolation of the factory made it easier for the Mejía family to maintain a rather paternalistic and personal control. Workers still remember how they were invited into the owner's house once a year, at Christmas; their children would find presents under a tree.

A union was formed in 1945, about two decades after the Cuzco factories were unionized. It was one of a number of unions organized by APRA and other parties in the southern sierra and elsewhere during the Bustamante y Rivero administration from 1945 to 1948. Their one attempt at a strike for higher wages led to a lockout in 1957. (This move, although illegal under the Peruvian labor code, presented no difficulties to the owners; one of the Mejías was a provincial representative to the national legislature at the time, and the *Ministerio de Industria y Comercio* rapidly discovered that the factory had entered bankruptcy.) The union has been quiet ever since. Labor practices that have disappeared from other factories continue there, notably frequent suspension of workers and payment for piecework rather than an hourly wage.

The general manager commented in the 1968 annual report, "It bears noting that the workers' union of our company has contributed to the social peace for our industrial center."[1] This social peace does not appear to inconvenience the owners greatly; they pay their workers less than a quarter of the average national wage in wool textile factories (Sociedad Nacional de Industrias 1969). Unlike many other textile mills, this factory has not had long interruptions in production caused by strikes.

THE FURRIERS

Local artisans make a series of products from the skins of alpacas under 3 months old. They tan these skins and sew them into rugs, slippers, toy animals, hats, and coats in order of decreasing importance. The skins have very soft fur which has not yet developed the woolly quality of the fleeces of mature animals. The production of the skins is seasonal, since alpaca births are restricted to a short period. Herders sometimes store the skins rather than selling them immediately, so there is a supply of skins throughout the year.

This is an old craft in the Sicuani area, but it began to expand around 1960. What local people refer to as the *"fábrica"* was opened in that year by a man born in Arequipa. He had come to Sicuani as a trader, made money buying and selling wool, and acquired some haciendas. He hired about 20 workers and purchased seven machines for sewing the skins. At that time, there were perhaps four or five individuals who sewed skins by hand in their homes. Several practices instituted in the *fábrica* have continued to the present among the furriers.

1. The owner buys uncured skins from Sicuani wool merchants rather than sending agents to the weekly markets or buying directly from *hacendados*. The production of his own haciendas is insufficient.
2. He hires workers to tan the skins, rather than sending them to a tannery.
3. Each worker is supplied with skins and patterns and expected to cut, sew, and finish the items.

[1] "Es justo remarcar que el Sindicato de Obreros de nuestra Compañía ha contribuido a que la paz social reine en nuestro centro fabril."

4. Workers are paid by a piece rate rather than an hourly wage. The owner originally gave a weekly salary, but the workers threatened to strike for a raise. He then shifted to a piece rate.
5. Each worker is permitted to contract helpers, generally individuals unskilled in this or any other line of nonagricultural work. The worker pays the helpers out of his own wages and teaches them the trade. The helpers, with a very few exceptions, are from the communities of the Río Vilcanota valley near Sicuani; they are often children.
6. New workers are hired from among the men who have worked as helpers.

The differences between the *fábrica* owner and the small shop owners (themselves former *fábrica* workers) lie in the marketing of the products, where the *fábrica*'s larger size offers more advantages. The *fábrica* owner took the items to Lima and Cuzco to sell to the large stores which sold to the public; later he marketed them through the state-run organization, *Artesanías del Perú* (AP), which maintained a chain of stores. Most of the small shopowners could not afford to travel, but AP refused nearly all their repeated requests to market their products, preferring to deal only with a few large producers rather than many small ones. The small shopowners hope that a new state-run organization, *Empresa Peruana de Promoción Artesanal* (EPPA), and the formation of the *Dirección General de Artesanías* of the *Ministerio de Industria y Turismo* will alter this pattern, but they do not appear likely to do so.

The small shop owners sell to traveling buyers who come from Lima and Cuzco. Some of these buyers have their own stores which cater to tourists, while others sell to such stores. Some shop owners receive advance orders, but cash advances are very rare. The furriers had a cooperative, founded in 1967 by a Peace Corps volunteer. It attempted to purchase products and market them in the cities, avoiding one level of intermediary. Other Peace Corps volunteers in Cuzco set up a store on the main square with a large sign in English announcing it as "The Coop Shop." It sold the products of a number of craft cooperatives in the southern highlands. The director of the store was a Sicuani furrier. When he was asked to account for S/100,000 missing from the account of The Coop Shop and claimed to be unable to locate any financial records, the Sicuani cooperative could not meet its own debts to its members and collapsed.

The division of labor in the furrier trade ensures that each worker knows all aspects of production except tanning. Tanning has a worker–helper and piece-rate system identical in structure to that of the furriers. The capital needed to open a shop has generally been low. Aside from the skins, which were fairly inexpensive, the only necessary investment is a special fur-sewing machine. These are manufactured in New York and could be ordered through the Singer agent in Sicuani for S/20,000, but inflation and new import restrictions raised the price in 1973 to S/40,000. The *Banco Industrial del Perú,* a state bank, has granted loans to many workers, enabling them to buy these machines and open their own shops. They often hired former helpers as workers. The number of shops has greatly increased; there were 80 in 1973, and new ones were still being opened.

Most shops are located in Sicuani, which has electricity to operate the sewing machines. A few shops that rely on foot-pedal machines or hand sewing are located in the communities adjacent to Sicuani, particularly San Felipe. In the past few years, some shops have sprung up in Puno, Juliaca, and Cuzco, but Sicuani is still the main center. It is close to supplies of skins, water for tanning, sources of cheap labor, and markets. The other towns have not yet presented serious competition, since the market is still expanding rapidly enough to absorb all the production.

There is variation among Sicuani shops in size and technique. Some are very small and still have not shifted from hand sewing to machine sewing. In some of them, the furriers do not work full time. The largest shops, though, have only three sewing machines. The largest work force is around a dozen, with 10 or so furriers and two or three tanners. There do not seem to be economies of scale beyond this point. The most successful shop owners invest their money elsewhere, often in commercial ventures such as hardware and stationery stores.

The furriers resemble the other urban artisans described in Chapter 8 in a number of characteristics, notably the shop organization and the worker–helper relation (Orlove 1974d: 196–199). One factor differentiating the furriers from other artisans in the marketing system is that the furrier does not sell directly or through a local intermediary; he sells through an intermediary from another city. He makes his products for a luxury market, rather than a market composed of a large number of individuals who regularly make purchases from him. (The demand for these items in the early twentieth century was small. Like the market for the hand-woven rugs that are still occasionally found, it consisted of town dwellers and *hacendados* wealthy enough to have a house of more than two rooms who wanted some decoration in the principal room.) Particularly for the rugs, the large items on which high profits are made, this market is composed largely of tourists, national and foreign. The local residents purchase the cheaper, more labor intensive items such

FIGURE 13. This woman is the wife of the owner of a medium-sized furrier shop in Sicuani. Note the partially sewn rug on the table and the pieces of patterns hanging on the wall. [Photograph by Laurel Nadel.]

as toy alpacas, small mats, and slippers. Lower profits are made on these, but tourists make up a large part of the market even for these items.

BAYETA

The province of Espinar and the southern part of the province of Canas form one of the principal *bayeta*-producing areas in the department of Cuzco. As with the ponchos and blankets woven here and elsewhere in the region, a good deal of the cloth is used for home consumption, but there is also considerable trade of *bayeta* to other areas. The gradual increase in the cash income of agricultural peasants in the irrigated river valleys as food prices in the cities and elsewhere rise has led many of them not to shift to manufactured clothes but to wear better traditional ones and to make them more frequently, of cloth increasingly obtained through cash purchase rather than barter. Owners of herds purchase *bayeta* more rather than weaving their own. There is also a considerable market for *bayeta* among sierra town dwellers.

Many *bayeta* weavers do not rely on the wool production of their own sheep (alpaca *bayeta* is not entirely unknown but quite rare); instead they purchase sheep hides from the petty traders at the weekly markets and shear them. The *bayeta* weavers do not purchase sheep hides directly from the peasants who sell them to the petty traders. Selling the shorn hides and the *bayeta*, they recover their initial investment and make some additional money. *Bayeta* making is an activity of the poorer peasants and herders who have less land, fewer animals, more time to dedicate to the craft, and a greater need for supplementary income. The more prosperous herders produce a larger share of the total wool output and a smaller share of the *bayeta*. The poorer herder's wool production is often insufficient for his *bayeta*. Chapter 8 discusses the prevalence in other trades of this pattern in which rural artisans are drawn from the poorer segments of the rural population but continue to engage in agriculture and pastoralism as well.

Unlike the textiles from the factory and the products of the furrier shops, *bayeta* is produced within kin groups. This pattern is also common among other rural artisans. One or two members of the household weave, although others may aid in the spinning. Frequently, older people weave the *bayeta* and give it to their younger relatives to sell. They are not paid directly in return but are supported as members of the household.

The residents of Hercca, a community near Sicuani, have specialized in buying and transporting *bayeta* from the main production areas in Espinar and Canas. They purchase it in the weekly markets and take it to Hercca. There they dye it with commercial aniline dyes and sell both the dyed and the natural at fairs and in markets throughout the area. They transport the *bayeta* throughout the department of Cuzco and to adjacent departments as well.

In a few cases, the organization of *bayeta* production is different. In the community of Huancané Bajo in Espinar, there are a number of

FIGURE 14. Bayeta is frequently made from pulled wool, or wool shorn from hides rather than from animals. The men in this photograph, taken in Lampa Chico, province of Chucuito, department of Puno, are using the lids of cans for knives; this practice is also common in the Sicuani region. [Photograph by Barbara Cody.]

peasants involved in the wool trade; a few have small stores. They buy wool at the weekly markets and from customers in their stores; some travel through the puna buying directly from the producers. They sell most of their wool to large buyers who attend the principal weekly markets (Orlove 1977b).

Many of these wool traders are involved in the *bayeta* trade. They are referred to as *bayeteros*. They turn the wool over to weavers who make the *bayeta* which they sell to the Hercca traders who come to Yauri every Sunday. In all cases, the weavers own their own spindles and looms; these tools cost at most S/300.

There are a variety of relationships between the *bayeteros* and the weavers. In some cases, it is simply one of employer and workers, with wages paid for piecework. The weaver is paid by the *vara*, the rate depending on the complexity of the weave. They receive between S/15 and S/50 a day, S/20 to S/30 being the most common wages. In other cases, *bayeteros* give raw wool to relatives, especially older ones living in other households. Payment is in cash and goods, usually foodstuffs and wool, and is not a direct piece rate. In still other cases, members of the *bayetero's* household work; he gives wool to his wife and children to spin and weave.

There are sometimes two stages in the division of labor. When skins are bought instead of wool, the *bayetero* must have them shorn. In some cases, the person weaving the *bayeta* will shear and spin. In other cases, an individual is hired only to shear the hides and spin the yarn. He stays in the *bayetero's* house and is given meals and coca leaf. He receives S/5 per hide, although hides differ considerably in weight. In other cases, members of the *bayetero's* household shear and spin, and the spun wool is then given to the weavers paid at a piece rate. Payment here is also indirect; the members of the household are supported by the *bayetero*.

COMPARISONS

These three forms of wool use are affected differently by falling wool prices. In the case of the textile mill, the price of wool varies from 40 to 55% of the costs of production, according to the annual reports. A fall in wool prices hence reduces the costs of production and production can be expanded somewhat. Since the workers are paid at a piece rate, it is possible to increase the number of man-hours worked without having to pay overtime or social overhead costs for new workers. The owners can raise production by refusing to grant the workers customary leaves of absence. There is a certain amount of unused capacity on the machines, so that production could be raised perhaps 30 to 40% without new major capital investment.

Falling wool prices would reduce local demand, since the peasants and herders who form a large part of the market would receive lower incomes. However, the factory could tap other markets. The production of mens' suitings appropriate for urban dwellers could be increased, and the proportion of the total production sold in Lima, currently around 10%, could grow. It would also be possible to increase smuggling to Bolivia, since the market in that country would not necessarily be affected by falling wool prices in Peru. About 30% of the production makes its way into Bolivia without paying duties, as the sales manager of the factory cheerfully admits and the market distribution pattern confirms; that country could absorb more. The factory has little direct competition, particularly for its yard goods and shawls. Unlike the other producers, it could retain its higher prices while costs fall, and take a larger profit.

The price of wool is about 55 to 70% of the costs of production of the furriers. Falling wool prices would reduce their costs of production. Production could increase in the shops; in this case as well, the payment at a piece rate makes it easy to obtain more labor from the workers. New units might also be opened; the smaller shops relying on hand sewing could proliferate, and the wealthier furriers could reinvest their capital in other shops rather than opening other stores. The organization of production assures that the existence of skilled workers is not a limiting factor.

However, the price of baby alpaca skins and the price of wool are only partly related. Skin prices tend to follow wool prices, so a fall in wool prices tends to lower skin prices, but this tendency varies in degree. The demand for the production of the furriers is relatively independent of wool prices, except in the case of a global economic depression, which would reduce tourism. The furriers have a world monopoly on alpaca-skin rugs. However, the market for such craft items is unstable. EPPA plans to expand advertising and marketing overseas, taking advantage of this monopoly. It could result in increased production in Sicuani. However, previous attempts by Peace Corps volunteers and AP to increase the sales of the items abroad have failed.

The price of wool forms about 75 to 90% of the costs of *bayeta* production. Falling wool prices would reduce these costs sharply. There are also few obstacles to increasing production. New units could enter

TABLE 1

Estimates for Wool Use in the Sicuani Region, 1972

Local production	
Sheep	1,460,000
Cameloid	1,343,000
Total	2,803,000
Local use	
Textile mill	
Total wool	750,000
Local wool	180,000
Arequipa wool	570,000
Bayeta	95,000
Furriers	17,000
Total local use of local wool	292,000 = 10.4% of total production

Sources: Textile mill figures from annual reports of the Fábrica de Tejidos Maranganí. Production figures from Sección de Lanas, Banco de la Nación, Sicuani. Bayeta figures include other domestic uses, especially the weaving of ponchos and blankets.

Note: Values expressed in pounds.

production as household producers shift from home to market production. Already existing units could expand by drawing more heavily on the labor resources of the household. With the large number of small units of production, the selling price of *bayeta* would quickly fall in line with wool prices. The demand for bayeta, however, would also drop among peasant consumers. The urban demand would remain steadier but could not take up much of the slack.

These alternative uses of wool have a limited ability to absorb local wool when demand in export markets falls and prices drop (see Table 1). The *bayeta* weavers would have the greatest reduction in cost but also suffer the greatest decrease in demand. To a lesser extent, this is the same problem with the other two uses: The fall in demand limits the ability to expand production. The solution would be to market more of the products outside the region, particularly in the case of the textile mill.

These alternate uses do absorb a certain amount of wool, particularly of the lower grades. It is difficult to purchase pulled wool in Sicuani for stuffing mattresses; it is all woven into *bayeta,* even when wool prices are low. However, these alternate uses offer little help to the alpaca herders. They hold their wool in the form of stocks until prices rise. The reports of the informants who state that they do this are confirmed by the records of both the Southern Peruvian Railway and the wool companies which show a greater movement of alpaca wool following price increases than could be accounted for by shearing alone.

These alternate uses of wool, then, compete relatively little with the export economy. They also offer little by way of counterbalancing the rather severe effects of a drop in wool prices.

8
Agriculture and Artisans

This chapter is the third of three focusing on production. The units examined in the last two chapters were directly involved with the production and processing of wool; this chapter investigates peasants, agricultural haciendas, and artisans who work with materials other than wool. It shows that the growth of the wool export economy has transformed these sectors as thoroughly as it has the sectors described in the preceding two chapters. The sectorial model is used to examine both the internal organization of each sector and its articulation with the social and economic system of which it forms part. In this case, the changes in relations between the herders and the external markets that purchase their wool have also altered the ties linking the herders with other economic sectors in the Sicuani region, notably the peasants and the artisans. These shifts among the joint production, barter, and cash modes of articulation in turn have affected the relations between these sectors. It is important to note the parallelisms and divergences in the paths of development of the agriculture and artisan sectors, since they are involved in different sorts of productive activities and operate under different ecological and technological constraints. National policy has affected the peasants profoundly and the artisans only minimally. The comparison and contrast between them is useful, then, since the modes of articulation with the wool-producing sector have changed in a similar fashion but operate on groups with different patterns of internal organization and external constraints.

AGRICULTURE

Environmental Constraints

The climatological and geological factors described in Chapter 6 affect agriculture as well as herding. These factors require some additional elaboration, because domesticated plants have different and, in general, narrower ranges of tolerance than animals. Animals can be moved to compensate for the rigorous climate, but plants cannot. The length of the growing season is an important variable in agriculture. As in the case of herding, the importance of these environmental constraints on the organization of production lies in the timing of the inputs of human labor and the structure of capital investment. Seasonal variations in labor requirements in agriculture are, of course, much greater than they are in herding. Almost all anthropological writing on agriculture in the Andes and elsewhere has focused on what can be called absolute timing—the placing of different agricultural tasks (planting barley, weeding maize, preparing *chuño,* threshing *tarwi,* and so forth) with respect to the calendar. The emphasis in this section is on what can be called relative timing—the sequence of the tasks, the length of period required to perform them, the intervals between them, and the extent to which they are confined to broad or narrow limits. The sequence may be pushed forward by early rains or threats of early frosts, or held back by the lateness of these factors. The absolute timing reported in most ethnographies covers the total range of time when any task may have been carried out in a period of a number of years. For this reason, such studies imply that this period is greater than is actually the case for any given year. The variation is not only over time but also over space; the sequence may begin at different moments in places relatively close to one another. This latter variation does not occur in herding. Capital investment will be treated as in previous chapters, concentrating on the marginal productivity of capital in individual production units and in the sector as a whole.

The principal limiting factors affecting the timing and location of agriculture are rainfall and frost. These two are related, as indicated earlier, since the lack of cloud cover during dry spells encourages heat loss from radiation, and hence heavier frosts occur. In the Sicuani area, rainfall decreases as one moves southwest, away from the tropical

FIGURE 15. Many of the agricultural tools in the Sicuani region are quite simple. These two men are using the *chakitaklla,* or footplow; they thrust down with their feet and pull back on the handle to turn the soil. The *ayllachu* or mattock in the lower left is used for harvesting potatoes, stripping bark off wood, and a variety of other purposes. Both tools have metal blades hafted to wood by sinews or leather straps.

forest. It also decreases somewhat as one moves south from the areas of heavier rainfall closer to the moist *páramo* of northern Peru to the drier zones in the south. The occurrence of frosts depends on altitude: Nocturnal heat loss is greater where the air is thinner. Finally, annual variation in day length increases with distance from the equator; the further south one moves, the greater the available energy from the sun, or insolation, during the rainy season and the greater the risk of frost during the dry season. Since the major rivers in the area flow north and northwest, the slower rates of maturation at higher altitudes in the upper sections of valleys are compensated for by greater insolation during the growing season. However, the risk of frost during the dry season is reinforced. These factors increase rather than decrease the length of the area in the river valleys where any particular crop may be grown (Gade 1975).

Finally, a number of local factors affect the distribution of rainfall and frost. These different microclimates can vary over distances as small as a few dozen meters; for instance, cold air sinks because it is heavier, and valley floors often have more severe frosts than adjacent slopes that are slightly higher (Peattie 1936: 79–106). Some mountains have localized rain shadows. The west side of a valley, warmed by the early morning sun, has less severe frosts than the east side. Local factors combine in a number of different ways.

Agriculture is different from herding in that there are several techniques involving large groups of productive units that mitigate the effects of these limiting environmental factors (Orlove 1977c). Irrigation is the most important of these. Water is diverted from streams and *bofedales* and led to pass through a series of large channels feeding into smaller ones that finally take it to individual fields. Local geological conditions favor the formation and maintenance of a number of small, independent irrigation systems. The Río Vilcanota valley is a particularly striking case. It was deepened by glacial action during the Pleistocene, and many aquiferous strata were exposed. There are a number of sources of water from these and from the numerous tributary streams. Since the valley is narrow, no part is very far from a water source. The irrigation canals are nearly all earth faced and need a certain degree of maintenance, since a relatively high slope produces erosion of the sides and a lower slope causes silting. Reeds and grasses clot the canals and need to be cleared. These tasks are handled by groups of a few communities or small groups of households. Irrigation is especially important for maize cultivation, since prolonged drought during the growing season sharply reduces yields. Maize is raised on unirrigated land in Canchis, but only in a small number of cases.

Stone-faced terracing is a second technique. Some terraces are being maintained; small additions are made on a few. The original terrace systems were used with irrigation, but even without it, productivity is raised. It appears that fertile alluvial soils were brought to fill the terraces. Terraces also have higher soil temperatures favoring more rapid germination and plant development. In general, the edaphic processes of terrace agriculture are poorly understood; no work comparable to that on southeast Asian wet-rice terraces (Geertz 1963b) exists for Andean terraces.

In contrast to the local herders who raise a small number of animal species with a few breeds of each, agriculturalists cultivate a large number of plant species and varieties. There are a dozen staple crops and many more raised as condiments and fodder. Some major crops, such as potatoes and maize, have over 20 varieties (Gade 1975). Each variety has somewhat different tolerances for soil nutrients, moisture, temperature, and insolation. Thus a wide variety of microenvironments can be used. In addition, the growth cycle of each crop and variety is somewhat different, permitting the labor input to be staggered over a period of time rather than being concentrated in a short one. In the annual cycle, some tasks are more restricted in time than others.

Initial preparation of the fields, particularly breaking the soil and clearing the vegetation which has formed over several years of fallow, can take place at any time during the dry season. In this instance, the peasants benefit from the relatively dry cold climate. In the moister, warmer sierra of northern Peru, clearing such scrub, or *monte*, is a more difficult task (Brush 1977). The final preparation of the field and the digging and plowing of furrows are performed immediately before planting or in direct conjunction with it. Planting takes place at the end of the dry season or at the beginning of the rainy season. Moisture, whether from irrigation or rain, must be sufficient to insure germination; the risk of frost (with respect to frequency, intensity, and duration) must be below a certain minimum to avoid killing a large proportion of the young plants. Informants state that *aporque* (*hallmay* in Quechua), or hilling up earth from the furrows to the mounds between them, should be performed for all crops. It is most important for tubers, maize, and broad beans and is sometimes entirely dispensed with for grains and some legumes. It is usually carried out once or twice during the growing season; like weeding, which is often done at the same time, it is not narrowly restricted to any particular moment. Harvesting should take place when the crops are mature but before losses set in. Again, these vary by species and variety; pea pods will split open and the entire crop will be lost, but potatoes can be left longer in the ground. Harvesting generally takes place over a relatively short period; the preparation of crops for storage (threshing and winnowing grains and legumes, husking maize for sun drying) usually has slightly less narrow limits, although freeze drying the tubers must take place in the early part of the dry season when the frosts are most intense.

The vast majority of the peasants in the Sicuani area plant several different crops and varieties each year. This diversity serves as a form of insurance; conditions that reduce the yield of one crop do not harm another. Sudden frosts that would kill small maize plants leave broad beans unaffected; heavy rains could rot potatoes without damaging barley. Another consequence of this practice, the spreading of labor requirements over a longer period, will be examined in more detail in the next section.

This description applies generally to all cultivation in the Sicuani area. However, one can distinguish among three distinct sorts of agricultural land. The first is the *bolsones,* or isolated patches of alluvial soil that are not contiguous with the valleys along the major rivers. There are some *bolsones* in the provinces of Canchis and Chumbivilcas, but they comprise a small fraction of the total cultivated area. In other parts of the sierra, such as the northern part of the department of Apurimac, such *bolsones* dominate, and long stretches of alluvial soil are not present. The other two types of land are more important. The second consists of flat stretches of alluvial soil lying along the Río Vilcanota and its tributaries. These soils are alluvial in origin and quite rich (ONERN 1969: 311–326). Both the richness of the soil and the availability of irrigation water facilitate continuous cultivation without fallowing. In similar land to the northwest of Sicuani around Andahuaylillas in the province of Quispicanchis, there is extensive double cropping; the risk of frost in the Sicuani area prevents this practice. Both planting and harvesting take place somewhat earlier to the northwest than to the southeast, for reasons outlined above; the delay is about two or three weeks from Checacupe to Marangani.

The third sort of land is composed of rolling grasslands and slopes, corresponding closely to what Custred calls the "lower puna" (Custred 1973). These soils tend to be not as rich (ONERN 1969: 310). Planting takes place with moisture from rainfall. The soil tends to lose much of its fertility after several years of continuous planting, so that fallowing is necessary to restore the nutrients. A thick sod cover forms. In some areas the *ichu* bunch grass returns. These lands also differ in the time of year when they are brought into cultivation, although the sequence is not as orderly as the slow progression up the Río Vilcanota valley.

Much of the land is farmed under the system of *laymi.* All *laymi* systems are found on lands belonging to individual communities. The *laymi* are sections into which the agricultural lands of a community are divided. They average between 50 and 250 hectares in area. Each one is sub-divided into a number of smaller, individually owned plots of land. Both the *laymi* and the plots have boundaries, but they are not fenced.

The *laymi* sections in a *laymi* system go through the same sequence of

FIGURE 16. There is a sharp contrast between the flat stretches of alluvial soils lying along the Río Vilcanota and the adjacent slopes. The rich soils and irrigation water permit continuous cultivation without fallowing. Different crops are planted in adjacent fields, unlike the *laymi* pattern which is practiced in the puna. [Photograph by Laurel Nadel.]

planting and fallowing. In a given year, all the plots in each *laymi* are either uniformly planted with the same crops or left fallow. For example, a community with a six-*laymi* system might have one *laymi* planted entirely with potatoes, a second sown with barley, and the remaining four fallow. The plots within the *laymi* are privately owned by individual peasants. During fallow periods, however, pasture rights are open to all community members. In the next year, barley would be sown in the *laymi* where potatoes were grown the previous year. The *laymi* where barley grew would then lie fallow, and the *laymi* which had been lying fallow longest would be plowed and planted with potatoes. The rotation would continue until, in the seventh year, the first *laymi* is again planted in potatoes. Ideally, the members of each household own at least one plot of land in each *laymi*, so that they have access to both crops every year. In some communities, there are two *laymi* systems in different areas. The particular sequence of crops and fallowing varies from community to community and between systems with two sys-

FIGURE 17. These terraced fields in the district of Tungasuca, province of Canas, are part of a *laymi* system. The lighter fields are planted in barley; the darker ones in the foreground are in fallow. Each plot of land is privately owned. The Río Apurimac can be seen in the lower left; the village of Surimana is near the right edge of the photograph. See also Figures 6 and 21.

tems. Several general characteristics were found in a study of 23 *laymi* systems (Custred and Orlove 1974). Potatoes are always the first crop planted when a *laymi* section is cultivated after laying fallow. Maize is never planted in *laymi* systems. Variation in the number of years that each *laymi* section lies fallow takes place only in systems with more than eight sections.

These *laymi* systems serve a variety of ends. By locating all the fields that are planted at any one time next to each other, they minimize the boundary of cultivated land and make it easier to keep animals out of the fields. They reduce damage to root crops from nematodes. Finally, they permit the coordination of decisions with regard to the timing of agricultural tasks by permitting older and more experienced peasants to suggest by example to others when to do such work.

Organization of Production

This section examines the social organization of production in the context of the material factors just described. As in the case of herding, access to labor is more complex than access to land, though the two are closely related. Capital investments are also more important.

All agricultural land is privately owned. Except for a few haciendas belonging to parishes and smaller plots attached to saints in churches, it is owned by individuals. The consequences of the agrarian reform law in the region are described in Chapter 10. Land is inherited partibly and bilaterally. It can be rented, bought, and sold, although there are some restrictions on the sale of land belonging to a *comunero*.

As in pastoral production, haciendas and communities may be distinguished in agricultural production. They are also composed of a number of relatively autonomous production units. There is considerable ambiguity in the use of these terms, since some communities have official recognition and others do not. The term *community* will be used to indicate the local terms *comunidad, parcialidad,* and *ayllu,* and *hacienda* will be used for *hacienda, quinta, fundo,* and *propiedad.* A number of individuals do not fit the standard ethnographic descriptions of these two institutions. Some *hacendados* are registered as community members, for instance, and others have less land than the wealthiest *comuneros.* Some *comuneros* belong to more than one community.

The two institutions may be distinguished, however, since haciendas usually consist of one block of land and holdings in communities tend to be fragmented. In the *quebradas, hacendados* do not participate in the *faena* work teams that maintain irrigation canals, and in the puna they plant as they wish, violating local *laymi* systems. The agricultural haciendas in the area, like the pastoral ones, are quite small by the standards found elsewhere in Peru and Latin America. There are only three haciendas larger than 180 hectares in the Río Vilcanota valley in the Sicuani region.

As in the pastoral sectors, there is inequality of wealth among *comuneros,* and peasants use some of the same mechanisms to obtain access to land and labor. One can distinguish among *comunero* households on the criterion of size. In some, the labor power of the members of the household is sufficient to work the land, and in others it is inadequate. Households that rely on *ayni* might be included under the former category, since this form of labor exchange operates on a basis of direct equivalence. This category includes tiny plots of land, under one-tenth of one hectare, which continue to be profitable. The labor necessary to work a field, roughly proportional to its area, can be concentrated in a few days of the year. Very small herds, by contrast, are not profitable; a shepherd must watch his flock every day whether it contains 100 animals or 10. Small herds are also more likely than larger ones to be eliminated entirely by natural disasters such as heavy snows or epidemics; small fields do not carry a corresponding risk. The upper limit of this category is about 1.5 hectares in the valley and 6 hectares in the lower puna, depending on the nature of the crops and the stage in the development cycle of the family (Chayanov 1966; Sahlins 1972).

An individual who owns more land than he can farm with the help of the members of his household may use a variety of forms to compensate for this deficit. The *mink'a* described in Chapter 6 is one; in the case of agricultural work, it is usual for payment to be in agricultural goods. The use of wage labor is usually included under the guise of *mink'a*, although landless migrant workers from Puno occasionally come through the area and receive piecework payment. Sharecropping (*a medias* or *waki*) is also found. An individual works a field that belongs to someone else and the two split the harvest. In different cases, the owner and the workers provide different proportions of the seed and tools. Although initial sharecropping agreements are made on a yearly basis, they tend to become deeply entrenched. In several instances, they have lasted for at least three generations. Rental is still another form of gaining access to land, in which an individual grants another the right to work a piece of land in return for a sum of money. Peonage on agricultural land is quite similar to the peon–*waqcho* system on pastoral estates in Canchis outlined in Chapter 6. The peon families live on the hacienda or the holdings of the wealthy *comunero*. They receive specified tracts of land, theirs to work on their own. They are expected to work for the landowner; a number of sources list the number of days per year (commonly 180), the tasks required, including work in the fields, transport of goods to market, domestic service, and so forth. These vary greatly from landholding to landholding, however, and the specific arrangements are not treated as legalistically as the ethnography indicates (Orlove 1975).

To examine these different patterns of labor relations, a rough continuum can be established,[1] according to the portion of the harvest

---

[1] I am omitting the Puno migrant laborers from this discussion, since they are few in number. The payment on a piece rate basis for agricultural labor is also quite uncharacteristic.

retained by the landowner and the portion received by the workers. In *mink'a*, the owner retains 70–85% of the harvest and the workers receive 15–30%. The shares under peonage are roughly proportional to the size of the fields controlled by each; it can vary from 10–50% for the workers and 50–90% for the *hacendado*. Each party ideally receives 50% in sharecropping arrangements, although the worker may contrive to withhold slightly more. In rental, the workers keep the entire harvest but give the owner 10–15% of its value, in effect retaining 85–90%. This continuum also corresponds to the control the two parties have over what crops are planted and the permanence of the relationship. As in the pastoral haciendas in Canchis, it is difficult to dislodge peons and renters. A worker's residence on a piece of land he works confers a certain degree of legitimacy on his presence that is not associated with pastoral herding.

These different arrangements are found in a variety of combinations. Larger units usually cannot work all their land in ways most profitable to the owner; they frequently mix peonage and *mink'a* with sharecropping, rental, or both. The smaller units are not self-sufficient but rely on arrangements with large landowners for additional income. In a number of such cases, the parcels are so tiny that the individuals who own them derive only a small portion of their livelihood from them.

In contrast to the pastoral situation, technological innovations and capital can be introduced piecemeal in agriculture. Horticulturists have investigated the plants domesticated in the Andes much more thoroughly than veterinarians have investigated the animals, and the amount of technological improvement is correspondingly greater. Many seeds of new varieties of crops can be purchased annually and planted without the problem of back-hybridization with unimproved varieties. Fertilizer and insecticide can be used by individual production units. Fertilizer in particular permits a more intensive use of the land by shortening the necessary fallow cycle in the puna.

Articulation with Pastoral Sectors

The environmental constraints imposed on agriculture in the Sicuani area permit several different forms of organization of production and labor, as described in the last two sections. The linkages between the agricultural and pastoral sectors also exhibit variation within the general system of constraints; they are connected by the joint production, barter, and cash modes of articulation.

The joint production mode, described in Chapter 1, is used by some herders who are also part-time agriculturalists, working fields in the lower punas near their pastures. Some herders in the punas in the northern part of the province of Canas have fields in the irrigated bottom lands of the Río Vilcanota valley near Combapata; this case and a similar one in the northern part of the province of Chumbivilcas are the only examples of the "vertical archipelago" pattern common elsewhere in the Andes (Brush 1976a, 1976b; Burchard 1972; Murra 1964, 1967, 1968, 1970, 1972). The lack of this pattern may be associated with the infrequency of *bolsones*. It is more common for fields and pasture to be adjacent and for fallow fields to be used for grazing. The different timing of the labor requirements of herd animals and crops permit this dual production strategy to be used (Rhoades and Thompson 1975). One member of the household, often a child, is left with the herds while the others work the fields. In some instances, the agricultural and pastoral tasks may be combined, as in freeze-drying tubers and meat to make *chuño* and *charki*.

The barter mode is used in the exchange of animal products for agricultural foodstuffs. This pattern has recently received a great deal of attention from anthropologists interested in the cultural patterns in the use of vertical ecological zonation in the Andes. There are several good studies of this topic (Custred 1973; Flores 1968; Mayer 1971), and the activities they describe for other parts of Peru are found in the Sicuani area as well. Goods are carried by the herders on llamas or donkeys. (In the Sicuani area, these journeys are now also made by railroad and truck; it is still the puna herder who travels.) Individual families of herders maintain trading partnerships with agricultural families. These ties often last as long as several decades. On occasion, the herders schedule their trips to arrive in the agricultural areas at harvest time; they help with harvesting, guaranteeing themselves a share of it. As described in Chapter 3, the rates of barter exchange show both short- and long-term fluctuation corresponding to supply and demand and to prices in the cash market.

The cash mode is established through marketing. The history and organization of the annual fairs and weekly markets that occur throughout the area are described in Chapter 9. Traveling buyers attend these events and purchase the products of the agricultural peasants and the *hacendados* alike. The produce is bulked in Sicuani and redistributed to the markets in the puna.

The connections between the herder and the agriculturalist are immediately evident in the first two instances, but not in the third. It could be suggested that both wool and foodstuffs enter a much wider economic system and do not interact directly. There are several sorts of evidence to justify the claim that the agricultural produce of the Río

Vilcanota valley and nearby lower puna zones goes primarily to a market of wool-producing herders.

The timing and location of markets support the hypothesis that these herders are the principal consumers of agricultural products. The main market in Sicuani meets every Saturday and Sunday. It draws several thousand peasants and hundreds of retailers and wholesalers who deal in foodstuffs. The largest portion of what is bought on Saturday is shipped by truck to Yauri, where there is a market every Sunday. Yauri is the center of a circuit of markets taking place on different weekdays in the province of Espinar. The Sunday produce goes to Juliaca, where the large Monday market draws on other Sunday markets as well. Some of the produce is shipped from Juliaca to Arequipa, but the bulk of it appears to be distributed through a set of smaller markets to the rest of the *altiplano* in the department of Puno (Appleby 1976a, 1976b). Both Espinar and the *altiplano*, as well as the smaller markets in the provinces of Canas and Melgar served directly from Sicuani, are puna grasslands where wool provides the major source of cash. Urban populations in these areas are low. The conclusion is that the major portion of the foodstuffs are sold to herders deriving their cash income from wool sales.

Movements in the prices of wool and agricultural foodstuffs also indicate this connection. The annual reports of the traffic department of the Southern Peruvian Railway, cited in Chapter 7, refer to the connection between rising wool prices and both greater volume and higher prices of foodstuffs sold in the markets. Urban newspapers carried reports from correspondents in puna towns that describe how the amount of agricultural produce brought to the marketplace falls when wool prices decline. A long article on Ayaviri was only one such case (El Sol [Cuzco] 19.9.31).

To reiterate a point made earlier, the difference between barter and market sale is that the social organization is different, since there are generally intermediaries in the latter but not in the former. They form a unitary economy rather than a dual one. These three modes of articulation between herders and agriculturalists represent different strategies on the part of both sets of actors, since individuals consciously choose among a set of perceived alternatives. The expansion of the wool export economy led to a series of shifts in the constraints on these actors that altered the proportion of different strategies and modes of articulation. There was a change from joint production and barter to barter and cash. An examination of the relative ease or difficulty of switching from one mode to another follows.

The shift from the joint production has the greatest permanence. In particular, an agriculturalist whose herd is becoming so small that it is difficult to maintain may choose to leave herding altogether or retain only a pair of oxen for plowing. Small herds, under 10 animals, are more likely to be eliminated by natural disasters such as heavy snow or epidemics. In addition, small herds waste labor, since at least one individual must spend time herding them.

It is quite simple for both pastoralists and agriculturalists to shift between the barter and cash modes of articulation. This is favored by an unusual characteristic of the Sicuani region: Cash crops are the same as the traditional crops consumed locally. A peasant living in the Río Vilcanota valley does not have to decide at planting time or even at harvest whether he wants to sell his broad beans or maize for cash, eat them, or trade them for puna products. The puna products can be preserved and stored. A herder can gather from conversations what market conditions are like, choosing to retain his products, sell them for cash, or barter them in agricultural areas. Prices are a major theme of discussion. In both cases, production can be divided between the two modes. This choice is made explicitly and consciously (Concha Contreras 1971: 54).

Changes in Internal Organization

The internal organization of the agricultural sector has been affected by external ties as well as by shifting modes of articulation with the expanding wool-producing sector. For reasons that are explained in more detail in Chapter 10, local branches of state agencies have worked with peasants more than with herders. Government policy has played a major role in the recent changes in agrarian social organization. These external constraints interact with local constraints in complex ways and have greater or lesser relative importance in different situations.

For instance, the splitting of communities was stimulated by the increasing willingness of state agencies to grant official recognition to these communities. The state agencies did more than merely ratify splits that had already taken place; they hastened the process. Groups that were tending to separate could focus on government-supported projects such as schools and cooperatives (Orlove and Custred 1974: 33–35, Orlove 1975). Splitting also has its roots in the shift in modes of articulation and the diminished importance of joint production. The interweaving of influences may be quite complex and operate in a manner unforeseen by the actors.

To take only one example of what is more fully discussed in Chapters 10 and 11, the *Servicio Forestal* of the *Ministerio de Agricultura*, through

FIGURE 18. Although large communities have split, the new communities still cooperate on certain occasions. This group of *comuneros* engaged in *faena* labor (see p. 127) are from the communities of Trapiche, Uscupata, and Pumaorcco, all of which were parts of the original community of Sencca. Each of the communities has a schoolhouse where the first two or three grades of primary school are taught; they are cooperating to enlarge the schoolhouse in Trapiche so that children from all three communities can attend fourth and fifth grades there. Note the man playing the conch shell horn, or *phututu*. [Photograph by Mark Curchack.]

its reforestation programs, was particularly important in an ecological aspect of the splitting of communities. Government officials could write reports referring to a satisfyingly large number of eucalyptus seedlings planted. The lack of access to animals might have proven serious to agriculturalists now cut off from them, since they had depended on dung for fuel and fertilizer, but the introduction of the eucalyptus in the agricultural zones compensated somewhat for this loss, since the rapidly growing tree provided twigs and branches for fuel, and its ashes served as fertilizer. (The species that predominates, *Eucalyptus globulus*, sends up new shoots after it is cut down and hence does not require replanting. In a real sense it is harvested rather than logged.)

A second change, the decline of the agricultural haciendas, was caused by a complex set of factors. With the growth of the cash mode of articulation, *hacendados* and peasants competed for labor, land, and water to produce marketable foodstuffs. The inability of the *hacendados* to maintain their control of any of these three resources was caused by political forms of intersectorial relations rather than by the more strictly economic modes of articulation. For instance, large sections of the Río Vilcanota valley owned by *hacendados* were planted in wheat through the 1920s; older informants recall the uniform golden color of the entire valley floor before harvest time in those years. Wheat can be grown without frequent irrigation, but the mills that grind it require a great deal of water. The *hacendados* owned the mills, and they had sufficient political power to assure that the peons and *comuneros* would maintain the canals that provided their mills with water. In later decades, the peasants took increasing control of the land, diverted the water from the mills, and shifted to crops that demand more water, such as broad beans and maize, which do not require milling and have a higher cash value. This change required greater access to land, water, and labor. The transfer of resources took a variety of forms, from passive resistance (a sharecropper retained a larger percentage of the yield, a tenant delayed in paying rent, a *comunero* sent a young son to a work party instead of attending himself) to open conflict (peasants armed with slings, rocks, and sticks drove *hacendados* off community lands [La Verdad 5.12.22, 16.7.23], peasants invaded hacienda lands and mills). Chapter 10 presents more fully the political context of the decline of the agricultural haciendas and the ascendancy of the *comuneros*.

Finally, the emergence of a set of *comuneros ricos* was brought about by shifts in both internal and external constraints (Fonseca Martel 1976). The agricultural sector is unlike the herding sector, where a considerable reorganization of a large number of productive units is required to raise the aggregate production, because the output of one agricultural unit can increase without changing that of other units. In part, this results from the greater marginal productivity of labor in local agriculture; an additional *aporque* of maize, more frequent weeding of a pea field, a slightly longer threshing of barley, all raise output. More important is the ease ("nonlumpiness" in economists' terms) of capital investment in seeds, fertilizer, and insecticide. Finally, there are some economies of scale. If a field is larger than .5 hectares, a team of oxen can be hired to plow it; the capital inputs become cheaper per unit area as the unit increases in size. These factors favor the concentration of wealth within the communities. An individual who has somewhat more land than others can use his position to get more; his profits are relatively higher. Wealth can be used to purchase land outright, but it can also translate into local political influence. A *comunero* with more money can hire laywers and bring gifts to judges and governors to obtain a distinct advantage in the settlement of disputed inheritances, damage suits, and disagreements over boundaries. These are common mechanisms of land accumulation.

The organization and collective activities of communities also favor the wealthier peasants, since they provide what might be called economic infrastructure for all peasant producers. The irrigation canal system and road networks are maintained by *faenas* and *cuotas*. The community also bears the costs of representing collective interests (e.g., defending lands and irrigation water against enchroachment by outsiders) by paying for legal fees and for trips of community leaders to the departmental capital to register complaints with the authorities.

These services are maintained by regressive taxation, however, to borrow another term from economists. All households pay the same *cuota*, regardless of their wealth or income; exceptions are made only for the aged and the widowed, who pay half and sometimes nothing at all. Similarly, the wealthier peasants can hire someone to work in their stead at the *faenas* or pay a fine for failure to attend. Hence, the costs are fixed, or inversely proportional to wealth. Leveling mechanisms, such as fiesta sponsorship, do not fully compensate for this inequality, as the life histories of some *comuneros ricos* show (Orlove 1974b). The benefits of membership, however, are directly proportional to wealth. An individual with twice as much irrigable land receives twice as much irrigation water. The peasants who own more land and those who have stores benefit more from the improved roads that link community and market town than the poorer peasants do.

The agricultural extension offices assist the rise of *comuneros ricos*. For instance, the Sicuani branch of the *Banco de Fomento Agropecuario* in Sicuani, established in 1956, makes short-term loans to peasants. Because its employees are concerned with avoiding making loans to individuals who will default on them, once a peasant has established credit with the bank, it is easy for him to get loans in following years. Local *Ministerio de Agricultura* officials similarly distribute their attention unevenly; they must have a few prize Indians to whom visiting officials may be taken. The history of the peasant cooperatives set up under the *Cooperación Popular* programs of the Belaúnde government is similar.

These changes in the internal organization of the agricultural sectors are closely linked to changes in other sectors, in this instance traders and bureaucrats. The second part of this chapter shows how the path of the sectors of artisans in some ways duplicates that of the agricultural sectors and traces the shifting modes of articulation between agricultural peasants and artisans.

ARTISANS

Environmental Constraints

In this context, the economic activity in which materials, whether still in natural form or already processed, are transformed on a small scale into other products for human consumption shall be taken as the work of artisans. The fabrication of new articles and the repair of old ones are both included, since these two activities are practiced by the same individuals in the same settings. The various specializations of artisans are known as trades.

The number of trades practiced in the area is very large. Space allows only illustrative descriptions of individual crafts, rather than systematic or exhaustive ones. The social organization of artisan production varies less than the specific techniques used. For more detail on artisans see Orlove 1974a; Valencia 1970; Verástegui Serpa 1972.

Artisans stand in sharp contrast to both herders and peasants in the nature of their productive activities. Their work is not tied to an annual cycle but to the period required to turn out individual products, which varied from a few hours (sandal makers) to a week or so (guitar makers). Some trades are limited by climatic factors in a general way: Adobe makers cannot set out their mud bricks to dry during the rainy season. In most cases, though, there are no environmental factors rendering production unfeasible at any time of year. Hence there are, with few exceptions, no labor peaks in artisan production. Artisan work is done when the opportunity cost of labor is low.

The location of production is based on convenience rather than necessity. It is easier for individuals living close to clay deposits to make pots than for those living at a greater distance, although pots can be fired in either place. In general, ease of access to raw materials and markets greatly influence the location of artisans. There are a number of *k'aspi ruwak* (literally, stick maker) in the community of Hercca in the province of Canchis. They trim young eucalyptus trunks into shape for roof poles. Hercca is located in a relatively sheltered and well-watered valley where eucalyptus grow abundantly. A road to the high, treeless punas of the provinces of Canas and Espinar passes through it, so that transportation costs to market are lower than they would be from more distant areas. In general, trades that purchase raw materials and wage labor and sell their wares for cash tend to be concentrated in the town of Sicuani. Similarly, crafts that rely on locally gathered or produced items and household labor and barter their wares are found in rural areas. The differences in organization between these urban and rural artisans will be discussed in the next section; the following section will examine their articulation with other sectors.

Organization of Production

The artisans of Sicuani are, with few exceptions, full-time craft practitioners. They work throughout the year. The shop form of organization is common to all of them. Each shop is an independent production unit run by one individual. He either rents it or, less frequently, works in rooms in his own house. He pays the local shop tax (*patente municipal*) and arranges for the sale of his products, either in his own shop or in a stall in the permanent market in Sicuani. In most cases, he sells them himself, although he may have an intermediary. Both urban and rural residents buy the products. The owner also obtains credit, buying tools in installments and receiving loans from relatives and other private individuals and, less frequently, from the state-run *Banco Industrial del Perú*. Urban artisans generally work with materials that have already been processed. The tailors sew factory cloth, tinsmiths rework old cans and sheet metal, carpenters work with wood transported from the tropical forest and already cut into planks, and bakers use commercial flour.

The owners themselves are artisans. They may work alone, but more frequently they hire other full-time artisans, known as *maestros*, and provide them with materials. Apprentices and part-time assistants are often taken on by both owners and *maestros*, though more frequently by the former. There are a few trades, notably tailoring and shoemaking, in which the *maestros* work in their own homes rather than in the owners' shops. The tools they use belong to the owner in some cases and to themselves in others. However, many *maestros* establish their own shops after working for an owner for several years.

In some cases, individuals give a payment to be accepted for apprenticeship. During the early part of apprenticeship they are not paid, although they may act as watchmen, receiving meals and a cot in the shop in exchange for protecting it against theft at night. After several months or years, they begin to be paid a piece rate, although they get less than a *maestro* is given. The piece rate continues to be the standard form of payment throughout an artisan's career. Daily and weekly wages (as well as scheduled working hours) are rare, for both *maestros* working full time and assistants taken on for short periods when demand is high.

All shop owners and *maestros* have learned their trade through a period of apprenticeship. Some artisans take their children and younger siblings as apprentices. A few families are famous for their trades, such as the Curie shoemakers, the Flores hatmakers, and the Tuero firework makers. These are atypical, however, since most apprentices work in the shops of individuals to whom they are not related. In certain trades, such as mechanics, it is unusual to find shop owners taking on relatives as apprentices.

It is also common to find assistants working in shops. They differ from apprentices in that they are not learning the trade but merely helping with certain tasks. They are not hired for long periods of time, and they have little expectation of remaining in the work for more than a few months. Assistants may be taken on as apprentices, but such cases are exceptional.

The division of labor within a shop is simple. In most cases, *maestros* are able to perform all the different stages in the elaboration of the final product. The more tedious and tiring aspects are usually relegated to the apprentice and assistants. In a number of shops, there is a division of production into several stages. The *peleteros* described in Chapter 7 are representative of this aspect. Shoemakers similarly are divided into several groups: those who cut out the leather for the uppers, those who sew the lining into the uppers, and those who fit the upper to the last and tack on the heels and soles.

In other cases, there is specialization within a trade. Some carpenters build furniture and others make coffins. Bread and pastries are baked by different individuals. Tailors show the greatest specialization: Men's suits, women's dresses and pants, peasants' shirts and vests, peasant women's skirts (*polleras*), and police uniforms are each sewn by separate groups of artisans. It is interesting to note that there is no division between what could be labeled traditional and modern trades. The interrelated patterns of the shop form of organization and the apprentice–*maestro*–shopowner career path are found among automobile mechanics and radio repairmen as well as carpenters and bakers.

Rural artisans differ in most of these features. Unlike the urban artisans who practice their trade full time, rural artisans also work as peasants and herders raising crops and animals. They fit their trades into the periods of the year when they are not occupied in the field or with their herds. Rural artisans work in their homes rather than in shops. The work groups are composed of relatives. They also own the tools and buy the raw materials they use, as do their urban counterparts, but they use much less capital, and raw materials are more often unprocessed, more often gathered rather than purchased. Characteristic examples are clay and volcanic rock temper for potters, llama wool, horsehair, and straw for rope makers, local wheat for bakers, and eucalyptus wood for carpenters. The rural artisans neither pay taxes nor receive credit. A member of the household markets the goods, usually at the annual fairs and weekly markets in Sicuani and the villages. They are more likely to barter their products than are the urban artisans. Some individuals, such as those who make rope and sacks from llama wool, are completely unwilling to sell their products for cash. Some people in Sicuani buy their products, but rural artisans rely on rural buyers more heavily than urban artisans do.

The individuals who assist the artisan are not paid for their work but receive goods and services as members of his household. The roof-tile maker does not pay his children for helping him carry clay from the deposit to his house or his wife for helping him fire the tiles. The money from the sale of the tiles goes for food, clothing, schoolbooks, and the like, consumed and used by members of the household.

The rural artisans learn their trades as they learn to perform agricultural and pastoral tasks, through daily contact with and imitation of their parents and other adults. Though not entirely unknown, apprenticeship and the hiring of part-time assistants are infrequent. Recruitment to work groups is much less formal than in Sicuani. It is more common in rural areas for relatives and, occasionally, friends to help an artisan if they happen to be present when he is working.

The division of labor within each productive unit and the specialization within a trade are also less complex than they are among urban artisans. The rural artisans show a capacity to innovate that belies their traditional and conservative image. Valencia documents this point for the artisans of San Pablo, showing how they adapt their products to a series of changes in their markets (1970: 69, 90 94, 104–117).

Articulation with Other Sectors

The three modes of interaction described for the agricultural sectors apply to artisans as well, and the previous discussion of these modes is generally applicable to them. The joint production mode is facilitated by the nature of artisan activity; the production of one item does not entail immediate further production, since both raw materials and tools can be stored. In a sense, peasants and herders engaging in household production of craft items such as textiles, rope made from *ichu* grass, and so forth, might be cited as examples of the joint production mode. Some activities done by artisans in one context constitute production for household consumption in another. The majority of peasant men can make adobes and build houses of them, just as almost all peasant

FIGURE 19. The preparation of *chalona* requires several steps. After incisions are cut in the meat, it is soaked in salt water, pressed under heavy weights, and salted. The men in this photograph are scraping salt off a sheep carcass. They will further dry the carcass by exposing it to sun and frost; they will use the salt again next year.

women brew *chicha*, a mildly fermented beer made of maize or barley. In Sicuani, individuals who perform these activities are artisans, called *albañiles* and *chicheras*, respectively; in rural areas they are not. A complementary example is the preparation of *chalona*, a form of preserved meat made by cutting incisions in fresh meat (usually mutton or alpaca), soaking it in salt water, pressing it under heavy weights, salting it, and drying it by exposure to sun and frost. *Chalona* can be stored for several years without spoilage. It is a basic ingredient of local cooking, both in town and in the countryside. Many people in Sicuani can prepare it, but do so only on a small scale for household consumption. In the countryside, making *chalona* can be considered an artisan activity, since it is often done in volume. On some occasions over 500 kilograms of meat are processed and sold.

Like peasants, many artisans combine these different modes of articulation. Joint production, in particular, fits in easily with other activities. Since artisan work can be fitted in around other tasks, there is a minimal opportunity cost to the individual (Kula 1970: 21–22, 53), and in many cases the capital outlay for tools is low.

In some cases, artisans switch between the barter and cash modes, as described for peasants. This is the case with potters. In other instances, it is more difficult. In particular, many urban artisans depend on cash for continued supplies of raw materials and labor. For this reason, the cash mode and full-time activity are closely linked. Artisans who stop working for a while are apt to lose their connections with both suppliers of raw materials and clients (Orlove 1974a: 201–202). If demand expands, the full-time artisans are capable of meeting much of the increase; they can hire part-time assistants and purchase more raw materials. Since wages are paid on a piece-rate basis, the tools can be used for longer hours without requiring additional expenditures for fixed capital, and labor costs remain proportional to the volume of output.[2] Similarly, the cost of raw materials remains closely proportional to the total output. In some cases, the price per unit is lower in the case of bulk purchases, but many artisans are not in a position to take advantage of this reduction; tailors must pay a standard price for cloth, as bakers do for flour.

Changes in Internal Organization

The expansion of the wool export economy brought increasing amounts of cash to the herders and disrupted the barter mode of articulation with other sectors. It also led to increasing specialization of herders as they abandoned other economic activities. As shown in Chapter 9, one consequence of the growth of wool exports was the increased volume of manufactured goods consumed by peasants and herders. In many cases, the traditional craft items were not abandoned for factory substitutes, however, but the amount of traditional items consumed went up instead. This point is made about *bayeta* in Chapter 7, but it is more generally true. Small wooden stools became a more frequent item in household inventories. Although fewer people go barefoot, not all of them have switched to manufactured shoes. The number of sandals made from rubber tires (*ojotas*), based on the llama leather *p'orqo* or *alpargata*, and in some cases artisan-made leather shoes, has grown as well. Collective levels of consumption have grown, as well as individual ones. Religious fiestas involve more expensive celebrations, and the number of fiestas grows as the communities that split off from others establish their own chapels; fireworks are now consumed in larger quantities.

---

[2] For instance, the demand for bread and cake for ritual purposes increases just before the fiesta of Todos Santos. The 150 ovens in Sicuani are used virtually around the clock for several days.

These changes have meant an expanded aggregate demand for artisan wares. Production by rural artisans has increased, but the growth in the output of urban artisans, tied directly to the cash mode of articulation, has been more striking (IBEAS 1968). The simple division of labor, the low initial capital requirements, and the unrestrictive guild organization have permitted new shops to proliferate.[3] Furthermore, the economies of scale are limited; the combination of these different factors, explained in more detail in Chapter 7 for the case of the *peleteros,* has had similar consequences for other trades. The lack of sources makes it difficult to say whether the expansion in production of rural artisans was produced by increased volume from previous units or the entrance of new ones into operation, but most likely both phenomena took place. The old forms of production continued, with a few exceptions.

These changes in the modes of articulation and the growth of the cash mode are not limited to the artisan sector, but they are tied to the growth of the market system. This topic will be investigated in Chapter 9.

[3] There are a few exceptions, where large initial capital requirements, greater required levels of skill, and closer regulation by the town government alter this pattern. Watch repair shops are one such example.

9

The Distribution System

The extensive commercial activity in the Sicuani area has been the object of comment by visitors to the area since the beginning of the century (Fuentes 1905: 5–6, La Verdad 10.9.39). There is now an extensive network of fairs and marketplaces. Small stores can be found in surprisingly large numbers in communities and villages. The Sicuani area contrasts sharply with other parts of the sierra, such as the southern provinces of the department of Ayacucho, where there is very little commercial activity. This variarion reflects fundamental differences in the relations between different sectors and the manner in which they articulate in the regional economy and society.

This chapter describes commerce as an economic activity, in much the same fashion as preceding chapters examined other sectors. It presents an explanation for the development of a high level of marketing activity in this century. The same factors that favor this activity in general also account for the particular forms of organization of the marketing system. This chapter looks at the different sorts of commercial transactions that take place and examines in general terms the two halves of the market relations, taken as aggregates: the purchasing power of the local population, on the one hand, and the organization of marketing units, on the other. The processes of their expansion is presented first in a general manner, and then with greater specificity.

The final section examines the sequence of stages through which the marketing system has passed, placing special emphasis on changes in the organization of the units and the institutions in which they operate. Several examples will illustrate the more general points.

MARKETING ACTIVITY

Marketing is fundamentally different from the activities described in the three previous chapters in that it forms part of the system of distribution of goods rather than that of their production. The joint production and barter modes, described in earlier chapters, also form part of this system. In marketing, intermediaries carry finished goods from one point to another. Small quantities of goods may be gathered into larger quantities to facilitate transportation or larger units may be broken down into smaller ones to favor sale. Cases where peasants, herders, and artisans sell their products directly to a consumer rather than barter them are relatively unimportant in the overall distribution of goods. Marketing units thus generally correspond to the cash mode of articulation.

Considering the Sicuani area as an entity, there are three possible combinations of producers and consumers: intraregional trade, where the producer and consumer are both from the region; interregional export trade, where the producer is from the region and the consumer is not; and interregional import trade, where the consumer is from the region and the producer is not.

Intraregional flows of agricultural products and artisan wares occur in many parts of Latin America. Local specialization in production may be articulated through a regional set of markets (Wolf 1967: 313–314). In the Sicuani area, such marketing forms a part of the cash mode of articulation for peasants, herders, and artisans. Much of this cash mode also is composed of interregional export trade, in which local products are shipped out of the region. The interregional import trade is also found in other parts of Latin America; Ortiz documents its importance in stimulating the formation of new markets in Colombia (Ortiz 1967).

These three types of commodity flow occur in almost all marketplaces. The organization of the markets serves two complementary functions: gathering and concentrating local products to be shipped out of the region, and bulk-breaking or wholesaling and retailing goods brought in from outside. Transactions wholly internal to the region involve removing local products from the former channel. The expansion of the marketing system in Sicuani reflects an increase in both internal transactions (with the replacement of the joint production and barter modes of articulation by the cash mode of articulation), and external transactions (with the increase of both the demand for local products in other areas and the local demand for products from other areas). The supraregional functions of the market continue to dominate the intraregional one, as they did when the joint production and barter modes provided for the distribution of goods.

Interregional import and export trade affect the local marketing system in different ways (Appleby 1976a, 1976b). The sale of local wool, meat, hides, and agricultural products has been the principal manner in which money enters the area. It permits the purchase of goods from other areas. Rises and falls in the sale of local goods lead to parallel shifts in the volume of local demand. The distribution of goods from other areas, though, in particular of manufactured goods from the coast and abroad, affects the particular forms of market organization more directly, for several reasons. The area has a negative net balance of trade. There are fewer transactions involved in shipping out local products than there are in bringing in manufactured goods; a peasant or a herder is likely to bring products for sale a relatively small number of times a year but return to the market more frequently to make purchases.[1] This pattern also reflects the fact that local production has a sharper seasonal peak than local demand.

PURCHASING POWER

Quantitative data to calculate precisely the aggregate demand and the shifts of "terms of trade" between manufactured goods and local goods are lacking. The danger of presenting a tautological argument is great. It is tempting to cite the growth of markets as evidence for an increase in purchasing power, and then to explain the growth of markets as a result of increased purchasing power. There is the consolation that data are virtually unobtainable.[2] However, this difficulty is not crucial. Although specific details are often absent, general patterns are clear and adequately documented. Various sources all indicate the in-

[1] In the case of a few products such as milk, eggs, and onions, peasants do sell their products more frequently in markets. These cases involve only a small portion of the peasant population and generally do not constitute a major part of their household income.

[2] This is the case in part because the consumption units are so numerous and scattered, in part because of the number of alternate means of transportation of goods, and finally because so few of the marketing units keep systematic records.

creasing volume and value of goods imported to the Sicuani region for local consumers.

Several factors account for the long-term growth in purchasing power of the Sicuani region, defined as the sum of the cash value of all market transactions in a given time. They generally can be subsumed under two analytically distinct categories: a shifting from joint production and barter modes of articulation to the cash mode and an increase in total demand.

1. *The increase of the cash mode of articulation.* As documented in Chapters 6, 7, and 8, herders and peasants began to obtain each others' products and the products of artisans by cash purchase, rather than through joint production or barter. The organization of production accommodated itself to this reliance on cash sale.

2. *Increased government expenditure.* Peruvian national budgets have increased sharply during this century. Although the portion spent in the sierra has remained low, the volume of government expenditures there has increased. Greater activity of government representatives and ministry officials has brought cash into the area in several ways (Orlove 1977d). Although employees saved a part of their salaries for investment in many cases, and sent the money out of the area to support relatives living in other cities, they nonetheless spent a part in the area. State programs also led to direct investment, particularly in the construction of public works. Through the *Banco de Fomento Agropecuario,* the *Banco Industrial del Perú,* and other agencies, the state has given money to peasants and artisans in the form of loans. These government expenditures had a multiplier effect (Schultze 1964: 56–61); when a school is built in Sicuani, a carpenter receives a contract for school furniture. He spends part of his earnings on shoes; the shoemaker has more available income, and so forth. Finally, certain government programs, such as road construction programs of the *Ministerio de Transportes y Comunicaciones,* provided peasants with cash income. Government expenditure raised income most noticeably in the town of Sicuani, but it also had an impact in the smaller villages and the countryside.

3. *Terms of trade.* As indicated in Chapter 3 and 4, the producers have received an increasingly larger portion of the export value of wool during this century. They have also begun to forego direct consumption for the sake of sale, particularly in the case of meat and cheese. These developments have mitigated the impoverishment that the general fall in the prices of raw materials with respect to manufactured goods might have engendered.

Price supports also favor the local producer. Peruvian governments have subsidized selected basic commodities, known as *artículos de primera necesidad.* This transfer of government revenue from export duties and foreign loans to consumers keeps the price of these basic articles well below international levels (Andean Times, 8 Feb. 1974, vol. 33, no. 1726, p. 4). Prices for certain domestically produced goods are likewise fixed. Although these policies seem largely directed at fore-stalling resentment among the more politically mobilized poor in coastal cities, where the purchase of such basic necessities forms a large por-tion of their household budgets, they have some favorable effect on disposable income in the Sicuani area. However, many of these items are beyond the accustomed living standards of the sierra peasants and herders. For instance, rice and cooking oil are luxury items usually reserved for festive occasions. Nevertheless, other items are cheaper. Wheat is maintained at about half the world price, although Peru relies heavily on imports for its supply of this commodity. Salt and sugar are other supported items in the rural diet. Frequent petty dishonesty permits storekeepers and market vendors to raise the prices of these goods 20 to 40% above government-fixed levels. None-theless, prices still remain lower than they would be if there were no regulation.

Finally, some manufactured goods have become much more inexpen-sive with respect to agricultural products and wool. One of the most striking examples is the development of the Peruvian plastics industry, with prices kept low by Peru's unusually favorable position with suppliers of raw materials for plastics, the low initial capital for entry into plastics manufacturing, and the high degree of competition among firms (Andean Air Mail and Peruvian Times, 8 Dec. 1972, vol. 32, no. 1665, pp. 9–48). Plastic bags and sheeting have found their way into many peasant and herder households; other items, notably shoes, jugs, and bowls, are also being purchased more widely.

It is difficult to evaluate the shifts in terms of trade without systematic quantitative data. Barring the discovery of a set of household budgets for previous decades, no definitive conclusions can be reached. Surveys in the past decade based on national statistics are unclear (Webb and Figueroa 1975). However, it appears that the terms of trade have at least been less unfavorable to consumers than elsewhere.

4. *The growth of remittances.* Quite small before 1920, migration out of the area has grown considerably. Much of the migration is temporary. Returning migrants bring cash to spend, at times conspicuously, on their kin, friends, and neighbors, at times more cautiously, in invest-ments such as land and houses. A number of informal and formal mechanisms require migrant *comuneros* to spend money in the area; they pay fines for *faenas* they have missed, they sponsor fiestas as

affirmation of their community membership, and so forth. Permanent migrants also make remittances to kin. Associations of migrants resident in cities, particularly Arequipa and Lima, give money to their communities of origin for the construction of roads, schools, and other public works.

Thus the aggregate purchasing power in the Sicuani area has expanded during most of this century. Southern Peruvian Railway reports, for example, suggest that the total volume of goods moving to the major market towns in the sierra has exhibited an upward trend in long-range terms, though with occasional setbacks because of declining wool prices, poor harvests, and what they term "unsettled conditions . . . due to political disturbances" (Southern Peruvian Railway 1964/65:12). This rise has been general throughout the area. Consumption rose even in such a poor part of the Sicuani region as the punas in the district of Tungasuca (Orlove 1975).

MARKETING UNITS: ORGANIZATION AND PROCESS

Aggregate purchasing power is a continuous rather than a discrete variable, and its increase has been gradual. Purchasing power translates into sales volume. The growth of distribution facilities, however, has not always been gradual. In particular, the institutional framework of marketing has changed in a discontinuous fashion, as quantitative change (increased demand density and sales volume) produced qualitative change (the emergence of new institutions). The general institutional framework in which these units operate has also changed, as annual fairs, weekly markets, stores, and permanent markets formed. These changes are examined by looking at the process of expanding total market capacity through the formation of new marketing units and the enlargement of existing ones.

Although the scale of a marketing unit is a continuous variable, three types of units can be distinguished on the basis of size, location, clientele, and suppliers. The first two operate primarily in Sicuani; there are a small number in Yauri and other towns. The wholesalers are relatively few. They purchase local commodities in large amounts and sell either manufactured goods in bulk or specialized merchandise such as medicine, stationery, or hardware. They deal with other traders. The more numerous retailers sell to consumers; they also purchase local commodities but on a smaller scale. The rural traders include itinerant vendors, sellers at fairs and weekly marketplaces, and proprietors of the tiny stores that have appeared in recent decades in the villages and countryside. Rural traders buy manufactured goods from urban traders; the size of their suppliers generally depends on the scale of their activities. They purchase wool, hides, and foodstuffs from the herders and peasants. It is important to remember that the units and sectors refer to activities; an individual in Sicuani can be both a wholesaler and a retailer, much as an individual in the countryside can be both a peasant and a rural artisan.

Vendors and stores can expand their operations by enlarging their stock, by increasing their rate of turnover, or both. Profits from operations can be invested in goods. A marketing unit can choose to continue purchasing the same goods (but in larger quantities so as to have lower unit costs) or to purchase more expensive goods with a slower rate of turnover (particularly when high rates of inflation discourage maintaining capital in cash). They can attempt to change their clientele, shifting from retail to wholesale.[3] In most cases, marketing units aim for security as well as expansion and try to maintain a steady clientele. Though important, this aspect of store-owner–client relations has been exaggerated in certain sources (Wolf and Hansen 1972: 120–123).

Individual marketing units may also raise their profits by changing location. A position on one of the streets in Sicuani or Yauri along which peasants pass on their way to the Sunday market is superior to one on a side street where only local residents are likely to come by.[4] A location near a police station is undesirable, since the police might come in and decide that the customers are drunk in order to collect fines or make them work in the police station for a few hours or days. Time is also often important. A store owner can send members of his household or employees out to take advantage of periodic marketing opportunities.[5] The owner of one of the larger stores in Sicuani kept the shop open seven days a week but sent one son with goods to the larger

---

[3] This distinction is difficult to maintain at times. A store in a town or village sells soft drinks at a given price (between S/3 and S/4 a bottle), whether by the bottle to customers there or in larger quantities to a regular customer who will take them to a peasant community and raise the price by S/.50 or S/1 a bottle. Marketwomen will sell bananas at slightly lower prices to someone buying several dozen to take to a weekly marketplace in the punas but will also sell bananas to individuals for consumption.

[4] The stores tend to fill up Sunday afternoons, even on the sidestreets; but business is more brisk in those with good locations. It is also more frequent for out-of-the-way stores to be occupied by a few people drinking beer while the stores on the main streets continue to do regular business.

[5] Only the largest stores in Sicuani have what could be dignified by the term shop assistants or clerks. In many cases, however, there are individuals attached to households, whether actual godchildren (*ahijados*), or merely young people treated as adopted children (*criados*) who help run the shops.

annual fairs and sometimes had a godson sell in the weekly street market in Sicuani on Sundays. In general, these adjustments of location and timing are necessary to take full advantage of the economies of scale in marketing.

The expansion of the volume of goods traded is also carried out through the entry of new trading units. It should be stressed that initial entry into small-scale trading is extremely simple and that there are rarely institutional barriers. At most, a new urban trader will have to pay a tax to the municipality, and a new rural trader will argue with the other sellers for a good spot in the plaza. These initial ventures may be very brief. A truckdriver returning to Sicuani from Quince Mil in the *montaña* brought his family a few dozen bananas; seeing that they would soon rot, his wife took them to the Sunday market and sold them. As this extreme but not unrepresentative example demonstrates, stocks are small. Among rural traders, a total stock worth S/250 for open-air vending and S/1000 for storekeepers is not at all unusual. Labor costs are virtually nil, since the marketers are largely self-employed and the opportunity cost of labor is low. Marketing brings supplementary income to many households, since women can care for their children while selling and even carry on other domestic tasks such as cooking. Retailers and even street vendors often leave their goods unattended. It

FIGURE 20. Initial entry into small-scale trading is quite easy. This woman is preparing *anticuchos* (grilled meat and boiled potatoes) for sale at a small fiesta in Sicuani. Investment in equipment and stocks in cases such as these is several hundred soles.

is up to the customer to locate the seller; theft is surprisingly rare. In the case of rural storekeepers and vendors at annual fairs and weekly marketplaces, time can be taken off from marketing to attend to agricultural or pastoral labor without permanent loss of clientele; both the marketers and their clientele are likely to be busy at the same time. Many rural traders, like the rural artisans, engage in other activities as well.

Many of the new units are formed by individuals with no previous marketing experience. They use capital saved from their own earnings or borrowed from friends, neighbors, or kin. Information about opportunities to make sales is easily accessible. The opening of marketplaces is announced through an active advertising campaign of flyers and radio announcements, as is each annual fair (see Appendix 3).

Certain features of house construction also favor the establishment of new units. New houses in Sicuani and the larger villages have rooms on the first floor opening directly onto the street. These can be used as stores. In the smaller villages and communities, individuals can construct additional rooms in their houses for stores. They build them after the model of urban stores, with counters, shelves, benches, and a cash drawer.

The demand for products is well known to the individuals involved in commerce. Since a large portion of the transactions takes place in public places, either in open air or in stores that face the street, marketers are aware of the conditions under which products sell well and of their usual prices. The state of markets is generally known, as well as the factors involved in fluctuations. For instance, the pilgrimage center in Huanca in the Río Vilcanota valley close to Cuzco draws so many people in September from the Sicuani area that attendance at the weekly markets in the area drops heavily. Market vendors tend to go there because of the large crowds of potential customers, peasants and herders find a number of products cheaper there, and many truck owners who regularly drive to the smaller marketplaces in the Sicuani area take passengers there instead.[6] Similarly, information about poor local harvests or falling wool prices that would reduce demand spreads quickly among the rural traders. The general activity in markets and particular price information is a frequent topic of conversation. The extreme crowding of buses and trucks also disseminates information. Seasonal fluctuations can be anticipated on the basis of individual experience: Pens and notebooks sell well when school opens; ritual items like

---

[6] Religious motivation is also important in pilgrimage attendance, and some centers such as Qoyllurrit'i have minimal economic activity associated with them.

candles, metal foil, and llama tallow are in demand at particular seasons.

In general, the situation is a sellers' rather than a buyers' market. Shortages are more frequent than gluts. A common sight is an individual going from store to store or market vendor to market vendor requesting, in a pleading tone, some particularly scarce item such as coffee, kerosene, *yauri* (baling needles), almonds, or white sugar. It is significant that the purchaser thanks the storekeeper rather than the reverse.

Certain mechanisms control the number of marketing units at any particular place and time. The general economic state of stores in a particular town, village, or community is evident to residents and visitors alike. Individual *comunero* storekeepers commented that they opened their stores because other communities similar to their own had busy stores but theirs had few or none.

Local demand also determines the number of trucks driving to any particular weekly marketplace, which limits the number of people who attend.[7] In general, individual traders carry a small amount of goods, and a large number of vendors attend even the smallest markets (Santa Bárbara is the only marketplace in the area that regularly has fewer than 20 vendors; most of them attract between 30 and 100) so that the presence of a few additional vendors or the absence of some regular ones does not disturb the usual activity.

The introduction of new products involves a risk, but such events are infrequent. In any case, there is a considerable population willing to buy new things that strike them as modern. For instance, new toys and children's games were successfully introduced in the early 1970s (Quino 1972: 32–35). Such items are often presented with relatively simple forms of advertising such as a man with a bullhorn or a brief series of radio campaigns (Andean Air Mail and Peruvian Times, 8 Dec. 1972, vol. 32, no. 1665, p. 27).

The profitability of a marketing unit depends on a number of conditions, including the initial capital, the contacts with suppliers (to ensure both a steady source of goods and relatively lower prices), and contacts with clients. These factors affect the size of inventories, the rate of turnover, and the differentials between buying and selling prices. The

[7] Vendors can also arrive on foot, carrying their goods on their backs or bringing them on a horse, donkey, or llama; in the valley marketplaces, they also arrive by train. The majority of them come by truck, since the trucks drive right up to the marketplace, avoiding the necessity of transporting goods from the station to the market. The vendors also have considerable control over when the trucks leave, which may vary by as much as an hour or two.

interrelations of these factors vary greatly in different types of marketing activity (see Chapter 4). In some cases, there is public access to the items to be sold; some factories maintain outlets in Sicuani, and others send traveling representatives. In other cases, particularly artisans, producers sell only to regular customers. In still other cases, the sale of goods is public, but the place of sale is outside the area. In these circumstances, it becomes important for the marketer to establish contacts either with people at the point of production who ship him goods or with distributors who sell goods to him in the locality. With the proliferation of middlemen, the number of links between producers and final seller can be larger, and the establishment of more direct ties can reduce prices. Oranges from the La Convención valley may be as cheap as S/.10 in Quillabamba and cheaper still in the groves. Many oranges come from La Convención to Cuzco by train, where they are resold to someone else who takes them to the Sicuani area. Several intermediaries may intervene before they are actually sold to the individual who sells them for S/.50–.70 to the consumer. In puna areas, they may be resold for S/1.00 apiece. Transportation costs account for only a fraction of this mark-up.

Furthermore, close ties with suppliers give an individual marketer better chances of receiving credit. Suppliers may be willing to accept partial payment in cash and receive the remainder later; in the case of large traders, they will accept checks. With the lack of effective collection mechanisms, credit is difficult to obtain.

The value of these links to suppliers is a major reason for the prominence of two related patterns in the formation of new marketing units: the importance of traders from outside and the tendency for employees and agents of wholesalers to become independent retailers or wholesalers. In the first case, similar phenomena have been noted in many parts of the world, especially Africa and Southeast Asia. Explanations tend to be structural (local people are embedded in a network of reciprocal obligations that impedes them from accumulating enough capital to operate businesses successfully) and cultural (local people have a set of values and orientations that do not permit them to engage in entrepreneurial activity). Nash shows that these two modes of explanation may be combined: The difference between local groups and trader peoples, such as the Hausa and overseas Chinese, is simply that their cultures are different, so that the trader people are free to enter into those new economic opportunities that other people cannot (Nash 1966: 83–87; Foster 1974). In this case, what might be called an articulational explanation accounts for the success of outside traders (Yambert 1974). A large number of the wholesale traders in Sicuani come from Arequi-

pa, which is a major distribution center for imported goods and manufactured items. Most of them were Peruvian, but there were four
Palestinians, two Czechs, and one Chinese. They arrived with more
capital and better connections than the local people. They could order in
bulk and found it easier to establish credit.

These wholesalers set themselves up in stores in Sicuani that are often
very busy, particularly on Sunday, the principal market day. Employees
and relatives helped attend to the customers, but relatives, often distant,
did not live with the owners but had households of their own. In
addition to employees, some of the stores had branches maintained by
agents. These were relatively few in number; several were found in
Ayaviri, Santa Rosa, and Yauri. In other cases, one man would own
several stores in town, each one run by an employee or agent; frequently these stores specialized in different kinds of goods.

Following the second frequent pattern, employees and agents of
wholesalers set themselves up as retailers or wholesalers on their own.
In some instances the split resulted from bitter conflict, but in many
cases the two separated amicably. The large storekeepers could either
find replacements for employees among local *sicuaneños* or bring individuals in from outside. Having already participated in the operation of
a large store, the employees had the necessary experience to work on
their own. They also had contacts in Arequipa from whom they could
get credit, paying for shipments with *pagarés*, or promissory notes.

This splitting off of storekeepers was only a replication on a lower
level of a process that had taken place before (see Chapters 3 and 4).
Many of the original storekeepers were themselves former agents of
firms, primarily Arequipa based, who had made themselves independent. The Arequipa firms themselves were similarly one and two steps
removed from the British trading firms that arrived early in the
nineteenth century or the German firms that came later, in the
nineteenth and early twentieth centuries. The strength of this group
will be discussed more fully in the following chapter.

STRUCTURE AND GROWTH OF
MARKETING INSTITUTIONS

The history of the marketing system in the Sicuani area
mirrors the growth of purchasing power and the shifts in modes of
articulation between sectors. The periods distinguished in this section
are approximate. It begins with 1900, since nineteenth-century sources

are sketchy. It seems likely that commercial activity increased greatly when the railroad reached Sicuani in 1897, linking it with the *altiplano*, Arequipa, and Mollendo.

1900–1940

Between 1900 and 1940, most commercial activity was concentrated in the town of Sicuani. Reportedly, over 5000 peasants and herders attended this market in busy weeks; the hills immediately east of Sicuani were covered with donkeys[8] and llamas. Many street vendors hawked wares. Stores bought a considerable amount of the peasants' and herders' agricultural produce and wool and sold manufactured goods. Some stores provided lodging (*alojamiento*), a rather kind translation for a bit of packed earth floor, on which peasants and herders could lay their blankets and ponchos. This benefit was part of the system in which personal ties linked individual peasants and herders to traders. Many herders came only once every few years, selling or exchanging their products for manufactured goods.

Transportation patterns formed an integral part of this system. The special train maintained by the Southern Peruvian Railway until 1954 for the Sunday market in Sicuani went "up the hill" (to borrow the terminology of the British railway staff) from Arequipa on Saturday with consumer goods and returned there on Monday with foodstuffs and wool. Significantly, no additional train was needed from Cuzco to carry the peasants and herders bringing agricultural products and wool from the Río Vilcanota valley and adjacent highlands. The majority of the local goods coming into Sicuani arrived on animals. Sicuani drained a vast area of southern Cuzco and adjoining departments. Peasants and herders journeyed along trails to this center which collected primary commodities for Arequipa and puna markets and distributed wares from the former. The train facilitated interregional trade, while intraregional trade remained difficult.

There were annual fairs in the area in Tungasuca and Coporaque. These date from the colonial period, when there was extensive trade in Argentine mules for work in mines further to the north and west (Concolorcorvo 1959). Historical accounts (Aparicio Vega 1965: 203) suggests that these fairs continued to be quite large in the early twentieth century, despite changed economic and political conditions. They

---

[8] The theft of these animals by Sicuani residents is the basis of their nickname, *asnu suwa* or donkey thief.

were the site of animal trading and the sale of some manufactured goods, as local informants report. Local writers, however, have glorified their importance.

Itinerant traders occasioned other small-scale trading activity. Many of these were agents of Sicuani storekeepers. In the Sicuani region, unlike many other parts of the sierra, there were no hacienda stores where the peons were forced to buy goods from the *hacendado* at inflated prices. Peons had direct access to marketing through the itinerant traders.

1940–1960

Changes in marketing patterns in this period are associated with new forms of transportation. In the colonial period, a road passed through the Sicuani area, coming from the *altiplano* through Ayaviri and Santa Rosa, entering the Río Vilcanota River valley at La Raya, and continuing

FIGURE 21. Changing modes of transportation have affected the distribution system in the Sicuani region. The Southern Peruvian Railway continues to transport large volumes of goods between the Sicuani region, the city of Cuzco, the altiplano, and the coast. This photograph was taken in the district of Marangani, province of Canchis. Note the tank cars and the *laymi* (p. 116) to the right.

FIGURE 22. Trucks have replaced llama caravans in many cases (see Figure 1). Several decades ago, herders such as these men would have transported their hides, sacks of wool, and other goods by llama caravans rather than by truck, as these men will do.

through Sicuani and Tinta. This road was still used in the nineteenth (Blanco 1835: 40–49, El Sol del Cuzco 23.7.1825) and early twentieth centuries, when there was scheduled horse coach service on it. It was improved during the 1920s at the same time that roads were being built in Espinar between haciendas and the capital city of Yauri. Road construction continued in a desultory fashion through the 1930s. Few other roads were begun. Only one main route, from Sicuani to Yauri through Descanso, and a set of feeder roads to the main Vilcanota valley road (Yanaoca–Pampamarca–Combapata and Acomayo–Sangarará–Chuquicahuana) were initiated. The only other important route linked Yauri to Llalli in the department of Puno.

The initial completion of a road is only one aspect of the extension of the transportation network. Roads must also be maintained, since landslides and flooding wreak havoc during the rainy season, and heavy traffic creates big holes in the dry season. Despite the often poor condition of roads, traffic began to increase in the late 1930s and early 1940s. (In 1942, there were enough truck drivers in Sicuani to form a *Sindicato de Choferes* or Drivers' Union.) The decade 1945–1955 seems to

FIGURE 23. Trucks offer the railroad considerable competition, as the complaint of the traffic department shows. Trucks in the Sicuani region are similar to this one, photographed in the district of Coata, province and department of Puno.

have been the period of final victory of the truck over the railroad, as the plaintive accounts of the Southern Peruvian Railway show:

> The man from the Sierra, who hitherto has been our client, looks around for a cheaper means of travel and therefore makes use of the bus route and if this is still too much for him and his family, he travels by lorry, incidentally a great discomfort but well able to put up with this inconvenience to save himself a few centavos. Actually this latter form of competition is our bugbear, as these lorry people carry passengers at cut-throat prices and possibly do not even cover running costs. The general run of lorry owner is devoid of economic sense and therefore any fare is good enough to obtain a full passenger load. Even when he is carrying goods, he makes it his business to carry the odd passenger either in front with him or on top of the cargo. [Southern Peruvian Railway, 1957/58, p. 8]

The railway had lost its traditional monopoly on the transportation of different items one by one: flour, sugar, beer, cement, "up" and wool, produce, even mineral ore, "down." Lower transportation costs and rising purchasing power converged to encourage the emergence of new

FIGURE 24. The *triciclo* has also facilitated the proliferation of retail stores in Sicuani. This man buys beer from a wholesale distributor and sells it to small stores.

marketing institutions. Though the Sunday market in Sicuani continued to be important, annual fairs sprang up at traditional religious fiestas in various towns during the 1940s. San Pablo, Sicuani, Tinta, Combapata, Langui, Yanoca, and Livitaca all established commercial fairs in conjunction with religious fiestas (La Verdad 7.1.42, Pampacucho 6.4.42, 20.6.42, La Verdad 31.7.42, 25.4.46, 23.5.46). Newspaper accounts document the rivalry between towns for successful fairs. They were organized by local notables, people from old *hacendado* families who controlled the appointive political offices and owned some property. Such people formed committees that spread information about the fairs, encouraged traders to attend, arranged for fair sites, and allocated space for animals to graze. The principal interest of these notables lay in promoting commercial activity in order to augment the income of their districts. The prestige of having a fair also gave the villages an aura of progress; the ones that failed to organize such fairs, such as San Pedro, Checacupe, and Pichigua, declined from their former importance.

The local elites gained little benefit from the commercial activity itself. In some cases, women from the respectable families ran a few of the larger stores on the main squares. The vendors at the fairs came mostly from Sicuani. Many were peasants who moved to Sicuani from nearby communities. The peasants who ran the smaller stores, with stocks of a few gallons of *aguardiente,* several pounds of salt, one or two dozen candles, and small sacks of sugar and coca, nonetheless did much business at this time.

In 1953, a roofed *mercado modelo* replaced the small daily market in Sicuani, supplying housewives with foodstuffs. Peasants continued to sell their products outside; women from Sicuani held stalls in the building stocked with specialty produce from Arequipa (tomatoes, fresh basil, celery, beets, and the like) and local foodstuffs provided by intermediaries.

Stores were also established in the district capitals at this time. Despite the very small size of their stocks, their appearance indicates both the lower transportation costs and the gradual shifts in rural consumption patterns. Stores began to proliferate to an even greater extent in Sicuani. Some of these were directed toward the urban market in Sicuani itself, which grew as the number of state employees and artisans increased.

1960–1976

A few weekly markets began in the same decade as the fairs, such as the one in Pitumarca (La Verdad 21.2.46) at the end of the valley furthest from Sicuani, but most of the weekly markets began in the 1960s: Langui, Layo, El Descanso, Checca, Quehue, Yanaoca, Tungasuca, San Pablo, Combapata, Tinta, Livitaca, Esquina, and Acomayo.[9] These markets followed a weekly schedule for the convenience of market vendors who left their homes in Sicuani each day to attend a different market. *Comunero* leaders stated they chose the day for new markets so as not to conflict with existing ones, knowing it would be futile to attempt to draw vendors on days when there were already markets elsewhere.

Sponsored by the cattle traders' association in Sicuani, *tabladas* or animal markets were set up in the mid-1960s in Tinta and Combapata

[9] Weekly markets first appear in Espinar much earlier; transportation is easier on the flat landscape (Orlove 1977c), and transport costs are lower since Arequipa is closer. Some of the marketplaces are in villages with very little activity of any sort except on market day. On other days, as one informant stated, *"Chawpi plazapi atoq waqashan"* ("The fox cries out in the middle of the square"). There are so few people in the village then that a fox could come in from the countryside.

on the weekly market days. Stores also began to appear in communities; there appear to be no cases of any older than the early 1960s, with the exception of the communities immediately adjacent to the town of Sicuani. Sicuani itself kept its importance as a commercial center, with increasing numbers of specialized wholesale stores (hardware, stationery, veterinary, dry goods) supplying artisans and smaller market vendors.

The growth of marketing shows an institutional pattern: Fairs appear earliest, then weekly markets, and finally stores.[10] This sequence corresponds to increasing frequency of sales and volume of purchasing power and decreasing mobility of traders. There are certain exceptions, notably the early importance of the weekly fair and stores in Sicuani. In part, this is attributable to unusual geographical conditions, Sicuani's position as railhead, and the fact that low opportunity costs of labor permitted stores to operate with reduced stocks. The relation of the marketing system to local power structures forms one important strand of Chapter 10.

---

[10] I am indebted to Gordon Appleby for many hours of conversation on the points in this section and others in this chapter, and for his extensive comments on an earlier version of this chapter.

10

Political Articulation in the Sicuani Region

INTRODUCTION

The previous four chapters have examined nine sectors in the Sicuani region: herders, pastoral haciendas, peasants, agricultural haciendas, urban artisans, rural artisans, wholesale traders, retail traders, and rural traders. They have focused on the economic activities performed by the units that compose these sectors. Ecological and economic constraints shape the organization of the units which, in turn, affects their interests. The previous chapters have examined three types of economic relations between sectors, the joint production, barter, and cash modes of articulation.

The material presented in these chapters serves as a background to the description of other forms of intersectorial relations in this chapter. These forms, discussed in Chapter 1, have both political and economic aspects. They involve competition over scarce resources and policy formation and implementation. The conflicts they engender affect the wealth and power of different sectors. This chapter thus complements earlier chapters by studying the political dimension of the economic relations among sectors.

This chapter also introduces a tenth and final sector, the administrative sector. It includes government employees and the personnel of the

Catholic Church; the members of this sector will be referred to as bureaucrats. This chapter examines the elites, which may be defined as the most wealthy and powerful sectors. Elites generally control important resources, shape policy to their interests, and have strong connections outside the region.

This chapter analyzes the shifts in power relations on the regional level, in particular the weakening of village elites and the end of their domination of the peasantry, the rise of a trader-dominated regional elite, and the growing importance of Sicuani as an administrative center. These changes all imply the increasing importance of the state in regional and local affairs caused by the growth of national government revenues and the power held by state employees.

BEFORE THE RAILROAD: THE LATE NINETEENTH CENTURY

Introduction

During this period, the Sicuani region was relatively isolated from national political processes. Power on the national level shifted among a few oligarchic parties in Lima or distant military leaders but had little direct effect on many parts of the highlands (Astiz 1969: 48–61). The Sicuani region was isolated even within the southern sierra. It produced a disproportionately low number of senators for the department of Cuzco.

Activity at the regional level was relatively unimportant during this period. The division of communities had not yet taken place, and many peasant communities had access to both valley agricultural land and puna pastures. Trade beyond the locality was limited to traditional barter and occasional cash sales. Political authority was concentrated in small village elites. Demographic patterns reflect this predominance of local activity; in 1876, Sicuani was not much larger than other settlements (see Appendix 4).

Economics

There was a *hacendado* elite in each of the villages, sharply differentiated from the peasantry by wealth and power. The population of the villages ranged from 150 to 2000, and of the elite from 20 to 120 (Fuentes 1905: 20). Peasants and herders lived in both the villages and countryside. In each village, there was a high degree of elite endogamy[1] with frequent cousin marriage. The intervillage elite marriages tended to be patrilocal, generating a pattern in which certain surnames were associated with specific villages.

The domination of this elite rested on their economic position as *hacendados*. They controlled the factors of production: labor, land, water, and capital. They owned haciendas in both the valleys and the punas. The size of the haciendas and the proportion of hacienda to community land varied in different parts of the region, but in general, both were smaller than in other parts of the sierra. At certain times of the year, the resident peons of the haciendas were insufficient in number to meet the labor requirements; larger work groups were needed. They were made up of peasants and herders from the communities who were paid in agricultural and pastoral produce and occasionally in cash. The elite also owned small gristmills located along the streams that flowed into the Río Apurimac, the Río Vilcanota, and their tributaries (Gade 1971). They charged the peasants, both hacienda peons and community members, for grinding their wheat, barley, and maize; the peasants had no alternatives to these mills.

For the peons, this system assured them access to land, and for the other peasants, hacienda labor represented the principal means of acquiring additional material goods beyond those produced or bartered by their households. Labor opportunities outside the immediate area were limited. There had been relatively little out-migration, and few local people had experience outside the area (Fuenzalida 1970b).

The economic activity of peasant and herders, then, was restricted by the elite's control as well as by the general isolation of the region. As described in Chapter 9, peasants and herders acquired a variety of products through the joint production mode of articulation with other sectors. Llama caravan trade led to the exchange of pastoral products for agricultural ones, and there was some sale of wool, primarily to traveling buyers and other rural traders. Many peasants and herders did not engage in cash sales more frequently than once every three or four years.

Politics

The positions of political authority in the villages were held by members of the elite. The number and specific titles of these positions

---

[1] There was a lower degree of endogamy in the peasant communities than at present, but few peasants chose spouses from more than 10 kilometers away.

varied with the size of the village and its status as *distrito* (district capital) or *anexo* (annex). The offices included *alcalde* (mayor), *gobernador* (governor), *juez de paz* (justice of the peace), and *comisario* (deputy officer). Individuals were formally appointed to these posts by the prefect in Cuzco or the subprefects in the provincial capitals, but in fact the prefects merely acknowledged and ratified the power that the elites already had. Their appointments lasted for a number of years; in some cases they were lifelong. The national government did not regularly give funds to these village officials. The district capitals had budgets financed through the collection or farming out of fines and property taxes, but these averaged a few thousand soles annually (Fuentes 1905: 6). Public works projects such as municipal buildings, roads, and irrigation canals were initiated and maintained with unpaid peasant labor, organized into *faenas* or public works groups by the village officials. The national government also delegated to the officials the responsibility for maintaining public order and apprehending criminals.

The peasant communities had no formal legal status, although they enjoyed a limited *de facto* recognition. Adult males passed through a hierarchically arranged series of civil and religious posts which required the sponsorship of feasts and religious celebrations (Fuenzalida 1970a: 95–100). The elders who had held these posts were recognized within the communities as authorities; they settled minor disputes and supervised community *faenas*.

In each community, a few older men acted as representatives of the village officials. It was their responsibility to ensure that men went from the communities to the *faenas* called by the officials. This direct penetration of community organization, the domination of the legal system, and the use of direct sanctions (fines, imprisonment, forced labor) by the elite limited the scope of peasant community activity.

The political power of the elite was used to maintain its economic position. Each community was responsible for the maintenance of the canal system that brought water to the haciendas and gristmills, whether or not the community also drew irrigation water for its own fields from it. A peasant who did not attend the work group when required was fined; those who did not pay their fines were jailed and forced to work until they paid the equivalent of their fines. The justices of the peace supported the hacienda labor system and the use of *faenas* by siding with the *hacendados*; they tended to settle disputes over water rights in favor of the *hacendados*.

Public office also provided direct economic benefits to the individual who held it. Fines were often collected illegally or arbitrarily. In some instances, the system of payment was institutionalized. Before Easter, a group of peasants would come to the villages from each community and, in conjunction with a ceremony known as *chaco*, bring several animals and some agricultural produce as tribute to the governor and the justice of the peace. The communities also sent young couples to work as *pongos* or unpaid domestic servants and laborers in the households of officials. Bribery and coercion were common. The justice of the peace would direct a litigant to care for his herds or work in his fields for several days before hearing his complaint. In some cases, this tribute and unpaid labor were as important economically to the elites as their haciendas were.

This local political and economic system was relatively closed. The urban sectors were small and relatively insignificant. Few economic opportunities existed for peasants outside the locality. They were unable to appeal to political authorities above the village level. Direct personalistic control by the elites made large-scale independent political organization within the communities virtually impossible. Political domination by the village elites reinforced their economic domination. The regional elites were relatively small. Like the village elites, they held appointive office, drew small tax revenues, owned haciendas, and used free peasant labor. They also engaged in minor interregional commercial activity.

THE EARLY TWENTIETH CENTURY: THE DOMINANCE OF TRADERS

A major series of changes came in the late 1890s. After the War of the Pacific (1879-1883) and the conflicts between different military caudillos that followed it, internal order was reestablished and both domestic and foreign trade grew. The arrival of the railroad in Sicuani in 1897 was more important for the region; it permitted new sorts of economic relations with other regions linked to the rise of the wool economy. The change in transportation networks brought the region stimuli that had reached western parts of the sierra much earlier. At first, much of the new activity was confined to the town of Sicuani while the villages and countryside continued under the domination of the local elites.

The result of the arrival of the railroad and the growth in the value of wool exports was not what might have been expected. The *hacendados*, who had dominated the region earlier, lost control, and the wholesale traders became the strongest sector in regional politics. In following their own interests, they sometimes defended other groups against the

FIGURES 25, 26. The annual tribute, or *chaco*, has not entirely disappeared. These men are taking fresh maize and a lamb to the *gobernador* of the district of Sicuani.

hacendados. The shift in power had other effects. The control exercised by the local elites had not extended beyond the villages; the new elites had power over several provinces. The regional level of articulation became more important than it had been before, and the local level less so.

The effect of rising wool prices on the agricultural and pastoral sectors was somewhat different from its effect on the trader sectors.[2] Different producers, both *hacendados* and herders, entered into competition for pastureland. The volume of commerce expanded as the rising value of wool exports permitted increased trade in the agricultural products of other regions and in manufactured goods. These two processes are linked, since the traders favored the peasants and the herders over the *hacendados*.

Wool exports favored several different economic sectors. A conflict emerged around two issues, however, the distribution of income from wool production in the area and general policies that affected the access of different sectors to the factors of production.

Production

One area of conflict occurred between pastoral sectors, the *hacendados* and herders in the punas. As shown in Chapter 6, the annual production of wool was relatively fixed. For this reason, one individual could increase his output only by decreasing that of another. This conflict took a variety of forms in different areas: *Hacendados* attempted both external encroachment onto herder lands (obtaining lands from communities) and internal enroachment (reducing *waqcho* herds on haciendas). They used a variety of techniques. In a few cases, they resorted to open force. Along the Río Ocoruro in Espinar, men on horseback drove peasants off their lands with guns. Such examples of the use of force, though striking in themselves, are relatively few in number. In some cases, peasants were willing to sell their land; others found themselves in debt to the hacendados, with their land as their only collateral. They lost their holdings when they defaulted on their loans.

Most *hacendados* made at least a pretence of going through official channels and obtained documents of sale. Deceit, however, was common. As one journalist stated,

> The notary publics, in whom the public commonly trusts, should be careful not to give bills of sale of property to the Indians while telling them that they are merely

[2] These price changes reached even remote areas, as documented in the discussion of price transmission mechanisms in Chapter 4.

authorizing legal representatives. This is one of the plagues that is eating up Indian lands and leading the Indian to a most detestable poverty.[3] [El Titan, 24.9.20]

This quotation has been supported by many informants' accounts. This legal formality was done not so much out of respect for herders but out of fear of other *hacendados* who could challenge the titles if no bill of sale could be produced. This was especially likely to happen because of the great frequency of disputed inheritances and contested wills. Some *hacendado* families began to spread their holdings beyond their immediate localities. The Caballeros, who originally held some property in the district of Langui in Canas, acquired holdings elsewhere in Canas and in parts of Espinar and Chumbivilcas. Similarly, the Aragón family of San Pablo in Canchis gained lands around Quehue and Checca in Canas.

Peasant political movements also limited the course of hacienda expansion. Cooperation between hacienda peons and *comuneros* permitted rustlers to steal animals from the large haciendas in the province of Canchis. The rustlers entered into agreements with both, giving them cash, animals, and other goods in exchange for information about the location of animals and concealment in the case of pursuit. These networks of support linked peasants in different districts and provinces (Orlove 1973). Rustling increased sharply during the 1920s when wool prices rose, as shown by local newspaper accounts (La Verdad 26.12.21, 7.4.22, 16.7.23, 8.9.23, 16.5.25, 12.3.27); this period overlaps the documented instances of hacienda appropriation of community lands (La Verdad 23.12.20, 27.9.22, 5.12.22, 7.8.26, 13.11.29). The bandits did not prevent *hacendados* from acquiring titles to community lands, but they did limit the reduction of *waycho* herds.

Political movements were larger and more successful in Espinar. The participants in the 1921 peasant rebellion were drawn from a number of communities in the eastern half of the province.[4] Although the rebels were defeated and the leader captured and executed, *hacendados* in what are now the districts of Ocoruro and Tocroyoc took no more peasant land. A movement in the province of Canas in the same year had a

---

[3] Que los señores notários públicos, como depositarios de la fé pública, tengan buen cuidado de que a los indígenas no se les engañe haciéndoles otorgar escrituras de venta de sus propiedades, diciéndoles que se está otorgando escrituras de poder; esta es una de las plagas que va consumiendo la propiedad indígena y conduciendo el indio al mas detestable pauperismo. [El Titan, 24.9.20].

[4] Piel states that it is not known whether various communities were involved (1967: 375); I established that they were in the course of interviews with surviving participants of the 1931 Molloccahua rebellion.

FIGURE 27. The man at the left of this group is a rustler. This photograph was taken in the Sicuani jail. Prisoners are provided with small areas in which to set up shops. In this manner, they can earn money to purchase food. Rustling continues to be carried out; after the agrarian reform (see pp. 181–183) the ex-haciendas, now cooperatives, remain the principal targets for the rustlers in the province of Canchis. The rustlers still enter into agreements with the herders.

similar effect. Ten years later, a rebellion in Espinar in the community of Molloccahua was more spontaneous and drew on a smaller area, but had a stronger effect. It included both community members and hacienda peons. Their killing of two policemen led to violent reprisals, but several *hacendado* families abandoned their lands. The expansion of haciendas in the districts of Yauri and Pichigua was effectively halted (Orlove 1974c).

Marketing

The growth of Sicuani as a commerical center led to the increasing importance of the cash mode of articulation between the different production sectors (Arguedas 1947). As wool producers withdrew from barter and joint production modes of articulation, they began to use cash more frequently to purchase agricultural produce and artisan goods. They were also wealthier than before; hence demand increased, stimulating retailing and artisan production. Population figures reflected this growth. Appendix 4 documents the changes in population in certain villages and towns. Sicuani began to take the lead, with a growth made up largely of artisans, traders, and individuals economically linked to them.

The position of the wool traders in the conflicts within the productive sector was indirect. As shown in Chapter 6, the annual wool production varied relatively little. In the first four decades of the century, traders purchased nearly all the wool in the town of Sicuani itself. It was brought to them either by the producers themselves or by the traveling buyers in the punas. Herder wool was somewhat more profitable, since the traders paid them lower prices than they paid the *hacendados*.[5]

The traders had a stronger reason for favoring the herders and peasants over the *hacendados*. The *hacendados* spent much of their money outside the area. The case of a member of the Aragón family who sent his children to study in Paris is extreme but not aberrant. Many *hacendados* took trips to Arequipa and Lima where they purchased imported goods. They also maintained residences in those cities. By contrast, the herder or peasant made purchases from the traders who bought their wool; they bought sugar, *aguardiente*, tools, cloth, and many other small items. One reporter, concerned about the negative effect on trade of a temporary scarcity of metal coins to which the peasants were still accustomed, stated:

> We know quite well that . . . the Indians are the ones who sustain commerical traffic [in Sicuani] as in all towns of the interior, whether as suppliers of wool, hides and grains, or as consumers of basic commodities . . . if the merchants do not agree to safeguard their own commercial life, the town will suffer the most painful consequences.[6] [La Verdad 27.2.15]

[5] The traders' expenses for bulking peasant wool and offering them lodging during the transactions were relatively low.

[6] Sabemos muy bien que . . . los indios son los que sostienen el movimiento comercial, como en toda población del interior, ya sea como expendedores de lanas, cueros y granos, o como consumidores de artículos de primera necesidad . . . si los comerciantes no toman un acuerdo para salvaguardar su misma vida comercial, dentro de poco . . . el pueblo sufrirá las más dolorosas consecuencias. [La Verdad, 27.3.15].

This does not reflect an arbitrary conservatism; the author continues, "Porque como estos [indios] no pueden recibir los cheques porque no saben leer y facilmente pueden ser víctimas de alguna picardía . . . "

The conflict between the traders and the *hacendados* was not always direct. Unlike those in many other parts of the sierra, the Sicuani *hacendados* did not maintain *mercantiles* or stores where their peons were obliged to make their purchases; there were only a few exceptions, such as Antayccacca in Maranganí. Similarly, disputes between land-owners and peasants in areas quite removed from Sicuani did not always concern the traders directly. However, certain basic conflicts had to come to a final resolution. The *hacendados* wanted to reduce the peasantry to an inexpensive and docile work force well under their control. To be able to work their lands, the *hacendados* needed regular labor and sizable work groups of additional workers at certain critical periods. They used several means to maintain their dominance over peon and *comunero* alike: They controlled the local judicial and legal machinery and had access to means of repression. They monopolized employment possibilities so that peasants looking for money had to turn to them. They were able to prevent attempts at political organiza-tion among peasants and herders; passive resistance, social banditry, and brief rebellions were the main forms of protest available to the peasants and herders.

The merchants ended the domination of these local elites, ensuring the permanence of their numerous peasant and herder clientele. The traders wanted to loosen the system of forced, unpaid labor, in part because they had ready access to cash and could afford to pay workers, servants, construction laborers, and others their very low wages and in part because they recognized that forced labor tended to keep peasants away from town and market for fear of being pressed into work gangs.[7] The traders gave the peasants access to source of cash other than the *hacendados*. Finally, by being located in the regional center, the traders were able to gain the support of judicial authorities and lawyers who were siding with the peasants in some of their claims against the *hacendados*.

To sum up, the regional society might take two possible directions with the expansion of the wool economy. The *hacendados* might come to dominate the punas, owning the lands and herds and monopolizing wool production; this control would leave relatively little room for the traders, who would purchase the wool and supply the *hacendados'* small local needs. Alternatively, the punas might remain in the hands of the herders, with a correspondingly greater volume of local purchases, to

[7] However, the merchants were willing to use peasant labor under the *Ley de Conscrip-ción Vial*.

the advantage of the merchants and agricultural peasants and artisans as well.[8]

Interrelations

The urban traders had several advantages over the *hacendados*. They were fewer in number and less fragmented. The *hacendados* were scattered throughout the entire region, each localized in the villages, and so it was difficult for them to make contact with each other. They tended to be suspicious of each other, each one fearing, with good reason, that the others were trying to enlarge their holdings at the expense of his own. It took a strong external threat, such as the Molloccahua uprising, to lead *hacendados* to cooperate (Orlove 1974c).

The traders also had more important links outside the region; and the *hacendados* were relatively weak in this regard. As pointed out earlier, there was a disproportionately low number of senators from the region. With their direct ties to the capital and the influence of the Arequipa firms, the traders had an additional source of power. As outsiders, many of them had kin in Arequipa. The number of *hacendado* families with Arequipa relatives, like the Pórcels of El Descanso and the Álvarez of Yauri, was much smaller.

The traders came to dominate the *concejo provincial* of Canchis and the *municipalidad* of Sicuani. Electoral governments favored them, since they offered personal favors to the voters who were concentrated in the town of Sicuani. They were able to use the *concejo provincial* to make some important policy decisions and to handle the larger budget of the *municipalidad*. This position gained them the support of the lawyers, who began to represent peasants and herders as well as *hacendados* in land disputes. As cases became prolonged and Sicuani acquired the reputation of being a center of litigation, this shift proved profitable to the lawyers. They found that the peasants could pay stiff legal fees when required.[9] A woman in Cuzco, recalling several months she spent

[8] The fates of the pastoral and agricultural sectors were, in theory, relatively independent. However, *hacendados* would attempt to own agricultural land as well as pasture, whereas the merchant would prefer to see relatively independent peasant groups in both the agricultural and pastoral sectors. The wool-producing sector strongly affected the agricultural.

[9] A small grain retailer in Sicuani owned a dog named Abogado (lawyer). I asked him why he gave his dog that name. He told me that the dog once secretly killed three of his chickens, eating one and destroying the other two so that they were useless. At that point he realized that the dog was like a lawyer, since, as he put it, *"come del poco que tienen los pobres."*

in Sicuani in 1942 as a child, said that the town was filled with *"bodegas y abogados"* (stores and lawyers).

The trader sectors were also favored by national trends. Wool was not the only export commodity to grow; sugar, cotton, and minerals experienced an even more rapid growth. Workers were needed in these sectors, particularly after the end of the importation of Chinese coolies (Piel 1970: 131). Some small-scale industrialization and a much larger growth of commercial and national bureaucracies led to rapid urbanization, especially in Lima. Migration met the need for a larger work force, as rural dwellers moved to the large export-oriented estates and the growing cities on the coast. People from the Sicuani region took part in this process.

The political system could not successfully accommodate the pressures generated by these economic changes. Leguía established himself as president from 1919 to 1930. Many of his innovations directly affected the relations of these different sectors in the Sicuani region. He created the Benemérita Guardia Civil, a police force that replaced the small and ineffective rural gendarmerie (García Márquez 1975: 117).

In response to a number of *indigenista* ideological currents, he permitted Indian communities to receive official recognition as corporate bodies with inalienable rights in their lands (Chevalier 1970: 189–193; Davies 1974). The bureaucratic procedures were simple; a group of peasants or herders who presented certain officials a list of community members and a sketch map of their lands were granted the special legal status of Indian community.

Finally, Leguía installed the economic infrastructure necessary for the expansion of the export economies. A number of its elements (e.g., port facilities, financial institutions) were located on the coast, but the sierra was affected by the *Ley de Conscripción Vial*, or Road Conscription Law, by which all adult males were required to provide between 6 and 12 days' labor annually building roads or pay a fine.

These changes were all used by the traders to win power in Sicuani and thus dominate the region, weakening the *hacendados'* position. The Guardia Civil did support the *hacendados* during the peasant rebellions and in the more routine task of capturing rustlers. It was not able to end rustling around Sicuani, however, as it did in other areas, such as nearby portions of the department of Puno. This occasional support was not sufficient to maintain the *hacendados'* position; the Guardia Civil did not favor *hacendados* generally, by forcing peasants and herders to perform *faena* labor, arresting tenants who did not pay rent, and so forth. The Guardia Civil's own use of petty graft, corruption, theft, and forced labor was a continuous drain on the peasantry, but it was not comparable to the large-scale consistent exploitation of the *hacendados*.

Sicuani newspapers often published the complaints of *hacendados* who resented the unwillingness of the peasants and herders to work as they once had; one *hacendado*, frustrated at the sight of Sicuani full of peasants on market day, called it "Lazyville" (*ociosolópolis*) (La Verdad 18.11.45). By way of contrast, *hacendados* in other parts of the sierra were able to use the Guardia Civil for their own ends. For instance, one *hacendado* in the province of Daniel Carrión, department of Pasco, not only had a police station established within his own hacienda but had sufficiently strong connections with the regional authorities to have a *cabo*, or corporal, whom he did not like replaced (Kapsoli 1972: 111).

Much as the relatively benevolent attitude of the authorities and the Guardia Civil permitted peasants and herders to regain some control of their labor, the *indigenista* legislation permitted Indian communities to receive official recognition of their lands, preventing further depredation of their lands by *hacendados*. To obtain this recognition, peasants entered into direct contact with representatives of the national ministries in Sicuani and Cuzco. They bypassed the village elites to receive support from higher-level officials. The Sicuani area resembled the rest of the department of Cuzco in taking early advantage of these laws, and a number of communities were recognized in the latter half of the 1920s (Orlove 1975). Some later governments continued these policies. They set up some agencies active in the region, such as the *Liga de Cultura Indígena* (La Verdad 11.4.31) and the *Brigada de Culturización Indígena* (La Verdad 23.11.39). Later governments added less exclusively Indian agencies, such as branches of the agriculture and education ministries.

The traders used the *Ley de Conscripción Vial* to their advantage. They dominated the *Junta Vial*, administering this law in Canas and Canchis, and built a road linking Sicuani with Cuzco and Arequipa, thus ending the virtual monopoly of the British-owned Southern Peruvian Railway in interregional trade. In other parts of the sierra, *hacendados* controlled the *Juntas Viales* and built roads linking their properties with provincial capitals and major market towns. The *hacendados* in Espinar used the law for this purpose, but in that province a German mining company had already built a road linking Yauri with the *altiplano* before World War I. This particular change in transportation networks further favored the traders over the *hacendados*; these roads remained after the law was revoked in 1930 and continued to be maintained.

Power Shifts

The traders used several sorts of institutions to consolidate and maintain their position. They regularly held important positions on the *concejo provincial*. They formed a *Sociedad de Comerciantes*, whose strength was in sharp contrast to the weakness of the *Liga de Hacendados*. The latter did not have regular elections or an established meeting place. It was unable to direct government funds toward projects that would favor the *hacendados*. Puno *hacendados* received sheep dip, and agricultural *hacendados* in the province of Anta near Cuzco were given threshing machines, but those in Sicuani received virtually nothing. The *obras públicas*, such as the construction of a roofed marketplace, favored the traders.

The mutual support between the traders and the representatives of the state ministries and agencies proved useful to both. Certain institutions helped to consolidate this support. Social and literary clubs were established in the 1920s and 1930s. They provided a context in which traders and bureaucrats could meet and discuss matters informally. These clubs were ranked according to the wealth and power of their members. Sicuani has been noted as a town where they are of unusual importance (Julio Cotler, personal communication). The large number of literary journals also demonstrates the vitality of these or-

FIGURE 28. This monument commemorates the foundation of the Rotary Club in Sicuani in 1937. The women in front of it are selling *llipt'a*, a substance made from the ash of *cañihua* stalks. Small quantities of *llipt'a* are chewed with coca leaf.

ganizations (Medina Díaz 1965). Until the 1960s, social activity in the Sicuani clubs was as extensive as in larger sierra cities such as Cuzco. This fact reflects the composition of the elite; in areas where hacendados predominate, individuals know each other, and kinship and *compadrazgo* links are more important. Traders and bureaucrats are more mobile and transient and do not have such well established networks. Clubs serve as a way for newcomers to gain entry into the provincial elite, a forum to mark people as acceptable, and a context in which to make contacts.[10]

To give one example of the operation of these links, the annual fair in Sicuani, which was the outcome of a long promotion beginning in 1926 (Pampacucho 6.9.42), brings a considerable amount of commercial activity to the region. The traders, with strong ties to Arequipa firms, have been able to get rebates from the Southern Peruvian Railway for both vendors and customers. The *Ministerio de Agricultura* also gives support by having its staff work on the fairgrounds, spreading information in the communities, and using its local agents to encourage peasants to attend.

Another example of the importance of these economic and political links between sectors is the espansion of the production of fireworks by specialized urban artisans (*pirotécnicos*) in Sicuani since the late nineteenth century. At that time, virtually all fireworks used in the area were imported from Japan. The demand for fireworks began to grow in the early decades of the twentieth century with the expansion and elaboration of patron saint fiestas at rural chapels. The rising demand for wool and foodstuffs had led to increased competition for land among peasants, herders, and *hacendados*, a competition that increased in turn the importance of a major aspect of the fiestas, the symbolic affirmation of the rights of individuals, as members of corporate groups, to use specific tracts of land. Because of the increased revenue from sales of wool and foodstuffs, peasants and herders had more cash to spend on the fiestas and purchased larger quantities of fireworks. The raw materials for the fireworks included explosives purchased from wholesalers who ordered them from Arequipa and *cañas* or reeds brought from the *montaña* by retailers and rural traders. Several families of *pirotécnicos* in Sicuani have supported themselves by making fireworks for several decades.

This expansion of fiestas in many cases was an important preliminary step to the official recognition of communities (Orlove 1975). Negotia-

---

[10] A few *hacendados* belong to the clubs, but they form a small portion of the total membership and are rarely elected to office.

tions with priests to introduce new masses into their ritual calendars gave peasants and herders experience in organizing new local activities and dealing directly with representatives of large bureaucratic institutions. This simple case of import-substitution industrialization illustrates in a small way the sharing of interests among peasants and herders, wholesale and retail traders, and urban artisans and bureaucrats.

More significant than fireworks is the development of education (van den Berghe and Primov 1977). It illustrates the composition of the elite and their links to the sectors directly engaged in production. Rural schools have been a focus of *hacendado*–peasant conflict in many parts of the sierra (Alberti and Sánchez 1974: 139–141). Since education gives peasants and herders better preparation for urban employment, they are more likely to leave the local area. Literate peons are more difficult for *hacendados* to control, since they are more open to political mobilization and can enter into contact with government officials and lawyers more easily on their own. The establishment of schoolhouses, like the expansion of fiestas, has been an important step toward the official recognition of many communities. The presence of schoolteachers breaks the *hacendados'* power monopoly. Although instances of *hacendado* opposition to rural schools are not entirely lacking in the Sicuani region, the *hacendados* have been less able there than elsewhere to prevent the spread of schools. Instead, there has been a strong drive toward education on all levels. Rural primary schools have been established in most officially recognized communities (PEIFEDER 1971). The traders have supported the night school in Sicuani organized by the urban artisans' association. The *Instituto Nacional Agropecuaria*, or INA, which offers a mixture of academic and technical training, is one of the oldest in the sierra. The secondary schools are also old and large. The *Ministerio de Educación*, the traders, and the *concejo provincial* have given active support to school construction and expansion. The elite has organized fund-raising drives.

The link between the urban and rural schools is strong. The INA draws over half its students from among the graduates of the rural elementary schools, and the secondary schools draw nearly that many (Payne 1968). This extensive education is advantageous to the traders, since teachers' salaries are spent locally. The wholesale traders run the eight bookstores that provide school supplies to the provinces of Canas, Canchis, Espinar, Chumbivilcas, and Acomayo, as well as parts of Quispicanchis and Melgar. Other urban sectors also benefit. Commercial activity comes to the small storekeepers as well as to the larger traders. The artisans also benefit; the tailors sew school uniforms, and the carpenters make school furniture. This example of the links among traders, bureaucrats, peasants, and herders in opposition to the *hacendados* is representative.

THE MID-TWENTIETH CENTURY: CHANGES IN THE ELITES

This general configuration has continued to the present. It is marked by an elite (wholesale traders and bureaucrats) and other urban sectors (retail traders and urban artisans) in Sicuani, and a countryside largely in the hands of communities composed of peasants, herders, rural traders, and rural artisans; the *hacendados* are weak. This section examines some aspects of the elite more closely and discusses changes in its composition in the 1950s.

The elite is strikingly impermanent. Many of its members are born outside the Sicuani region, primarily in Arequipa. They encourage their children to leave the area, and many of them also move out. This career pattern has different roots for the wholesale traders and the bureaucrats. The importance of outside connections for traders has been explained in Chapter 9. Consequently, most of them come from outside the region and return to their places of origin. This is especially true of the largest traders, who are often agents and in some cases employees of outside firms.

The same pattern applies to the bureaucrats. There are relatively few positions with high pay and considerable influence in Sicuani; they include the prelate and the heads of the regional offices of the *Ministerio de Educación*, the *Ministerio de Agricultura*, the *Banco de Fomento Agropecuario*, and the *Guardia Civil*. These offices tend to be occupied by men in their 30s and 40s who expect transfers to Cuzco, Arequipa, or Lima. Although they may no longer be in charge of entire divisions in their new positions, they will still have made important advancements. This "up-and-out" pattern also applies to lower-level bureaucrats, and only a few positions tend to be permanent. These include secondary school principals and important judges.

The Sicuani cemetery offers evidence of this transience. There are only four or five large tombstones, two of which have tumbled down. In other towns, well-attended graves indicate a more permanent elite, whose children remain and offer public testimony of the importance and wealth of their predecessors by maintaining their graves.[11] In Sicuani, ancestry and inheritance of wealth is not so important a basis for elite membership as in centers more dominated by *hacendados*.

Another factor favoring this circulation of elites is the lack of sizable capital investment opportunities in the Sicuani region. In other words, the elite leaves because there is no place for them to invest their profits in Sicuani. For instance, traders reach diseconomies of scale with excessively large inventions. Even real estate investment is relatively limited around Sicuani. Retail traders and urban artisans invest in inventories and artisan shops, but larger-scale investments (such as the textile mill described in Chapter 7) are relatively few. Some of the enterprises, such as the mineral water and soft drink bottling plants in San Pedro, can be handled by a manager, with only brief, infrequent visits by the owner. Some enterprises are favored by Sicuani's distance from other towns, such as the radio and gasoline stations. A few involve land-intensive use of small plots in the valley near the town: There is a small dairy farm, two chicken farms, and a brothel. Given this lack of opportunity, most of the elite invest outside the area and provide their children with professional educations that entail settling in large cities.

These limitations on investment seem to be partly the outcome of national political processes. The *Sociedad de Comerciantes*, the *concejo provincial*, and other groups have put on long campaigns to get support for a cement plant and a large tannery. Government aid would have been necessary, either in the form of direct investment in construction and operation or in loans to private individuals through development banks. Without such aid, private investment is limited to small factories such as the bottling plants. Government aid to this small-scale industrialization in the south, however, goes primarily to Arequipa and, to a lesser extent, to other cities. Political influence determines the location of investment, as Dew documents in the case of a cement plant (1969: 106–108). The elite, then, would be willing to commit itself more thoroughly to the Sicuani region, but it does not find it profitable.

One sign of this commitment is the strength of what I will call the campaign for the formation of the department of Vilcanota, or the Vilcanota campaign for short. This campaign has one central issue: that the Sicuani region should become a department. The earliest instances of this campaign for which I have records took place in the 1920s (La Verdad 19.4.22), and it continues to the present. The provinces to be

---

[11] The internal psychological state of the children at the time of the funeral is not necessarily an explicit or cynical calculation of strategies, but the consequences of their actions are the same.

included vary; they are usually Canas, Canchis, Espinar, and Chumbivilcas and at times Melgar, Cailloma, Carabaya, Acomayo, and part of Quispicanchis. This campaign is only one instance of the attempts of different administrative units to move up the ladder of district–province–department; the threats of the department of Loreto to secede from the Peruvian nation are only an extension of this. The *departamentalización* would give Sicuani a certain degree of fiscal independence from Cuzco as well as a greater number of administrative offices, important for patronage. It reflects annoyance at Cuzco's collection of tax revenues from the area and the apportionment of these revenues, intended for the entire department, only to the city of Cuzco. The elite organized large public rallies on occasion for this campaign and dedicated special issues of local periodicals and, more recently, radio programs to it. It is a common theme of political speeches. Pressures from peasant groups in the 1960s also led to the expansion of government services (Orlove 1977d). Belaúnde's rather mild agrarian reform law followed considerable rural agitation in different parts of Peru and led to further turmoil. The La Convención valley was the scene of repeated peasant strikes and land invasions in the early 1960s. University students and peasants from Canchis who had taken part in these movements organized hacienda invasion near Sicuani in 1964, with the support of the *Federación de Campesinos del Cuzco* (Peasant Federation of Cuzco). Peasants from adjacent communities and haciendas occupied both the lands and a mill belonging to the *hacendado*. The *Guardia Civil* was called out and killed more than 100 peasants. This episode occurred after the main thrust of peasant movements elsewhere in the sierra (Handelman 1975: 62–154) at a time when the policies of repression of the movements and the expansion of government programs in politicized areas were becoming more clearly formulated than they had been earlier. The regional elites may have perceived the relatively low risk of a major social upheaval and the possible benefits of an enlarged administrative sector. These movements led to the formation of a *Zona de Acción Conjunta* (joint action zone). A number of state agencies collaborated on these joint programs associated with Belaúnde's political party.

The wholesale traders had found an additional urgent reason for the Vilcanota campaign. The sharp fall in wool prices after the Korean War led to a reduction in the number of firms operating in Arequipa. These firms adopted a more cautious purchasing policy. Nearly all the wool in Sicuani is now purchased by the agents of five Arequipa firms (see Appendix 5), operating on short-term credit. Independent wool buyers, who were also wholesalers of manufactured goods, were virtually wiped out as a group. In other words, some units in one sector of the elite, the large wholesalers, shrank. The national government responded by enlarging the other, the bureaucracy. Although Sicuani has not become the capital of a department, the campaign has not been a complete failure.

A new department was not created, but a number of offices usually found only in departmental capitals were established, as discussed in Chapter 5. With proposals for the consolidation of departments being issued occasionally,[12] it seems unlikely that a new department will be created. Yet while some of the 23 departmental capitals are losing importance, as supradepartmental agencies are created (paralleling the division of Peru into five military regions), Sicuani receives new offices.[13]

The Catholic Church in the Sicuani region has tended to follow these shifts in the composition of elites and the political relations among

[12] Huancavelica seems a particularly likely candidate for future extinction.

[13] The penetration of bureaucratic agencies to distant portions of the Sicuani region and the ambiguity of peasant response is demonstrated by this *huayno* from the remote district of Velille, province of Chumbivilcas, collected in 1973. It is ironically dedicated to a document, submitted on the official stamped and lined paper available in bookstores.

In the translation, the sentences in English are numbered to correspond with the verses of the *huayno*.

> *papelcha sellado, papelcha rayado,*
> *papelcha sellado, papelcha rayado,*
> *mayta juzgadopiraq muyuriyushanki*
> *mayta juzgadopiraq muyuriyushanki.*
>
> *desdecortemanta orinchay yanasqa*
> *desdecortemanta orinchay yanasqa*
> *chay sumaq tata pusamuychiq nispa*
> *chay sumaq tata apamuychiq nispa.*
>
> *rinayta munaspaqa pasanayta munaspaqa*
> *rinayta munaspaqa pasanayta munaspaqa*
> *josecha avilata apachimachunku*
> *pedro avilata apachimachunku.*
>
> *papelcha sellado, papelcha rayado,*
> *papelcha sellado, papelcha rayado,*
> *mayqen tribunalpiraq tukuyá tapunki*
> *supremo tribunalpiraq p'antayá tapunki.*

(1) Oh little document, to which court will your turnings take you? (2) From the court you have been left below somewhere to darken, while they say, "This nice notable will lead you [to where you are going]." (3) If I want to go to see you, may you be taken to José and Pedro Ávila [local notables]. (4) Oh little document, you ask in which tribunal you will end up, you ask if there will be a mistake in the supreme tribunal.

sectors. At the end of the nineteenth century, parish priests were drawn from the local *hacendado* families. Most of them were secular rather than regular; that is, they were attached to specific dioceses rather than religious orders.

The bishop had administrative authority over them but exercised relatively little influence. They derived their incomes from payments for the performance of the sacraments and from Church haciendas. In a number of cases, the priests became involved in village politics. In the first decade of this century, the parish priests in Quehue in the province of Canas were active in the campaign to raise the village from the status of an *anexo* of Checca to an independent district (Orlove 1974d). The parish priest in Yauri helped organize *hacendado* vigilantes during the Molloccahua uprising of 1931 (Orlove 1974c). The expansion of community fiestas helped support the priests, but their incomes and land-holding appear to have declined much as those of the *hacendado* elites with whom they were associated. The peasants in the district of Tungasuca in the province of Canas, for example, stopped providing unpaid domestic service to the priests (Orlove 1975). The growth of the cash mode of articulation, the increase of alternative economic activities, and the rise of the powerful trader sectors all contributed to the decline of peasant support for local priests.

The position of the Church in recent decades is once again congruent with the dominant power relations in the region. The 1959 encyclical, *Princeps Pastorum*, of Pope John XXIII directed religious orders in developed nations to devote a greater portion of their activities to the Third World. In response, a number of prelatures and dioceses were created in that year in southern Peru with the assistance of specific orders; Ayaviri received the support of the Order of the Sacred Heart, Juli of the Maryknolls, and the prelature of Sicuani was established with the support of the Chicago Province of the Carmelite Order. This prelature is composed of the provinces of Canas, Canchis, Espinar, and Chumbivilcas.

The formation of the prelature brought an influx of funds and personnel to Sicuani. The prelate constructed a large residence on the edge of town after living several years in the former residence of the Mejía family at the textile factory in Marangani. The parish house in Sicuani was also refurbished. A number of foreign priests and nuns joined their Peruvian colleagues in Sicuani. They were active in education and public health (Payne 1968). A number of them taught in the public high schools (the *colegios nacionales*) and worked in the government hospital. They drew salaries and support from their orders, and so they did not rely, except secondarily, on the performance of the sacraments to make a

FIGURE 29. The image of a saint housed in a chapel in an outlying neighborhood of Sicuani is made to bow to the more powerful saints in the cathedral on the main square. The continued importance of the cathedral and its saints is part of the centralization of power structures in the Sicuani region.

living. Direct contacts with peasants and herders were made by some of the priests and nuns in both Sicuani and other villages with several ecclesiastical personnel, such as Langui, San Pablo, and Yanaoca. They trained peasant catechists in current Catholic practice and doctrine in an effort to reduce or eliminate traditional rituals of dubious orthodoxy, and they undertook small development projects, such as improved sanitation, increased use of fertilizer, and pig-raising programs.

In both Sicuani and the villages, then, the priests cooperated with government agencies. Their position was similar to that of other bureaucrats; they were part of a highly centralized system with a regional center in Sicuani, they concentrated their resources in Sicuani rather than in rural areas, they drew salaries from outside the region, and they had small peasant clienteles in rural areas. The importance of the ties of the Church to other powerful sectors in Sicuani is revealed by the individuals who challenged this relation. In 1973, an American priest and nun were strongly encouraged to leave the prelature. They were part of a group of foreign missionaries who had helped to create a *comunidad de base* or center in Sicuani where a number of discussion groups and meetings were held. This center succeeded in developing a parish council with growing participation of urban laity and peasant catechists. The involvement of this group with the rural sectors drew some of the principals to move out of town. The priest had established a center near Sicuani for peasant catechists where issues of social justice as well as Catholic doctrine were discussed. Support from outside was curtailed, and the peasants reconstructed and expanded the center in the style of their own houses, using their own resources. The nun, who was a nurse, set up a clinic in a peasant community in one of the side *quebradas* of the Río Vilcanota valley. She had left the hospital because she believed that the majority of the medical problems in the region were in the countryside rather than in town. She trained local peasants in first aid procedures and sponsored meetings in which the social and economic causes of health problems were discussed. Both the priest and the nun began to ride bicycles rather than cars and adopted a simpler lifestyle than many other religious personnel.

Under pressure from the large traders and other bureaucrats, high Church officials directed them to leave. Their open support of the peasantry and their questioning of the existing social order were one challenge to the established relations among sectors; their disregard of the centralized bureaucratic structures was equally serious. The priest wanted funds for the reconstruction of the cathedral on the main square of Sicuani to be diverted to the smaller chapels in the poorer outlying neighborhoods; the nun wanted rural clinics to be relatively autonomous from the central hospital in Sicuani. The content and form of their activities thus challenged the logic underlying the Vilcanota campaign and the position of the elite in Sicuani.

Sicuani's transition from a commercial to a mixed commercial and administrative center has not been an uncomfortable process for the wholesale traders, many of whom found opportunities to adapt as individuals. One wool merchant purchased a large building near the railroad station and converted it into a hotel, hoping that commercial travelers would stay there. When commercial activity declined, he rented it to the *Ministerio de Agricultura* for their offices. They pay him a larger rent than would normally be given for such a building, receiving his good will and that of his friends in return. The wife of another wool merchant runs a cafe on the main square; she charges high prices for her pastry and coffee, and the clientele consists largely of sophisticated young ministry employees, who find the other restaurants unsuitably provincial.[14]

---

[14] There are parallels with the functions of the social clubs which the younger bureaucrats find too stuffy and *burgués*.

More important is the money the government invests in agricultural and educational programs. Some of it returns directly to the wholesale traders. Loans from the *Banco de Fomento Agropecuario* are spent on fertilizer and seed at the shops known as *agro-veterinarias*. In other cases, the money comes indirectly. School-building programs lead peasants to purchase school supplies. This closeness of interest often leads to the cooperation documented above.

With these changes, the regional elite remains as a set of inter-mediaries. The commercial aspect still continues, though confined to a narrower set of channels. Sicuani is now a wholesale center. The elite articulates the rural traders in the new marketplaces and community stores with Arequipa and Lima firms. As bureaucrats, the elites link national institutions and local-level peasant organizations. At times, this articulation takes the form of personal vertical mediation; more often the ties are shorter in duration and more impersonal. The impor-tant articulation continues to be on a regional level; local landowning elites have virtually disappeared.

Following the 1968 coup, the military government completed the process with a land reform that finally eliminated the already enfeebled *hacendados* and organizational changes that have increased the number of bureaucrats. The trader–bureaucrat alliance has completely de-stroyed the *hacendados*. The peasants once again face a unified elite, but on a regional rather than a local level. This elite draws its power from its contacts with Arequipa and Lima rather than from independent power bases. The responses of the peasants to this elite will open the next period of the history of the region. The next section of the chapter, based on visits to Sicuani in 1974 and 1976, interviews with individuals who have traveled there, and published sources, reviews the impact of the military government there.

THE SICUANI REGION IN THE MID-1970s

Like the rest of Peru, the Sicuani region has been greatly affected by the military government which took power in 1968. The fact that the changes there have been less dramatic than in many other areas illustrates several themes of this book: the weakness of the *hacendados* in the region and the focus of governmental attention on other richer, more productive areas. It also demonstrates the importance of viewing the internal dynamic of the Sicuani region as well as the external one.

The military government has been the subject of extensive debate, since it resists simple classification into one of the well-known types of

FIGURE 30. These buildings in the district of San Pablo, province of Canchis, illustrate the relative position of two elite sectors. The older building in poor condition, to the right, belongs to an old family of agricultural *hacendados*. The newer building with its more solid balcony, roof, and walls houses government offices.

Latin American regimes. Particularly in its early years, observers were puzzled by the odd mixture of left-wing nationalism and militarism. Despite the obvious crises of the previous government (Bourricaud 1967), they did not expect a military coup to be followed by nationalization of major foreign firms and progressive reforms of industry, finance, education, agriculture, mining, fishing, and other economic and social sectors. Massive state investment appeared to indicate a commitment to industrialization based on the public sector. The government's nationalistic insistence on its uniqueness and proclamations of its independent foreign policy did not clarify its fundamental directions; students of the government had to puzzle through a variety of new forms of economic and political organization to assess the validity of official declarations that Peru was neither capitalist nor communist and that its military government was based on the full participation of the masses (Cotler 1970, 1972). The interested reader is referred to two recent edited volumes on this government (Lowenthal 1975; Chaplin 1976); the British weekly journal *Latin America* also provides useful information.

Since 1974, many observers note a retreat from the commitment to the role of the public sector in the national economy and the transfer of power to the masses. The decline in international copper prices and the lack of petroleum in the Amazon basin exacerbated the economic difficulties Peru shared with many other Third World countries, and the government was unable to continue its investment policies. Changes in leadership and the withdrawal of support from key institutional innovations have provoked much comment (Fitzgerald 1977). Despite these differences from the early revolutionary days, there is much greater resemblance between the Peru of Velasco and the Peru of Morales Bermúdez than between the governments of Cámpora and Videla in Argentina, Torres and Banzer in Bolivia, or Allende and Pinochet in Chile.

The task of this section, however, is to review changes in the Sicuani region rather than in Peru as a whole. The most important reform for the region was the agrarian reform promulgated on 24 June 1969. It established procedures for the government to expropriate privately held land and transfer it to agricultural workers. Subsequent laws established and modified the complex juridical and administrative structures that oversee these transformations. Most of the expropriated land was granted to production cooperatives and to SAISs (*sociedades agrícolas de interés social*), large associative units linking cooperative and peasant communities.

The large, heavily capitalized, productive sugar plantations on the coast were the first units to be expropriated, and this interest in the most productive areas and crops continued later. Wool no longer contributes a major share to the nation's exports, and the southern sierra has some of the least productive agriculture in the country. The agrarian reform thus did not reach the Sicuani region until 1973. The administrators of the agrarian reform found that haciendas were neither large nor numerous in the Sicuani region as in many other regions. Most of the haciendas were pastoral; and by 1976, the punas of the region had been converted into cooperatives and, particularly in Canchis and Canas, SAISs; the expropriated *hacendados* were given bonds as indemnifications. The ex-peons retained their *waqcho* herds. These expropriations thus occurred during the period of economic difficulties for the government, so it invested less in these cooperatives and SAISs than it had earlier in economically and politically more important regions.

Many important decisions in the cooperatives and SAISs remain in the hands of the administrators, who retain close ties to the ministries to whom they report as well as to the ex-peons. The cooperatives and the SAISs have the potential for introducing significant changes into the productivity of the pastoral sector. Unlike the *hacendados* and the prereform herders, they potentially have the access to the capital and political power necessary to introduce fencing (which would permit further selection of stock, the use of veterinary medicine, and the sowing of pasture). Thus, economic change and further transfer of power to the herders depends on the responses of the peasant and herder sectors to policy at the national level. In the meantime, the countryside of Sicuani appears much less transformed by agrarian reform than that of many other regions, since the *hacendados* were already so weak and since the state has provided relatively few resources to the new units.

The state has also proposed the reorganization of wool marketing through the establishment of enterprises for this purpose. Both the sheep wool marketing organization, INCOLANA, and the corresponding organization for alpaca wool, ALPACAPERU, are social property enterprises that are to be characterized by workers' self-management through the purchase of shares by workers' councils. These enterprises have special access to loans and other forms of government assistance. The government hoped that these two marketing organizations would eventually market the entire Peruvian clip, much as marketing boards have come to do for cotton and other crops (Yambert 1976). They would collaborate with the cooperatives and the SAISs. In addition, INCOLANA and ALPACAPERU would promote technical improvements in production practices and in the classification of wool and in other social property enterprises, such as textile factories. The establishment of ALPACAPERU in 1975 took place on the fifth anniversary of the formation of a large SAIS; the director of the National Social Property Commission (CONAPS, Comisión Nacional de Propiedad Social) proclaimed, "Peruvian participatory socialism is expressed in this simple act" (INCOLANA EPS 1976: 3).[15] The recent decline in support for social property enterprises may delay these further goals and the completion of a participatory socialism. In the meantime, INCOLANA and ALPACAPERU act as additional wool buyers in the Sicuani region; like the private buyers, they have a series of suppliers whom they pay in cash. These firms have shown great initial success, due to high prices for wool on the international market, the establishment of direct links with European textile firms, and their ability to give producers higher prices than their private competitors (Latin America Commodities Report 11 Feb. 1977). These enterprises retain a considerable potential for transforming the regional economy in much the same way as the

---

[15] "En este sencillo acto se expresa el socialismo participatorio peruano."

cooperatives and SAISs do. It remains to be seen whether a large center for the classification of wool will be established in Sicuani.

Finally, the government has opposed certain practices of retail traders. It has proposed the establishment of boards to receive consumer complaints against unfairly high prices, speculation, and hoarding. A few traders have been fined for such practices. Government-subsidized stores called *tambos* would market manufactured goods directly to the consumer, avoiding the entire chain of intermediaries. The *tambos* are still few in number.

In short, the government has attempted to replace the *hacendados* and wholesale wool traders and limit the retail traders. It has been successful only in the first of these tasks, because the *hacendado* sectors were weaker than the traders and because the government directed greater effort toward it. The Sicuani region is thus changed less notably than other regions. The growth of the administrative sectors and the decline of the *hacendado* sectors had already been well-established trends; the military government carried them further, but their full consequences remain to be seen.

The opening of a series of copper mines in Espinar and Chumbivilcas could also affect the region dramatically. Small, privately owned Peruvian mines began operation in 1973, and Japanese and Canadian mining companies and the Peruvian state-owned MINEROPERU have also shown an interest in the area. Some engineers have projected the number of mineworkers in 1985 at over 5000, although the current decline in world copper prices may limit the investments necessary for this expansion. Such a number would imply a reduction in the number of men working in the peasant and herder sectors, although their remittances might increase the total income of these sectors. The additional income would stimulate trade, but it might also serve to link the provinces of Espinar and Chumbivilcas more strongly to Arequipa. In this manner, it might weaken the influence of Sicuani traders over these provinces. The mines would also affect the political relations among sectors. Strong unions might establish ties with peasant and herder organization; official bodies to represent the workers, such as the *comunidad minera* or mining community, would tend to support the bureaucrats. Increased attention to the mineworkers might also affect urban artisans in Sicuani and textile workers in Maranganí. The interaction of future government programs and the potential expansion of the mines is difficult to forecast. Existing relations among sectors will channel the influences of these new forces, as they have done in the case of the wool export economy.

SUMMARY

One of the richest wool-producing areas in the sierra, the Sicuani region was also one of the last to be thoroughly integrated into the wool export economy. The arrival of the railroad in 1897 ended its isolation in the eastern part of the Andes. By that time, the export houses based in Arequipa had come to dominate the wool trade through links with foreign banks, shipping lines, and wool purchasers. They used these advantages to control the wool shipped from the Sicuani region. Closely linked to them, the Sicuani traders held considerable power in the region.

This late incorporation of the Sicuani region into the Peruvian wool export economy also meant that the expansion of this economy there came during a period of relatively strong national governments, particularly with the *oncenio* of Leguía's rule. The national government worked to prevent the consolidation of a regional *hacendado* elite that would have exclusive control over the local populations. This experience offers a sharp contrast to the situation in Puno and other departments in the southern sierra. They received the impact of the wool export economies earlier, when national government were much weaker, and could not check the power of regional *hacendado* elites as effectively.

For these reasons external to the region, the *hacendados* in Sicuani had little opportunity to retain their earlier control; their counterparts elsewhere had greater success. The internal dynamics of the region are of equal significance. The traders and bureaucrats came to form the regional elite, through their economic and political ties with local groups of producers on the one hand and with government agencies and commercial firms in Cuzco, Arequipa, and Lima on the other. Their defeat of the *hacendados* was carried out in an alliance with other rural sectors. The specific form of articulation between sectors within the region led to the stagnation of wool output and the lack of a more productive, capital-intensive pastoralism such as that found in Puno, Junín, and elsewhere in South America. It also generated considerable commercial activity. The peasants and herders in the Sicuani region were able to use this to their economic and political advantage; their lot has been much less harsh than that of their counterparts in many other parts of the Andes.

11
Conclusions

THE SECTORIAL MODEL AND THE SICUANI REGION

The Sicuani region has changed greatly in the past hundred years. The alpacas and sheep still move up and down the mountains in annual rhythms imposed by the rains and the frosts, but the people whose lives are tied to their wool have experienced major social, economic, and political transformations. These processes of change are complex, and their linkages to the growth of the wool export economy may seem unclear. This final chapter analyzes the underlying patterns of change by using the sectorial model to demonstrate the fundamental importance of the wool export economy in the region. This analysis indicates certain weaknesses of the theories of modernization and dependency.

The fundamental components of the sectorial model are material resources and human activity. Units are the minimum set of interdependent roles associated with the performance of activities. Their organization and interests are shaped by the resources they control, the goals they seek, and the constraints they face. Sets of units engaged in similar activities form sectors. The sectorial model examines processes of cooperation and competition within sectors and between them. The specific content of intersectorial relations varies from case to case.

Externally generated processes of change complement this internal dynamic.

The history of the Sicuani region presents a useful case for the application of this model. Because of the importance of the wool export economy and Peruvian governmental agencies, this history challenges the ability of the model to examine major processes of transformation that are significant on a global scale. The character of the region as a well-defined entity also favors the utilization of the model. Geographical boundaries have strongly constrained economic and political activity by increasing interaction within the region and restricting ties outside it to a few specific channels. The geographic distribution of resources also emphasizes the regional nature of economic and political activity. The sectors in the Sicuani region are referred to either by the name of the members of the component units (e.g., urban artisans) or by the name of the units themselves (e.g., pastoral haciendas). There are 10 sectors: herders, pastoral haciendas, peasants, agricultural haciendas, urban artisans, rural artisans, urban wholesale traders, urban retail traders, rural traders, and bureaucrats. Certain specialized urban retailers who deal in expensive items, such as books, stationery, hardware, medicine, and agricultural chemicals, are included as urban wholesale traders. Clergy and other full-time personnel of the Catholic Church are considered members of the bureaucracy.

The sectors may be grouped into sets by the criteria of location and occupation (see Table 2). Urban sectors, based in Sicuani, include the urban artisans, the wholesale traders, and the retail traders. The smaller towns and villages and the countryside contain the rural artisans, the peasants, the herders, the agricultural and pastoral haciendas, and the rural traders. The bureaucrats, as employees of national and international organizations, are considered extralocal. It should be recognized that many *hacendados* maintain urban residences. The occupational criterion establishes the categories of agricultural, pastoral, artisan, trader, and administrative sectors.

These sectors compose the regional economy. There are several kinds of relationships between sectors, as described in Chapter 1. Three of these are termed "modes of articulation"; they refer to the patterns of movement of goods between sectors and, to a lesser extent, the performance of services by units in one sector for those in another. They are the joint production mode, the barter mode, and the cash mode. These goods and services may be consumed directly by the unit that obtains them. In other cases, these goods serve as intermediate products; for example, an urban artisan unit such as a *peletero* shop may obtain alpaca skins from rural trader unit or a herder unit. These relations are

TABLE 2

Sets of Sectors

I. Locational groupings		
Local sectors		
Urban	Rural	Extralocal sectors
Urban artisans	Rural artisans	Bureaucrats
Wholesale traders	Peasants	
Retail traders	Agricultural haciendas	
	Herders	
	Pastoral haciendas	
	Rural traders	

II. Occupational groupings				
Agricultural sectors	Pastoral sectors	Artisan sectors	Trader sectors	Administrative sectors
Peasants	Herders	Urban artisans	Wholesale traders	Bureaucrats
Agricultural haciendas	Pastoral haciendas	Rural artisans	Retail traders	
			Rural traders	

generally comparable to an input–output analysis of an economy. There are several cases of the need for intermediate products. These are most clear in the case of the artisan sectors, which must obtain raw materials. Rural artisans tend to use the joint production mode, and urban artisans rely on the cash mode. Trader sectors, which must also obtain their products from other units, use the cash mode, occasionally supplemented by the barter mode. Wholesalers supply manufactured goods to retailers, and they both supply rural traders; locally produced goods flow in the opposite direction.

These patterns have been described in more detail in Chapters 4 and 9. In addition, agricultural and pastoral sectors provide each other with necessary resources. Agriculturalists often use dung as fertilizer, since the natural processes that restore fertility to soil are slow, and artificial fertilizer is expensive. Pastoralists graze their animals in fallow fields, particularly in the lower *punas*; they often include such grazing in their patterns of transhumance (Orlove 1977a).

The activities in which the units and sectors engage bring them into other forms of articulation. Resource competition is an important basis for such relations. Agricultural haciendas and peasants enter into conflict over the control of arable land and irrigation water, as pastoral haciendas and herders do for grazing land, particularly the valuable dry-season pasture or *bofedales*. Labor is also scarce in certain contexts; Chapter 6, for example, documents the competition between herders and pastoral haciendas for labor at the time of the annual shearing at the beginning of the rainy season. These forms of competition are often found within sectors as well as between them. Conflict over land and water occurs among peasant households as well as between peasants and *hacendados*. Later sections of this chapter will demonstrate that the hacienda sectors are particularly marked by internal conflict.

Finally, sectors may disagree on policy issues. For instance, urban sectors tend to prefer policies that lower the prices of food and wool and raise the price of manufactured goods, while rural sectors want the reverse. A number of other issues involve the selective enforcement of laws, such as those establishing minimum wages and forbidding unpaid Indian labor.

THE IMPACT OF THE WOOL EXPORT ECONOMY

As documented in Chapter 10, the *hacendado* sectors were dominant in the late nineteenth century. Through their control of economic and political resources, they dominated the peasant, herder, and rural artisan sectors. The trader and urban sectors remained on a relatively small scale. Interregional trade had not yet achieved the importance it would later hold. A large proportion of the units supplied themselves with products from other sectors by the joint production mode of articulation. The town of Sicuani had about the same population as the other villages in the region.

The arrival of the Southern Peruvian Railway in Sicuani in 1897 consolidated the ties of the region to the Peruvian wool export economy. This shift from a relatively closed economy to one oriented toward export markets engendered a complex series of changes. New units, primarily trading firms, entered the region. They provided new resources, particularly cash and manufactured goods. The acquisition of these resources became the goal of many units already established in the region and others that emerged in the climate of economic expansion. They offered opportunities for the sale of wool that altered the system of constraints in the region.

The pastoral units were the most immediately effected, since they were the only ones that produced wool. The higher prices offered for wool encouraged many units to attempt to increase their production. They sought to increase the size of their herds, and some of them selectively culled the animals that produced lower-grade wool. Grazing land became more valuable than it had been before, so many units restricted the access of others to their pasture. They relied on the cash and barter modes rather than the joint production mode to supply themselves with agricultural products. Since the pastoral units had more cash at their disposal, they often adopted the cash mode of articulation.

In this way, the increase in demand for wool affected sectors that did not produce wool. The shift away from joint production meant that agricultural and artisan sectors also came to rely on the barter and cash modes. The latter mode encouraged the continuing expansion of the trader sectors. The traders increasingly channeled foodstuffs out of the Sicuani region to the altiplano as well as to the higher punas of the Sicuani region; they also brought foodstuffs in from lower *quebradas* to the north and west. The traders thus helped convert agricultural production into a complementary economy, in that the demand for foodstuffs became increasingly tied to the state of the wool economy. The monetarization of the regional economy and the higher income levels also raised the demands for artisan wares. The volume of artisan production increased as the number and size of artisan production units grew. Some artisans, especially rural ones, continued to barter their products, but most of them sold them for cash, further expanding the trader sectors.

Summarized in this fashion, the growth of the wool export economy in the Sicuani region appears to have favored all sectors. The increased income of the wool producing sectors led to the creation of complementary agricultural and artisan economies, as pastoralists specialized in the production of wool. This shift from joint production mode of articulation between sectors towards the cash mode also favored the traders. These patterns follow certain elements of the modernization paradigm, which argues that monetarization reduces the limits tradition places on innovation and increases the number of economic opportunities. It leads to the differentiation of economic activity, which causes greater interdependence and higher levels of productivity and consumption.

However, the wool export economy generated conflict as well as cooperation. It led to shifts in the relations between sectors by increasing the importance of resource competition and policy issues, the two additional forms of articulation described in Chapter 1. The reactions of different units and sectors to these shifting patterns of alliance and conflict altered the power within the region exercised by extra-regional units, particularly national governmental agencies. These other forms of conflict and cooperation between sectors will be reviewed in turn. These intersectorial relations have generally served to reduce intrasectorial conflict and competition; the *hacendado* sectors are the only major exception. The sectorial model thus permits the analysis of particular responses to the global processes of the expansion of export economies and the growth of nation-states.

Intersectorial Conflict

PASTORAL HACIENDAS AND HERDERS

Pastoral *hacendados* and herders competed for land and labor. As the demand for wool increased, pastoral units attempted to expand their production and found that they could not raise the value of their clip without enlarging the area of land to which they had access. As explained in Chapter 6, environmental constraints place a high threshold on initial capital investment in wool production. Without large sums of money and considerable political influence, pastoral units cannot fence their land; this step is a necessary antecedent to the introduction of improved breeds of animals, the sowing of higher quality pasture, and the systematic use of veterinary medicine. In short, to increase the value of the wool the pastoralist has to increase its volume, which entails obtaining more land to graze larger herds. Because of the strong environmental constraints on the timing of labor inputs into pastoral activities, haciendas and herder units often competed for the limited supply of herder labor. This pressure was particularly severe at the time of shearing and at the annual slaughter.

This conflict took a variety of forms. Both the incursion of a *hacendado*'s animals onto a herder's lands and the reverse occurred frequently, as did the theft of animals, sometimes justified as compensation for alleged damages. Some *hacendados* used fraudulent contracts; for instance, some illiterate herders would agree to sell their lands, believing that they were only renting them. The conflict also led to infrequent but dramatic outbursts of open violence.

These two sectors also entered into conflict over policy issues. They wanted different sorts of public works projects. Both were interested in the expansion of the transportation networks, for instance, but the *hacendados* typically wanted roads built to their haciendas to facilitate the movement of their animals and goods. The herders preferred to link villages with other roads to allow the establishment and expansion of marketplaces. In a number of cases, these roads were built with the unpaid labor of herders. The herders were more interested in the establishment of rural schoolhouses than the *hacendados* were; the latter educated their children in towns and found that a more highly educated work force was likely to be a more discontent one. Like the conflicts over land and labor, these policy disagreements brought units into contacts with lawyers and judges. They each wanted the administrative apparatus oriented in their favor.

AGRICULTURAL HACIENDAS AND PEASANTS

The conflict between these two sectors generally paralleled that between the pastoral sectors, since the quantity of land is finite and labor is scarce at certain times of peak demand. However, the differences between agricultural and pastoral production alter the nature of the conflict. Because of its scarcity and its multiple uses, water is a highly contested resource in agricultural areas, particularly in the valleys in the Río Vilcanota and the Río Apurimac. As described in Chapter 8, the *hacendados* favored diversion of water to their mills. This use constrained peasants to grow crops such as wheat, which did not need much water. These crops frequently required milling before consumption. The peasants preferred diverting the water to their own lands for irrigation. This use of water permitted the production of crops such as maize and *habas*, which did not require milling and also had higher value. Furthermore, the fact that animals, unlike crops, can walk affects the manner in which the conflict was expressed; accusations of petty incursions into agricultural land and theft of crops were less common than the corresponding complaints in pastoral areas, but litigation over land was more common.

The patterns of conflict over policy issues were also different. The thresholds for initial capital investment in agriculture are not high, so that government extension agents can become more directly engaged in offering loans for fertilizer and insecticide, encouraging eucalyptus reforestation, and the like. Hence the *Ministerio de Agricultura* is more directly involved in agricultural production than in herding, and there was more conflict over the orientation of its policies.

HACENDADOS AND URBAN TRADERS

Resource competition was a relatively minor aspect of this conflict. Although *hacendados* and traders occasionally competed for government revenue, the funds they received came from different budgets, so that an increase for one sector was not directly tied to a decrease for another. Competition for funds from a single agency, as was the case in the conflict between agricultural *hacendados* and peasants, tends to be more acute.

The *hacendado*–trader conflicts were based on policy issues; they involved the formal and informal exercise of influence over decision making in Sicuani. The traders recognized the large potential market among the peasants and herders. They knew that the success of their enterprises depended on the sale of goods to local consumers as well as on the purchase of goods. They wanted to ensure large attendance at the markets in Sicuani, so they were against the forced recruitment of peasants and herders to public works projects. The *hacendados*, who did not share these concerns, adopted the opposite view.

The traders also favored higher levels of government spending, which increased commercial activity; the *hacendados* were more selective in their interests, as their opposition to the expansion of schools shows. The two often differed on specific projects; for instance, the traders wanted roads to connect Sicuani with Cuzco, Arequipa, and the altiplano, whereas the *hacendados* wanted to link their properties into the transportation system. The traders preferred urban improvements in the town of Sicuani, since paved squares and streets encouraged commerce, but the *hacendados* sought improvements for the district capitals and their lands.

These policy issues also led on occasion to an opposition of the *hacendados* to the rural traders, though it was weaker than their conflict with the urban traders. Particularly since 1960, *hacendados* occasionally opposed the formation of marketplaces in peasant communities. They preferred them to be held in district capitals, since the peasants and herders were required to pay taxes to the district councils controlled by the *hacendados*. The traders could avoid this obligation in the community marketplaces. These conflicts have been particularly marked in the province of Espinar.

URBAN TRADERS AND ARTISANS

A fourth potential conflict based on resource competition did not emerge. There are several sets of artisans and workers in the Sicuani region who use wool: the rural *bayeteros*, the urban *peleteros*, and the textile mill workers. It might have been possible for them to compete with urban wholesalers and retailers for supplies of wool; the traders would want to sell the wool to Arequipa firms, and the artisans would want to retain it in the region for their own use. However, this competition never materialized, for reasons described in Chapter 7. The *bayeteros* use wool shorn from hides, of such low quality that the Arequipa firms ordinarily do not want it. These firms also do not purchase large numbers of baby alpaca skins, the basic material of the *peleteros*. The textile mill purchases most of its wool outside the region. There is little overlap between export wool and artisan wool, and so the competition does not arise.

Intersectorial Alliances

These alliances are the obverse of the intersectorial conflicts. Like the conflicts, they are based on material resources and interests. They occur between sectors that do not compete for resources. These sectors have similar economic interests, and they prefer similar sorts of government politics. The degree to which these alliances are conscious and explicit varies from context to context. The support may be unintended at one moment; later it may become a more purposeful cooperation or collaboration.

WHOLESALE TRADERS AND RETAIL TRADERS

The large and small urban traders do not enter into competition. The wholesalers supply the smaller ones in Sicuani and other villages, and the retailers supply the urban population and some peasants and herders. The purchasers of specialized products, such as hardware, stationery, medicine, and pesticides, buy from the wholesalers. The wholesalers tend to supply the larger rural traders and the retailers to supply the smaller ones. The activities of these two sectors lead them to have common interests. As traders, they would like to see the commerce of the region expand, so they favor certain policies: improved transportation networks, lower railroad and truck freight charges, government support of annual fairs, and low taxes on commercial enterprises.

URBAN ARTISANS AND RETAIL TRADERS

Although these two sectors have different occupations, there are important similarities in their activities. They both work full-time in shops. They pay taxes to the town council. They sell their wares in their shops, although some also maintain stalls in the principal market. These similar activities lead to shared interests, including urban improvements, such as the paving of streets to facilitate sales, adequate urban services such as water and electricity, and low prices for foodstuffs and goods brought in the region from outside, such as kerosene. In some cases, they are linked by the joint production mode of articulation; some artisans are also shopkeepers.

RURAL ARTISANS, PEASANTS, AND HERDERS

Some similarities in activity overcome the differences among agriculture, herding, and the crafts in which rural artisans engage. Artisan work tends to be seasonal, as do agriculture and herding. The household form of organization predominates in all three cases. The units exchange their products through barter and cash sale in marketplaces and often engage in the joint production mode of articulation among themselves. They obtain necessary inputs because of their membership in communities; the peasant's irrigation water, the herder's pasture, and the potter's clay are all owned collectively rather than individually. Hence they share interests and favor similar policies, such as government defense of community ownership of resources, government maintenance of roads and rural schools, and extensions of marketing systems. Many of them belong to officially recognized peasant communities and other peasant organizations.

AGRICULTURAL AND PASTORAL HACIENDAS

A fourth potential alliance based on common interest did not emerge. These two sectors enter into little competition over land, water, and labor, because of the different edaphic and climatic requirements of crops and animals and the different timing of labor inputs. Their organization leads them to have similar interests, such as attacks on the titles of peasant communities to their lands. These interests lead them to take specific positions on a number of issues: They are opposed to extensive rural education programs, *Banco de Fomento Agropecuario* credit policies that favor small producers over large ones, and government intervention into employer–worker relations. In some cases, they are linked by the joint production mode.

This potential alliance *between* the two sectors did not emerge, however, because of conflict *within* each of them. This conflict within units and within sectors is partly based on resource competition. As described in earlier chapters, *hacendados* pay their peons with usufruct rights to plots of land and grazing rights. In both cases, an individual *hacendado* could increase his income by reducing the size of his peons' plots and herds. He also comes into conflict with his peons over the allocation of labor; the periods of peak labor demand for the *hacendado* and the peons come at the same time. The activity and organization of haciendas, then, generate conflict within the units (see pp. 93–95). Competition between haciendas is also strong, especially in the case of pastoral haciendas, where boundaries are poorly defined. Disputed land sales and inheritances are common causes of litigation between *hacendados*. These conflicts are especially strong, since there is little immediate basis for cooperation between *hacendados*; they do not use resources collectively and are seldom united into corporate groups.

Internal conflict within other sectors is not as marked. Peasants and herders also compete for land and labor, but this competition does not generate such severe conflict, for several reasons (Whyte 1975). The units are not marked by such severe internal dissension. They also share collectively owned resources, such as pasture and irrigation water. There are other projects, such as the construction of schoolhouses, which entail the cooperation of sets of units and sometimes even several communities.

There is even less conflict within the artisan and trader sectors because of the increase in demand for their activities and products and the relatively unlimited supplies of the resources they use. There is more room for an additional bakery or store in Sicuani or in a village than there is for an additional hacienda in the punas. There is less competition within a unit because there is much less inequality between its members. The gap in wealth, power, and life chances between a *hacendado* and a peon tends to be much greater than that between a shopkeeper and his assistant or between an artisan and his apprentice. This difference is caused by the larger scale of haciendas and the greater occupational mobility within artisan and trading units.

Sets of Sectors

These conflicts and alliances, then, are the result of the expansion of the wool export economy in the Sicuani region and its effect on the preexisting relations among sectors. As individual actors and units followed their interests, they entered into these characteristic relations with other actors and units, altering the relations among sectors. In other words, the processes of decision making and economic and political activity generate the structure of relations among sectors. An examination of these intersectorial relations reveals three sets of sectors: the hacienda sectors, the other rural sectors (peasants, herders, rural artisans, and rural traders), and the urban sectors (wholesale traders, retail traders, and urban artisans). The other rural sectors and the urban sectors are both opposed to the *hacendados*, but there are no ties of conflict between these two sets of sectors. There were also no alliances between them, as discussed in the previous section; alliances emerged only with their contacts with a fourth set of sectors, the bureaucrats.

The structure of relations among sectors in turn generated other processes, altering the positions of different sectors. The evolution and expansion of complementary agricultural and artisan sectors, the shifts in land tenure patterns, and the growth of the marketing system are the clearest examples of predominantly economic changes. The structure of relations among sectors also generated changes which had a more markedly political aspect. It shaped the ties of bureaucrats to other sectors. The patterns of opposition led all three regional sets of sectors to seek additional support from outside the region. As documented in Chapter 10, they all attempted to establish links with government bureaucrats. This effort weakened the *hacendados*, whose dominant position rested on their power monopoly. The direct access of other sectors to governmental agencies threatened their regional hegemony. This process led to the rapid increase of government influence, as each set of sectors tried to outdo its opponents in establishing ties to agencies. The *hacendados* found it necessary to seek these ties to defend their short-run interests, but this tactic led to their eventual downfall. The urban sectors and nonhacienda rural sectors were successful in defeating the *hacendados*. This victory, however, entailed strong alliances with the bureacrats who increased their economic and political importance in the region. The discussion of the roles of education, marketing, and the Vilcanota campaign in Chapter 10 illustrate these points.

The common opposition to *hacendados* and the alliance with bureaucrats also established a balance between urban and rural interests. The potential conflict between them has not developed as much as might have been expected. Their interests are opposed on a number of issues, since they compete for government revenue and disagree on price policies. The urban sectors want low prices for wool and food and high prices for manufactured goods, while rural sectors prefer the reverse. However, their long experience in fighting the same opponent, the *hacendados*, has led to a degree of compromise on these issues. It has also established an economy in which some interests are shared; if the urban traders and bureaucrats were to weaken the peasants, herders, and rural artisans too greatly, they would be destroying their own clientele. Finally, the urban and nonhacienda rural sectors perceive that they can each get more resources from the government if they collaborate in trying to increase the activities of the government in the region. The support for the Vilcanota campaign illustrates this trend. The complete destruction of the *hacendados* with the agrarian reform has not changed this pattern and, to a certain extent, may reinforce it.

The wool export economy, then, brought the decline of the hacienda sectors and the rise of the trader and administrative sectors. The economic and political position of other urban and rural sectors improved as the importance of commerce and governmental agencies grew. The structure of intersectorial relations thus begins and ends with process. It is generated by decision making and economic and political activity, and it establishes the internal and external dynamics that determine the growth and decline of different sectors and the shifts in the regional economy and society. The structure of intersectorial relations is the context of much of the interaction between individual activity and the systems of constraints.

These processes have been examined in earlier chapters and summarized in this one. The changes in the regional economy and society, however, may be illustrated by two events, the two general strikes in Sicuani in the twentieth century. A brief discussion of the strikes will demonstrate the shifting lines of alliance and conflict between sectors. In 1946, the Southern Peruvian Railway, owned by a group of British bond holders, proposed to increase its rates for passengers and freight. At that time, the railroad carried most of the long-distance traffic to Sicuani, so an increase in railroad rates would have meant higher prices for items of daily urban consumption, such as rice and sugar, and for raw materials for urban artisans, such as commercial flour for bakers. A strike committee was formed to oppose this increase. It included representatives of guilds of urban artisans and associations of traders, notably the *Asociación Fraternal de Artesanos Grau*, the *Sociedad de Comerciantes*, and the *Union Sindical Provincial*. These groups had held a number of demonstrations in the following months. Local authorities, including the mayor, also supported the strike. Strikers halted trains and trucks around Sicuani and ensured that storekeepers and artisans closed their shops. There were no acts of open violence. The strikers sent telegrams to Lima to inform national leaders of their complaint against the Southern Peruvian Railway. At this time, during the Bustamante y Rivero administration, APRA, and several left-wing parties had a number of members and sympathizers in the national congress. The strike lasted only one day and met its goals: Price increases were arrested for a period of several months.

The organizations that supported the strike made a number of strong statements in favor of the peasants and herders, criticizing unpaid peasant labor on government projects and the exploitation of peasants by *hacendados*. The *Unión Sindical Provincial* encouraged the formation of peasant unions and may have assisted the few communities that received official recognition in the late 1940s (see Appendix 4). However, there was virtually no peasant participation in the strike; it was an urban strike, organized by urban sectors to defend their interests.

The peasants and herders had to defend their interests through other means. In cases of extreme conflict which would have corresponded to strikes, such as the rebellions of 1921 and 1931, they had to act alone.

Urban sectors offered them assistance in less extreme circumstances by representing their interests to administrative and judicial agencies in Sicuani.

The 1973 general strike offers an interesting comparison. Like the 1946 strike, it was a brief event in which strikers halted traffic and stopped commerce without open violence. It took place at a time when left-wing parties exercised significant influence in Lima. Several organizations which had been holding demonstrations in the previous months formed the backbone of the strike and received the support of the mayor and other local authorities. The strikers informed authorities in Lima of their demands and succeeded in having them met. However, the demands of the strikers and the sectors from which they came were different.

The principal issue of the strike was government aid to the Sicuani region. The most specific complaint was the failure to deliver the 20,000 bags of cement promised to pave the streets of Sicuani. In addition, the strikers wanted a new hydroelectric plant to provide power to Sicuani and adjacent rural areas, additional roads, more elementary, secondary, and technical schools in Sicuani and the countryside, a more generous credit policy of the *Banco de Fomento Agropecuario* and the *Banco Industrial del Perú* toward peasants, herders, and artisans, an expansion of the hospital, increased government aid to peasant communities, and a variety of other public works projects. Many speakers at public meetings suggested that official institutions attempted to manipulate the people rather than offer them genuine participation in the government.

The strike committee included a number of organizations[1] that represented the urban artisans and traders who had been the main base of the 1946 general strike. There were a number of other groups as well, some of which dated from the political mobilization of the 1960s (Handelman 1975; Whyte and Alberti 1976). Organizations of peasants and herders were well represented among the speakers and crowds at the demonstrations; a number of speeches were made in Quechua. Student organizations, drawing members from both urban and rural areas, were quite active. In short, rural sectors were more directly represented in the strike, and the demands of the strike included rural as well as urban issues. Some of these demands were met, and the strike was partially successful. The 20,000 bags of cement were delivered, and there was some additional government aid to the area. It is difficult to assess what the levels would have been if the strike had not taken place, but interviews with officials and peasants suggest that the general tone of

---

[1] In order to protect my sources, the names of the specific organizations are not given.

resentment at government neglect increased the aid. Informants frequently quoted a familiar proverb, *"La huahua que no llora no mama"* ('The baby that does not cry does not suckle').

The differences between the two strikes indicate the changes that took place in the Sicuani region in the intervening 27 years. In 1973, as in 1946 and earlier, peasants and herders could not always rely on the urban sectors to defend their economic and political interests, but this support came more readily and more frequently than it had earlier. The shift in demands shows that the connection between urban and rural sectors that developed with their common attack on the *hacendados* had grown stronger. This attack entailed the establishment of alliances with government agencies and a growth in the influence of those agencies in the area. Government salaries and revenue supplemented trade, previously the mainstay of the economy of Sicuani and the basis of increased prosperity in the countryside. The shift in the target of the strikes demonstrates this change. It may suggest that the urban and nonhacienda rural sectors, who were able to set aside their differences in the struggle against the *hacendados,* may continue in their alliance to receive greater support from the national government and orient government policies to meet their needs.

MODERNIZATION, DEPENDENCY, AND THE SECTORIAL MODEL

The previous portions of this chapter have analyzed the changes in the Sicuani region by using the sectorial model. The processes that took place there—the incorporation of the region into an export economy and the growth of national governmental institutions—are changes that the theories of modernization and dependency both examine. It is therefore of interest to review the predictions these theories would make for the Sicuani region and check their accuracy. The failure of these theories to account for major features of the history of this region, particularly the nature of alliance and conflict and the role of the state, is fundamentally caused by the manner in which they explain phenomena. By assimilating a variety of processes of change into single types, they neglect the basic elements of these processes that generate diversity.

Modernization theorists would have seen the arrival of the railroad and the expansion of commerce as sources of modernization in a traditional society such as that of the Sicuani region in the late nineteenth century. They would have predicted that an increased use of cash would have led impersonal relations to replace personal ones in the marketplace, permitting higher levels of economic innovation and activity. The commercialization and innovation would lead to increased economic and social differentiation which in turn would produce greater interdependence and solidarity. Social conflict would tend to decrease.

Some of these predictions, particularly those concerning the increase of economic activity, are correct. However, others are incorrect; market relations remain personal, and the higher levels of conflict suggest that social solidarity did not increase. Many other features which have been labeled traditional have remained; artisan production has withstood the competition of manufacturing, and religious fiestas continue to be celebrated. Regional ties have grown stronger rather than weaker; the expansion of links to the national government has led to an increase rather than a decline in sentiments favoring the *departamentalización* of the Sicuani region.

Dependency theorists would take a different tack, focusing on the importance of the wool export economy. They would see the production of raw materials as the basis of the domination of this hinterland region, and they would argue that other aspects of the economic and political structure would serve to maintain this domination. They would see the Sicuani region as an internal colony, subject to the double domination of the industrialized nations and the national Peruvian bourgeoisie. These two would be assumed to share interests because of the essentially dependent nature of the Peruvian economy.

This theory would predict that regional society would crystallize into two classes, the wool producers and a regional elite. The state would side with the regional elite in assisting the transfer of surplus to the metropolis. Hence, the model would argue that regionalism would be strong rather than weak. The producers would therefore be under a triple domination: international, national, and regional. They would attempt to oppose this domination, but their efforts would fail until a revolution destroyed the bonds of dependency. The theorists would see such movements in the strikes against the British-owned Southern Peruvian Railway and the national government and in the peasant movements of the 1920s and 1960s, each of which attacked one of the aspects of domination.

According to this theory, the relations between the two classes in the region would be determined by the position of Peru as a dependent nation which exports raw materials. A number of relations would remain problematic. It is unclear whether the artisans would be absorbed into a nascent proletariat or merge with the regional bourgeoisie, or whether the rural traders would become the allies of the dominant export interests or the dependent workers. Most important, the position of the regional elite would be assigned to it by the nature of relations between nations and Peru's dependency: The regional elite, dependent on the national elite, would have to exploit the peasantry. Dependency theory would predict only two sets of sectors; the sectorial model reveals four: *hacendados,* other rural sectors, urban sectors, and bureaucrats. Hence dependency theory would suggest that the most important split in regional society would be between elite and peasantry, and it would be difficult for this theory to conceptualize and examine splits between different elite sectors. It is precisely these splits, the conflicts between traders and *hacendados,* that are at the root of the dynamic of the Sicuani region.

Modernization theory, then, would accept the notion of sectors but argue that the corollary of increasing differentiation is increasing interdependence and harmony. It would suggest that intersectorial conflict would decline. Dependency theory would also accept the notion of sectors but argue that the sectors would coalesce into two classes. It would claim that the major conflict in regional society would occur between the two classes.

This problem with the analysis of intersectorial relations weakens the analyses that these theories make of the role of the state. These analyses are further hindered by the tendency of both theories to view the changing position of the state as part of general trends on the national level. Modernization theorists would argue that it grew in a fashion complementary to national economic development to support the interests of the entire society. Dependency theorists would say that it was a creation and instrument of dominant nations and classes to support their interests over the dependent majority, so that the state is imposed upon the region from outside. The sectorial model shows that sectors within the region brought in government agencies to further their own interests, so that the growth of the state must be seen in terms of a dynamic internal to the region as well as external to it. Although the national economy places constraints on the actions of the state, the interests the state supports cannot be predicted beforehand, as the theories of modernization and dependency would suggest; the state does not automatically support either the interests of all sectors or only the interests of dominant sectors. The sectorial model thus offers a more coherent and complete analysis of the history of the Sicuani region. It is able to do this because it does not attempt to assimilate this history to a single process, as the theories of modernization and dependency do. Instead, it presents export economies and national governments as crucial forces but shows that the forging of a world-system is a process of integration rather than homogenization.

The theories of modernization and dependency present the transformation of the world as a single, inescapable destiny that will befall all humanity, although they disagree as to whether it is a fortunate or a tragic one. The sectorial model, by viewing individuals as actors, shows history as something they construct. People are faced with forces not of their own making, but they respond actively to these forces rather than receiving them passively. Their reactions are based on their particular circumstances as well as their common position in export economies and nation-states. The variety of local conditions thus generates a variety of responses to these global forces, so the interlocking of alliance and conflict, of internal and external dynamics, proceeds differently in different cases. The sectorial model shows that what is universal about the people of the Sicuani region is their uniqueness. It argues that to understand them, as to understand other peoples who have become incorporated into export economies and nation-states, is to understand the diversity of the encounter of a global system with many particular realities. It allows us to comprehend our world as our world is: unitary but not uniform.

APPENDIX 1

Wool and Wool-Bearing Animals

There is a certain amount of disagreement over the range of fibers to which the term "wool" may be applied. Some sources restrict it categorically to the coat of the domestic sheep (FAO 1971). Other animals, including the native American cameloids (the llama, alpaca, vicuña, and guanaco), are said to have fur or hair. In other cases, the term seems all-embracing; a minor customs official, exhibiting the characteristic inconsistency of government record keepers, classified not only cameloids, but also the *Ceiba pentandra* tree as wool bearing, although this plant was not listed in wool export figures for other years (Superintendencia General de Aduanas 1904). Further information on this tree may be found in Levi-Strauss (1950:474).

At times, the claim for the uniqueness of sheep wool is made arbitrarily (Hultz and Hill 1931: 195, 253), but more often it is justified by use: Some writers state that the only fiber that will felt is that of the domestic sheep or that it exhibits great elasticity. The arguments based on the structure of the fiber reduce to ones of use: The microscopic platelets on the surface explain felting much as the lack of an inner core or medulla produces elasticity.

The structure and use of these fibers differ in degree rather than kind. All the fibers are formed in a similar fashion, from dead epidermal cells sloughed off into follicles. The properties of elasticity and felting are exhibited by other animal fibers such as those of the llama and goat (FAO 1971: 53–54). The simplest position with regard to the technical writers who make varying claims about the status of the fibers of the camel, alpaca, llama, vicuña, goat, yak, and musk ox is to follow ordinary language use, and to refer to fibers that are customarily spun and used for yarn in knitting and weaving as wool, retaining the word "hair" only for camel hair. Some of the confusion in usage is caused by the fact that many animals have two coats: a soft inner one for warmth and insulation and a stiff outer one for protection of the skin. The wool corresponds to the inner coat. The technical term *kemp* will be used for the stiffer hairy fibers of the outer coat often found mixed with wool.

Wools in general share a series of qualities that make them useful. They are resilient and elastic and stand wear well. They provide good insulation because of the air trapped between the fibers. Their ability to absorb water and form felt permits a variety of fabrics to be made from them. There is great variety of fabrics to be made from them. There is great variation in wools among different species of animals and among breeds and varieties of each species; this variety is another advantage. Peruvian wool comes from four animals, the sheep and three of the native cameloids, the alpaca, the llama, and the vicuña. Peru has a virtual world monopoly on the cameloid wools, but it is a minor producer of sheep wool.

Little scientific work of a biological or veterinary nature has been done on the cameloids, with the exception of a few studies by IVITA (*Instituto Veterinario de Investigaciones Tropicales y de Altura*). Alpacas are less well understood than sheep; it was only discovered in 1971, for instance, that the two varieties of alpaca originally called breeds are only varieties, since the offspring do not always resemble the parents (Fernández Baca 1971: 9).

Alpacas average 90 kilograms in weight. They have a strong tendency to engage in herd behavior. A few dominant males initiate herd movement and other activities. Fertility rates are low; between 50 and 70% of the mated adult females give birth. Females occasionally produce more than one ovum, but no cases of multiple births have ever been recorded. The loss appears to be caused by abortion in the first month of pregnancy rather than by failure to conceive. Mortality rates among the newborn are also high. Between 15 and 25%, and in some years nearly 50% of the neonates die in the first three months of life.

Alpaca wool is soft, lustrous, and very fine. It is much less greasy than sheep wool and contains only small amounts of kemp. Annual wool production in adult animals averages 1.3 kilograms. Wool growth is stimulated somewhat by shearing. Wool grows at different rates on different parts of the animal. The wool of older animals is coarser.

The colors of wool include different tones of white, cream, fawn, tan, gray, brown, and black. Some alpacas are of a uniform color, usually white, but many have piebald coats with patches of different colors. There are different qualities of wool, notably the crimpy and curly *huacaya* and the straight and lustrous *suri*. Darker shades tend to be finer than ligher shades.

Environmental factors also affect the quality of the wool. Alpacas thrive at high altitudes, 4000 to 5200 meters being the optimum range. The greater cold at higher altitudes seems to stimulate wool growth. At lower altitudes, especially below 3400 meters, external parasites such as lice and mange make the wool short and uneven and reduce yields. These parasites often infect entire herds, since all the animals share common sites for dust baths. In many instances, the effect of the environment on the wool is mediated by its relation to the general health of the animal. At low altitudes, alpacas are subject to intestinal worms, and pulmonary infections become a problem at very high altitudes. Excessively soft and moist ground promotes foot infections. Certain diets are insufficient in nutriments. The alpacas must also eat the dry, tough grasses found at high altitude, since their teeth continue to grow throughout maturity and thus need a degree of wear.

Llamas differ from alpacas in a few ways. The neck and head are shaped differently, making them easy to distinguish at great distances. They are bigger, averaging 115 kilograms. They are also sturdier and much less susceptible to disease at low altitudes.

Their larger size and more robust build allow them to be used as pack animals. They can carry up to 35 kilograms. Though they travel only 25 kilometers per day, their ability to graze on sparse pasture makes them irreplaceable at high altitudes. It is not necessary to invoke cultural conservatism, as some observers have done, to explain the continuing use of llamas rather than European pack animals in much of Peru and Bolivia. Their wool is not as fine or soft as that of the alpaca, and it has more kemp. However, it is extremely durable.

Vicuña wool is extraordinarily fine and soft, although mixed with kemp. Unlike the alpaca and the llama, the vicuña has not been successfully domesticated, except under special conditions on an experimental basis. Vicuñas are much smaller than the other cameloids and yield less wool, often under 250 grams annually. They live in territorial herds, adequately described by Koford (1957). Although in preconquest times the vicuñas were rounded up, sheared, and set free, they are now hunted, and the population has decreased greatly. There are now almost no vicuñas where Koford reported large herds. Hunting vicuñas and exporting their wool is illegal in Peru, although some is smuggled to Bolivia and exported.

The close phylogenetic relation among these species is shown by the fact that hybrids are fertile. Llama–vicuña crosses have been bred, but the crosses of these two with the alpaca are more common. The llama–alpaca, or *huarizo,* has wool that is intermediate in quality between the two, and the animal is more resistant to disease than the alpaca. The alpaca–vicuña, known as the *paco–vicuña,* has also been produced. Reports described them with great optimism as having the wool of the vicuña and the relatively easy handling of the alpaca, but they are not yet herded on a commercial basis. *Huarizos* are more common.

In contrast to these cameloids, sheep have been the subject of a great deal of work in selection of new breeds and in veterinary and biological research. Unlike the cameloids, which are found outside the Andes only in zoos, sheep are raised throughout the world. There are well over 100 breeds (Lipson 1953: 2). Each has a characteristic wool, varying along a number of characteristics: fineness, length, weight, uniformity, greasiness, and color. Breeds also differ with regard to other physiological and behavioral characteristics, so they have different environmental ranges, depending on temperature, humidity, rainfall, and available food. Only a few of these breeds are represented in southern Peru, primarily the Criollo, or native sheep, the Merino, and the Corriedale.

These three breeds share a number of traits characteristic of their species. As in the cameloids, herd behavior is pronounced, but it has a different source. Rather than following a few dominant animals, individual sheep tend to imitate neighboring animals. At times this characteristic is advantageous; sheep huddle in cold weather. A herd of llamas can easily be managed once the one or two head animals are controlled (Concha Contreras 1971: 48); this is not the case with sheep.

Estrus in ewes is triggered in certain months by changes in the number of hours of daylight. Males initiate intercourse only with estral ewes. Since the gestation period varies little (150 days), the birth of the new lambs occurs in a relatively short period of the year that coincides with the greater availability of pasture. In the tropics, day length is nearly constant, and estrus among ewes does not exhibit regular annual periodicity. If they are not impregnated, ewes return to estrus in 2 to 3 weeks (Rafez *et al.* 1969: 320). Lambing occurs throughout the year. This fact disappointed sheep raisers in northern Australia, who expected the success of ranchers further south to be duplicated in all parts of the continent (Galloway 1961: 3–5). In Peru, it is taken as a matter of course that lambs are born throughout the year and that mortality of neonates is high in certain months.

The wool of domesticated sheep differs from that of wild sheep in several ways. Modern sheep have white fleece, unlike wild sheep which are colored. Domestic sheep do not molt; wild sheep shed their entire coats each spring, and many primitive breeds lose a large amount of wool. Domestic sheep have little or no kemp; the kemp of wild sheep is coarser and more extensive. If domestic sheep are not maintained by selection of stud rams and culling of ewes, they slowly revert to these feral characteristics.

This reversion can be seen in the Criollo sheep. They are the descendants of the Merino and Churrua sheep introduced by the Spanish in the sixteenth century. In adapting to the Andean environment, they changed in certain ways. These sheep are small and have relatively little wool; they are quite hardy. Both kemp and dark wool fibers have reappeared.

Merino sheep were reintroduced in the southern highlands in the late nineteenth or early twentieth century. This breed is noted for its fine, crimpy wool. The Spanish monopoly on this breed ended in the eighteenth century, and the expansion of the Merino, first in Europe and later in the Southern Hemisphere, followed the increasing demand for raw material by the mechanized textile industry. New breeds were developed from Merinos in Europe, Australia, and New Zealand; the latter two have been the primary sources for Peru.

The wool varies in length and thickness in different parts of the fleece, making the sorting slow, difficult, and labor intensive. The adaptation of Merinos to the Spanish climate provided certain advantages for those who wished to introduce them to Peru. The breed has a strong tendency to flock. Though small, the animals are active foragers

TABLE 3

Important Breeds of Sheep in the Sicuani Region

Breed	Adult weight (lbs.)	Annual wool production (lbs.)	Infant mortality (% of lambs born)	Number of lambs surviving per 100 ewes mated
Criollo	99.0	1.25	8.0	84
Merino	134.4	4.46	19.9	59
Corriedale	148.3	4.74	18.7	63

Source: Chuquibambilla archive (ca. 1948).

(Hultz 1940: 6) which enables them to find pasture in years of mild drought. Merinos are subject to disease, however, particularly foot rot and eye infection. Fertility is low, and infant mortality is high because the lambs are born without fleece (see Table 3).

Corriedale sheep were developed in New Zealand around 1960 as a cross between Merinos and Lincoln sheep, a British mutton breed. Corriedales mature more rapidly than Merinos and grow to a larger size. Their wool is not as fine or crimpy, but it is longer, more uniform, and considerably less greasy (Kershaw 1953: 4). As a producer of both wool and meat, it is known as a "dual-purpose" breed (Hultz 1940: 119). Its docile temperament makes it easy to herd and gives it a tendency to fatten. It is adapted to a moister climate, and it can be accustomed to the altitude and rigorous climate of the highlights better than most other breeds.

APPENDIX 2

Peruvian Wool Export Statistics

I am very grateful to Shane Hunt for his kind permission to include unpublished export figures in this book. They are taken from his 1973 paper. For more detailed discussion of the composition of twentieth century wool exports and their breakdown by species, grade, and port of embarkation, see Bertram (1974).

Hunt describes the difficulties of using Peruvian sources to study nineteenth century export levels (Hunt 1973: 32–41). He shows that the five principal trading partners (Britain, France, Germany, the United States, and Chile) purchased over 99% of the wool exported in years for which there are reliable and comparable figures.

TABLE 4

Nineteenth-Century Peruvian Wool Exports

Year	Peruvian sources			Foreign sources		
	Sheep	Alpaca	Total	Sheep	Alpaca	Total
1830				0	3	3
1831				0	0	0
1832				1	11	12
1833				5	7	12
1834				0	78	78
1835				0	0	0
1836				2	433	435
1837				0	869	869
1838				12	1045	1057
1839				55	975	1030
1840				39	1257	1296
1841				65	1426	1491
1842				20	713	733
1843				28	1150	1178
1844				277	0	227
1845				1	1207	1208
1846				28	1128	1156
1847				41	1644	1685
1848				140	1663	1803
1849				52	1439	1491
1850				756	743	1499
1851			1155	775	908	1683
1852				682	932	1614
1853				860	911	1771
1854				910	567	1477
1855				1030	585	1615
1856				1026	1296	2322
1857				1397	1014	2411
1858				974	1168	2142
1859				1647	1115	2762
1860	654	1046	1700	1371	1059	2430
1861				1451	1266	2717
1862				1483	1214	2697
1863				1489	1258	2747

Note: In metric tons.

(Continued)

TABLE 4 (*Continued*)

Year	Peruvian sources			Foreign sources		
	Sheep	Alpaca	Total	Sheep	Alpaca	Total
1864				1772	735	2507
1865				1511	1082	2593
1866				2237	1522	3759
1867				2797	1436	4233
1868				1317	750	2067
1869				1282	1351	2633
1870				2264	1508	3772
1871				2012	1399	3411
1872				1789	1598	3387
1873				1332	1767	3099
1874				1238	1558	2796
1875				1865	1638	3503
1876				1434	1413	2847
1877	1483	1583	3066	1494	1500	2994
1878				1277	1774	3051
1879				1181	1665	2846
1880				522	641	1163
1881				713	805	1518
1882				586	1441	2027
1883				822	638	1460
1884				2184	3072	5256
1885				1212	1708	2920
1886				1022	1754	2776
1887	1331	627	1958	1159	1938	3097
1888				855	1797	2652
1889				1320	2048	3368
1890				1086	1413	2499
1891			2831	1429	1813	3242
1892			3130	1223	1841	3064
1893				1651	2042	3693
1894				1374	2053	3427
1895				1228	1653	2881
1896			2544	1469	1649	3118
1897	1666	2104	3770	1393	2064	3457
1898			3489	924	1763	2687
1899			3435	1104	1921	3025
1900			3535	969	1922	2891

TABLE 5

Twentieth-Century Peruvian Wool Exports: Export Values in 1953 Prices

Year	Wool	Year	Wool
1900	84.4	1932	108.3
1901	—	1933	155.8
1902	90.1	1934	141.1
1903	—	1935	172.1
1904	70.8	1936	177.0
1905	101.4	1937	140.9
1906	112.3	1938	132.7
1907	95.2	1939	145.3
1908	78.4	1940	141.9
1909	90.9	1941	120.7
1910	118.2	1942	96.3
1911	96.1	1943	116.0
1912	97.0	1944	134.2
1913	114.3	1945	127.7
1914	112.2	1946	104.5
1915	149.6	1947	65.3
1916	153.0	1948	68.0
1917	186.0	1949	131.0
1918	150.5	1950	209.0
1919	117.3	1951	152.2
1920	90.9	1952	145.2
1921	47.9	1953	146.8
1922	121.2	1954	138.6
1923	136.7	1955	109.4
1924	193.2	1956	144.4
1925	138.7	1957	177.9
1926	126.5	1958	130.7
1927	151.9	1959	183.1
1928	153.0	1960	127.6
1929	121.7	1961	129.8
1930	79.5	1962	162.3
1931	89.2		

Note: In millions of *soles*.

TABLE 6

Price Ratios

Year	Wool
1913	4.5
1929	8.6
1939	9.9
1950	56.6
1953	100
1954	118.8
1959	135.5

Note: 1953 = 100.

Text of an Announcement of an Annual Fair

CRAN FERIA Regional Agropecuaria en el Pueblo Benemérito de TINTA DEL 22 AL 26 DE AGOSTO DE 1972
Que se realiza todos los años conmemorando la Fiesta de:
San Bartolomè Patrón Titular de la Villa Martir
El Concejo Distrital y el Vecindario en general, se complacen en invitar al público, productores y comerciantes de la Región, a concurrir a esta feria anual, que ha organizado con el plausible propósito de cimentar y afianzar las actividades económicas y productivas de Tinta y pueblos vecinos.
Se efectuará compra y venta de cereales, productos de la región y del Valle de la Convención habrá trenes y carros directos que unirán con el Cusco, Sicuani y Yanaoca otros lugares circunvecinas.

[The announcement continues to describe other events, including a horse race, a bullfight, and an "almuerzo lunch danzant."]

La cuidadanía de Tinta expresa su anticipada gratitud a los concurrentes a la Feria
Tinta, Agosto de 1974
LA COMISION

APPENDIX 4

Demographic Statistics

The tables in this appendix require special caution in their use. The figures contain a number of inaccuracies. The distinction between urban (*urbano*) and rural (*rural*) leaves a great deal to the interpretation of the census taker. The general nature of this distinction appears to have shifted over time; the 1876 census terms a large number of rather small population nuclei as "urban." I rejected the alternative of listing the population of the district, provincial, and departmental capitals as urban, since the 1961 and 1972 censuses do not list all the *centros poblados*, as do the earlier two censuses. These latter censuses frequently appear to equate administrative centers with urban settlements, reflecting the tendency by which increased penetration of national administrative agencies and marketing systems favored some hamlets over others, leaving the small local elites (who were previously considered urban) to collapse into peasant status (Orlove 1975). The application of racial categories in the 1940 census must have confused the census takers further and brought further inconsistencies in the applications of the terms *rural* and *urbano*.

The earlier censuses sometimes include estimates of uncensused populations; for this reason, the total populations in a district, province, or department may sometimes exceed the sum of its rural and urban populations. The 1876 census mentions that several census takers quit their positions, leaving the officials charged with providing the figures no alternative but to make rough guesses. Later censuses, though possibly more accurate, are less frank, and similar events most probably took place.

Finally, administrative boundaries shift in a somewhat irregular fashion. At times, one district divided into two; thus Túpac Amaru [Tungasuca] split from Pampamarca, Quiñota from Llusco, Suyckutambo from Condoroma. On other occasions, several districts cede territory to a new one: Kunturkanki received lands from Langui, Layo, and Checca. It is not always possible, therefore, to prepare a list that neatly indicates the bureaucratic mitosis of administrative reorganization, and I have generally left blanks for units that had not yet been formed.

Nevertheless, the census figures are of some value. The figures for urban populations may best be used to show shifts in the relative positions of different centers from census to census, rather than to measure rates of urban population growth. The total figures yield aggregate rates of increase that should be used judiciously.

TABLE 7

Population of Peru

Year	Urban	Rural	Total
1876			2,699,945[a]
1940	2,240,348	3,976,619	6,216,967
1961	4,698,178	5,208,569	9,906,747
1972	8,058,495	51,479,713	13,538,208

[a] This figure includes 47,266 inhabitants of the provinces of Tarapacá and Arica which Chile annexed as a result of the War of the Pacific.

TABLE 8

Population Data for Southern Peru

Place	1876			1940			1961			1972		
	Urban	Rural	Total	Urban	Rural	Total	Urban	Rural	Total	Urban	Rural	Total
CUZCO	19,096		229,635	123,882	362,710	486,592	198,341	413,631	611,972	256,640	456,278	712,918
Cuzco		4,150	23,246	44,954	9,677	54,631	87,752	7,336	95,088	130,942	11,089	142,031
Acomayo			17,516	10,456	18,941	29,397	9,518	21,236	30,754	11,863	17,366	39,249
Acomayo	4,310	1,887	6,197	2,128	3,199	5,319	1,874	4,005	5,879	1,795	3,734	5,529
Acopía							1,436	2,739	4,175	1,361	1,354	2,971
Acos				1,735	2,602	4,337	1,327	2,692	4,019	1,808	1,954	2,762
Mosoc Llacta										537	566	1,103
Pomacanchi	3,470	1,649	6,197	2,715	7,726	10,441	2,983	4,813	7,796	2,663	4,549	7,212
Rondocán	2,410	298	2,708	401	4,018	4,419	778	3,846	4,224	365	3,794	4,159
Sangarará	2,874	618	3,492	3,485	1,396	4,881	1,520	3,141	4,661	3,354	1,159	4,513

(*Continued*)

Source: Demographic sources for the colonial period include Aparicio Vega (1968) and Concolorcorvo (1959).

[a] The district of Pampamarca formed part of the province of Canchis until 1971, when Espinar split off from Canas. Pampamarca was given to Canas to console the Yanaoca elite for the loss of the valuable punas to the south.

[b] The district of Combapata was separated from Tinta.

[c] The district of Pitumarca was created from Checacupe.

[d] In the 1876 census, Santo Tomás and Llusco were enumerated jointly.

[e] The province of Espinar was separated from Canas in 1917.

[f] The shifting fortunes of the Grau family are reflected in the changing names of a province; the province split sometime after 1940 to become two provinces.

[g] The province of Melgar was created after the 1876 census.

TABLE 8 (*Continued*)

Place	1876			1940			1961			1972		
	Urban	Rural	Total	Urban	Rural	Total	Urban	Rural	Total	Urban	Rural	Total
Arta			17,248	7,627	31,750	39,377	10,290	34,800	45,090	11,517	34,893	46,410
Calca				4,723	29,055	33,778	8,080	31,240	39,320	10,635	35,789	46,246
Canas	4,171	31,805	35,976	4,058	22,781	26,839	3,629	24,975	28,604	3,544	27,754	31,298
Yanaoca	1,018	2,763	3,691	1,384	5,854	7,238	1,146	6,529	7,675	1,090	6,986	8,096
Checca	388	3,320	3,708	860	4,156	5,016	150	4,013	4,163	97	4,432	4,529
Kunturkanki							165	2,876	3,041	268	3,745	4,013
Langui	629	2,421	3,050	769	3,081	3,850	393	2,062	2,455	382	2,219	2,601
Layo	302	1,855	2,157	131	3,972	4,103	128	3,928	4,056	207	4,407	4,614
Pampamarca[a]	1,026	1,406	2,432	816	3,779	4,595	1,041	1,023	2,064	864	1,254	2,118
Quehue				98	1,939	2,037	112	2,152	2,264	129	2,212	2,341
Túpac Amaru							494	2,392	2,886	507	2,499	3,006
Canchis	11,412	24,118	35,530	15,521	49,438	64,959	21,650	48,838	70,488	23,397	52,389	75,786
Sicuani	2,299	10,114	12,413	6,335	21,526	27,861	10,664	21,903	32,567	12,956	22,756	35,712
Combapata[b]				1,224	3,050	4,274	1,491	3,081	4,572	1,129	2,993	4,122
Checacupe	3,175	2,636	5,811	1,280	3,412	4,692	1,297	3,403	4,700	1,804	2,682	4,486
Marangani	459	3,821	4,280	596	6,752	7,347	1,017	6,163	7,180	760	8,843	9,603
Pitumarca[c]				2,162	3,614	5,776	2,352	3,456	5,808	1,924	3,807	5,731
San Pablo	2,156	2,667	4,823	1,392	5,136	6,528	1,885	4,656	6,541	1,641	5,040	6,681
San Pedro				880	2,475	3,355	902	2,468	3,370	925	2,626	3,551
Tinta	2,297	3,474	5,771	1,653	3,473	5,126	2,042	3,708	5,750	2,258	3,642	5,900
Chumbivilcas	4,564	13,654	22,115	3,676	41,789	45,465	5,168	45,862	51,030	5,760	52,712	58,472
Santo Tomás[d]	1,974	4,559	6,533	877	10,874	11,751	1,659	11,635	13,294	2,095	14,438	16,533

Capacmarca	494	700	1,194	741	2,729	3,470	920	3,299	4,219	746	3,334	4,080
Colquemarca	984	5,538	6,119	580	6,747	7,327	388	6,911	7,299	561	7,452	8,013
Chamaca				209	3,930	4,139	117	4,651	4,768	160	4,868	5,028
Livitaca				407	6,882	7,289	337	7,570	7,907	345	8,444	8,789
Llusco[d]				612	5,960	6,572	1,139	6,316	7,455	712	4,882	5,594
Quiñota										311	2,668	2,979
Velille			ca5,000	250	4,667	4,917	608	5,480	6,088	830	6,626	7,456
Espinar[e]	1,018	9,950	10,968	2,909	28,416	31,325	5,627	31,355	36,982	5,991	35,532	41,524
Yauri				1,487	10,977	12,464	2,834	9,926	12,670	4,066	11,867	15,933
Condoroma				46	840	886	1,292	873	2,165	211	843	1,054
Coporaque	493	7,664	8,157	419	9,891	10,310	471	10,826	11,297	327	10,737	11,064
Ocoruro	175	797	972	186	1,220	1,406	176	1,115	1,291	215	1,376	1,591
Pallpata				173	1,998	2,171	601	3,876	4,477	917	3,423	4,340
Pichigua	148	3,125	3,273	598	3,490	4,088	253	4,739	4,992	189	5,375	5,564
Suyckutambo										66	1,911	1,977
La Convención	659	9,517	10,176	2,689	24,554	27,243	10,550	51,351	61,901	14,212	69,052	83,264
Paruro	11,239	5,561	16,800	5,848	23,285	29,133	6,870	24,858	31,728	8,443	23,363	31,806
Paucartambo	3,281	10,862	14,143	2,423	18,553	20,976	2,951	23,504	26,455	3,692	26,429	30,121
Quispicanchis	10,155	8,906	20,371	7,911	46,000	53,911	14,419	47,581	62,000	15,856	46,175	62,031
Cusipata	2,478	3,777	6,255	1,618	11,948	13,566	1,197	3,623	4,810	1,021	3,596	4,617
Quiquijana							1,422	8,021	9,443	1,372	7,956	9,328
Urubamba	8,700	7,814	16,514	11,087	18,471	29,558	11,837	20,695	32,532	10,768	23,913	34,681
APURIMAC	119,426			36,936	221,158	280,213	57,116	231,107	288,223	71,595	236,210	307,805
Antabamba	7,114			4,000	9,643	14,812	5,827	9,537	15,364	8,442	7,673	16,115

(Continued)

TABLE 8 (Continued)

Place	1876			1940			1961			1972		
	Urban	Rural	Total	Urban	Rural	Total	Urban	Rural	Total	Urban	Rural	Total
Aymaraes			18,186	7,570	28,851	39,542	10,332	28,820	39,152	13,789	24,649	38,438
Cotabambas^f			28,646				4,937	33,997	38,934	5,259	35,179	40,438
Grau^f				7,725	56,457	69,683	7,982	20,328	28,310	7,564	20,212	27,776
AREQUIPA			160,282	155,046	107,933	263,077	250,746	138,135	388,881	433,186	97,342	530,528
Arequipa			61,989	93,476	35,333	128,809	172,528	49,849	222,377	320,570	30,374	350,944
Castilla			23,223	9,216	14,003	23,219	10,752	16,556	27,308	10,879	17,436	28,315
Caylloma			19,111	13,875	13,659	27,534	15,431	17,201	32,632	20,145	13,822	33,967
Condesuyos			10,999	6,136	9,458	15,594	5,977	10,302	16,279	7,472	9,232	16,704
La 'Jnión			19,299	5,839	14,622	20,461	6,874	14,381	21,255	10,748	8,157	18,905
PUNO			256,594	71,263	477,108	548,371	124,147	562,113	686,260	186,838	592,756	779,594
Melgar^g				11,516	29,681	41,197	14,475	33,726	48,201	19,386	33,171	52,557
Ayaviri				5,675	5,064	10,739	7,553	4,516	12,069	9,719	3,749	13,459
Antauta				59	2,383	2,442	295	3,245	3,540	432	3,280	3,712
Cupi				151	1,017	1,168	162	1,258	1,420	158	1,287	1,445
Llalli				393	996	1,389	479	992	1,471	1,256	832	2,088
Macari				607	3,349	3,956	678	3,702	4,380	993	4,139	5,132
Nuñoa				1,627	4,843	6,470	2,137	5,613	7,750	3,001	4,702	7,703
Orurillo				766	7,044	7,810	732	9,085	9,817	989	9,555	10,544
Santa Rosa				1,767	3,218	4,985	2,054	3,191	5,245	2,369	3,032	5,401
Umachiri				471	1,767	2,238	385	2,124	2,509	469	2,604	3,073

224

TABLE 9

Date of Official Recognition of Peasant Communities

Year	Canas	Canchis	Espinar	Chumbivilcas	Four province total	Rest of Cuzco	Cuzco total	Rest of Peru	Peru total
1926	7	2	6	8	23	17	40	18	58
1927	—	10	—	7	17	16	33	21	54
1928	7	7	18	3	35	8	43	55	98
1929	4	9	7	3	23	11	34	47	81
1930	—	—	—	3	3	—	3	28	31
1931	—	—	—	—	—	—	—	23	23
1932	—	—	—	—	—	—	—	11	11
1933	—	—	—	—	—	—	—	35	35
1934	—	—	—	—	—	—	—	7	7
1935	—	—	—	—	—	—	—	73	73
1936	—	—	—	—	—	5	5	50	55
1937	—	—	—	—	—	—	—	64	64
1938	1	—	3	1	5	—	5	72	77
1939	—	—	—	—	—	—	—	34	34
1940	—	—	—	—	—	3	3	91	94

(*Continued*)

Note: Comunidades indígenas until 1969, then *comunidades campesinas.*
Source: Directorio de Comunidades Campesinas. Lima: Sistema Nacional de Apoyo a la Mobilización Social, Oficina Nacional de Apoyo a la Mobilización Social, Dirección General de Apoyo a Empresas, 1974.

[a] Chaynapampas' date is typed ambiguously in text (p. 89). Counted as 1969.
[b] Pampamarca Urinsaya's date of recognition is unclear (p. 70). Counted as 1973.
[c] SINAMOS directory claims 19 *comunidades* in Cuzco province but only 18 are listed. This reduces Cuzco department and Peru totals from the listed 439 and 2390, respectively. Other department totals are correct.

TABLE 9 (*Continued*)

Year	Canas	Canchis	Espinar	Chumbivilcas	Four province total	Rest of Cuzco	Cuzco total	Rest of Peru	Peru total
1941	—	—	—	—	—	—	—	66	66
1942	—	1	—	—	1	2	3	46	49
1943	—	—	—	—	—	3	3	63	66
1944	—	—	—	—	—	2	2	67	69
1945	—	1	—	—	1	1	2	62	64
1946	1	2	—	—	3	4	7	87	94
1947	—	—	1	—	1	2	3	57	60
1948	—	—	—	—	—	4	4	40	44
1949	—	—	—	1	1	1	2	14	16
1950	—	—	—	—	—	—	—	8	8
1951	—	—	—	1	1	—	1	22	23
1952	—	—	—	—	—	1	1	11	12
1953	—	—	—	—	—	1	1	7	8
1954	—	—	—	—	—	—	—	14	14
1955	—	—	—	—	—	1	1	10	11
1956	—	—	—	—	—	7	7	62	69

Year									
1957	—	1	—	—	1	4	5	32	37
1958	—	1	—	—	1	1	2	25	27
1959	—	—	—	1	1	—	1	12	13
1960	—	—	—	2	2	1	3	21	24
1961	—	—	—	—	—	4	4	34	38
1962	—	4	—	1	1	15	16	18	34
1963	4	10	—	1	5	8	13	25	38
1964	3	11	—	—	14	24	38	91	129
1965	15	15	—	—	14	22	36	79	115
1966	6	6	—	2	32	35	67	70	137
1967	1	2	—	—	12	15	27	113	140
1968	—	1	—	1	4	8	12	78	90
1969	—	—	—	—	1	3	4	38[a]	42
1970	—	—	—	—	—	—	—	—	—
1971	—	—	—	—	—	—	—	5	5
1972	—	—	—	—	—	—	—	7	7
1973	2[b]	—	—	2	2	5	7	38	45
	51	83	35	35	204	234	438	1951	2389[c]

SOURCES

Resumen del censo general de habitantes del Perú hecho en 1876. Dirección de Estadística. Lima: Imprenta del Estado. 1878.

Censo nacional de población de 1940. Dirección Nacional de Estadística. Lima: Ministerio de Hacienda y Comercio. 1949. vols. 1, 7, 8.

Sexto censo nacional de población levantado el 2 de julio de 1961. Resultados finales de primera prioridad. Dirección Nacional de Planificación. Lima: Instituto Nacional de Planificación. 1964

Resultados provisionales del censo de población del 4 de junio de 1974. Lima: Oficina Nacional de Estadística y Censos. 1973.

APPENDIX 5

Sicuani Wool Statistics

The figures for wool shipments from Sicuani included in this appendix are taken from two sources. I compiled statistics from the *Sección de Lanas, Banco de la Nación*, Sicuani, for the years 1971 and 1972, and used a secondary source for the years 1958, 1960, 1962, 1964, 1966, and 1968, despite its improbable and inconsistent reporting for 1958 and 1960. That source is Gutiérrez Galindo Blas and Cucho Moscoco Hernán, *La comercialización de lana y fibra en Sicuani,* in *Tres estudios en Canas-Canchis,* Instituto Indigenista Peruano, Proyecto de Desarrollo e Integración de la Población Indígena del Consejo Nacional de Desarrollo Comunal, Sub-proyecto de Investigación (Zona: Canas-Canchis; Lima: Ministerio de Trabajo, 1969).

I observed the recording of data in the *Banco de la Nación* on several occasions and noted inaccuracies caused by haste. Wool merchants also told me that they did not report all their wool sales. Hence there was underreporting of wool shipments. Inconsistencies in labeling of llama and *huarizo* wool is another difficulty. Nevertheless, I believe that the important nature of these data warrants their inclusion, despite these flaws.

TABLE 10

Volume of Wool Shipped from Sicuani, 1958–1968

Year	Alpaca	Sheep	Other[a]	Total
1958	1,765,631	0	0	1,765,631
1960	956,910	0	0	956,910
1962	1,185,410	36,491	89,880	1,311,781
1964	1,246,253	272,892	96,807	1,615,952
1966	953,885	115,531	19,348	1,088,764
1968	1,246,162	300,033	14,497	1,560,692

Note: In pounds.

[a] Llama wool and mixed consignments. After 1970 llama wool is often classified as alpaca wool, and occasionally as sheep wool, but only rarely as llama wool.

TABLE 11

Value of Wool Shipped from Sicuani, 1958–1968

Year	Alpaca	Sheep	Other[a]	Total
1958	0	0	0	0
1960	0	0	0	0
1962	17,438	218	598	18,254
1964	20,198	2,125	829	23,152
1966	11,638	911	127	12,676
1968	20,069	1,799	160	22,028

Note: In soles.

[a] Llama wool and mixed consignments. After 1970, llama wool is often classified as alpaca wool, and occasionally as sheep wool, but only rarely as llama wool.

TABLE 12

Volume of Wool Shipped from Sicuani in 1971

Month	Alpaca				Sheep	Total
	White	LF	Shades	Total		
Jan.[a]	10,000	20,000	12,805	42,805	15,567	58,372
Feb.	58,666	12,233	63,438	134,337	3,567	137,904
Mar.	28,179	4,313	21,408	53,900	38,197	92,097
Apr.	46,946	11,988	45,385	104,319	129,961	234,280
May	30,512	4,326	29,104	63,942	99,017	162,959
Jun.	17,950	2,817	14,087	34,854	47,593	82,447
Jul.	17,708	3,177	17,242	38,127	15,284	53,411
Aug.	15,495	1,515	19,072	36,082	77,018	113,100
Sep.	10,433	1,545	14,960	26,938	35,270	62,208
Oct.	26,103	5,417	29,114	60,634	80,846	141,480
Nov.	41,152	12,634	31,852	85,638	102,764	188,402
Dec.	83,672	13,630	62,824	160,126	126,544	286,670
Total	386,816	93,595	361,291	841,702	751,628	1,613,330

Note: In pounds.

[a] No shipments were recorded before 15 January.

TABLE 13

Value of Wool Shipped from Sicuani in 1971

Month	Alpaca				Sheep	Total	Value of wool shipped by railway
	White	LF	Shades	Total			
Jan.[a]	155	28	96	279	156	435	0
Feb.	905	176	451	1,532	41	1,573	47
Mar.	461	65	164	690	362	1,052	293
Apr.	909	177	406	1,492	1,115	2,607	540
May	340	47	202	589	1,024	1,613	647
Jun.	396	49	191	636	606	1,242	151
Jul.	322	325	147	794	157	951	466
Aug.	252	185	141	578	867	1,445	537
Sep.	216	24	122	362	400	762	407
Oct.	524	77	237	838	598	1,436	744
Nov.	806	231	236	1,273	1,045	2,318	1,119
Dec.	1,414	252	476	2,142	1,493	3,635	1,118
Total	6,700	1,636	2,829	11,205	7,864	19,069	6,069

Note: In *soles*.

[a] No shipments were recorded before 15 January.

TABLE 14

Volume of Wool Shipped from Sicuani in 1972

Month	White	LF	Shades	Total	Sheep	Total
		Alpaca				
Jan.	179,091	40,136	240,889	460,116	103,023	563,139
Feb.	37,523	8,765	26,183	72,471	54,362	126,833
Mar.	15,960	4,295	107,969	128,224	169,756	297,980
Apr.	67,094	8,892	126,934	202,920	110,846	313,766
May	9,925	0	69,007	78,932	92,795	171,727
Jun.	5,897	428	10,798	17,123	67,449	84,572
Jul.	8,076	182	1,214	9,472	52,834	62,306
Aug.	8,404	1,500	43,700	53,604	128,070	181,674
Sep.	1,800	300	14,600	16,700	164,021	180,721
Oct.	32,305	300	800	33,405	43,460	76,865
Nov.	16,313	1,700	24,540	42,553	68,950	111,503
Dec.	106,672	8,584	112,154	227,410	74,786	302,196
Total	489,060	75,082	778,788	1,342,930	1,130,352	2,473,282

Note: In pounds.

TABLE 15

Value of Wool Shipped from Sicuani in 1972

Month	White	LF	Shades	Total	Sheep	Total
		Alpaca[a]				
Jan.	3,263	692	1,532	5,487	1,078	6,565
Feb.	1,042	172	300	1,514	654	2,168
Mar.	177	118	1,866	2,161	2,190	4,351
Apr.	2,032	265	3,267	5,564	1,339	6,903
May	268	28	1,217	1,513	1,554	3,067
Jun.	156	11	204	371	1,020	1,391
Jul.	175	5	20	200	487	687
Aug.	231	22	365	618	1,473	2,091
Sep.	45	7	179	231	1,703	1,934
Oct.	928	8	12	948	491	1,439
Nov.	471	14	712	1,197	1,067	2,264
Dec.	207	22	855	1,084	1,315	2,399
Total	8,895	1,364	10,529	20,888	14,371	35,259

Note: In *soles*.

[a] The records of values of alpaca wool are incomplete for the months of January, November, and December.

TABLE 16

Volume of Alpaca Wool Shipped from Sicuani, by Export Firm

Year	Michell	Ricketts	Patthey y Corzo	Sarfaty	Sota	Tingolana	Clamasa	Gibson
1958	164.801	189,339	67,457	214,605	0	0	0	0
1960	121.740	124,333	72,229	71,896	0	0	0	0
1962	267.140	167,891	101,436	237,645	71,978	0	0	0
1964	468,237	232,226	14,643	210,579	61,874	0	0	0
1966	244,317	211,410	70,445	181,957	21,273	251,226	0	0
1968	373,527	14,011	69,182	28,500	49,586	180,730	428,568	15,623
1971	314,942	28,669	0	87,636	11,388	202,800	0	0
1972	266,089	69,966	0	336,817	4,009	265,700	137,615	0

Note: In pounds. This table is based on the stated recipient of wool shipments, and hence does not include wool shipped to other agents or suppliers of the firms.

TABLE 17

Number of Individuals Who Ship Wool from Sicuani

Year	Number
1958	26
1960	16
1962	12
1964	9
1966	9
1968	14
1971	17

APPENDIX **6**

Land Tenure Patterns and Livestock Holdings

I accompanied one of the interviewers who gathered data for the *II Censo Nacional Agropecuario*, on which these tables are based. Underpaid, inexperienced, and hurried, he nonetheless interviewed with a certain degree of care, for which I do not believe my presence was solely responsible. I noticed several inaccuracies in his recording, and there were obvious contradictions between interviewees' responses and other sorts of evidence. Several informants also told me that they had been warned that the census would be the basis for new taxes. The data presented here must therefore be used with a great deal of care. The lack of information on cameloids is both unfortunate and characteristic. There are between 300,000 and 400,000 alpacas in the provinces of Canas, Canchis, Espinar, and Chumbivilas.

TABLE 18

Land Tenure and Livestock Holdings in Cuzco and Apurimac

	1	2	3	4	5	6	7	8
Departments								
Cuzco	123,328	30,878	92,405	2,113,497	327,510	1,545,013	61,615	370,492
Apurimac	64,451	18,432	46,019	576,938	292,285	509,539	66,679	173,867
Provinces of Cuzco								
Cuzco	4,029	1,276	2,753	15,601	7,444	33,241	1,548	12,262
Acomayo	8,062	1,543	6,519	19,473	11,164	87,675	3,285	10,708
Anta	10,777	2,833	7,944	96,839	39,100	54,374	7,427	34,259
Calca	9,679	2,100	7,579	255,737	23,255	68,914	6,298	43,321
Canas	7,245	1,055	6,190	116,393	24,779	195,782	1,665	11,404
Canchis	15,188	6,659	8,529	184,241	27,132	135,055	948	25,195
Chumbivilcas	12,987	3,024	9,963	463,336	58,943	265,827	6,746	26,085
Espinar	6,189	1,633	5,186	311,074	41,691	344,015	73	12,842
La Convención	12,223	794	11,429	161,859	20,889	20,997	6,439	103,293
Paruro	8,900	2,278	6,622	76,806	21,337	66,476	4,868	20,367

(Continued)

Source: Datos Oficiales del II Censo Nacional Agropecuario, 1972, 1973. Oficina Nacional de Estadística y Censos. Lima: Ministerio de Agricultura.

Note: The number variables are as follows:

1. Number of production units (*unidades agropecuarias*) below .5 hectare in area
2. Total area of production units below .5 hectare in area
3. Number of production units above .5 hectare in area
4. Total area of production units above .5 hectare in area
5. Number of cattle
6. Number of sheep
7. Number of pigs
8. Number of chickens

TABLE 18 *(Continued)*

	1	2	3	4	5	6	7	8
Provinces of Cuzco (cont.)								
Paucartambo	6,283	1,375	4,908	172,808	15,194	72,298	9,527	18,406
Quispicanchis	13,726	4,295	9,431	214,037	20,357	145,779	8,227	27,338
Urubamba	7,365	2,013	5,352	25,473	16,225	54,580	4,564	29,954
Provinces of Apurimac								
Abancay	8,218	2,724	5,494	96,610	51,770	39,674	8,163	30,081
Andahuaylas	27,279	7,827	19,452	75,440	107,253	234,108	46,482	89,605
Antabamba	3,687	462	3,225	71,340	23,905	36,559	651	4,851
Aymaraes	10,462	2,529	7,933	285,459	55,545	55,550	3,859	23,125
Cotabambas	8,171	2,622	5,549	20,713	23,993	77,673	4,497	15,348
Grau	6,634	2,268	4,366	27,356	29,819	65,975	3,017	10,887
Districts in selected provinces in Cuzco								
Canchis	15,188	5,659	8,529	184,241	27,132	135,055	948	25,195
Sicuani	5,374	2,987	2,387	51,869	10,412	37,002	221	14,346
Combapata	1,034	294	740	12,651	1,733	7,443	25	1,739
Checacupe	885	299	586	7,138	1,233	7,141	92	1,569
Maranganí	2,230	810	1,420	66,966	5,593	27,953	13	1,292
Pitumarca	1,645	607	1,038	23,077	1,144	22,159	246	1,292
San Pablo	1,964	750	1,214	20,462	3,749	21,414	134	1,543
San Pedro	756	436	330	506	1,251	3,373	70	1,258
Tinta	1,300	486	814	1,572	2,017	8,570	147	2,196
Canas	7,245	1,055	6,190	116,393	24,779	195,782	1,665	11,404
Yanaoca	1,874	280	1,594	10,052	4,250	43,232	856	3,499
Checca	986	116	870	29,787	5,322	38,966	57	1,130

(Continued)

TABLE 18 (*Continued*)

	1	2	3	4	5	6	7	8
Canas (cont.)								
Kunturkanki	974	82	892	29,793	5,629	36,751	16	1,289
Langui	562	80	482	6,619	2,399	14,711	21	1,050
Layo	1,026	209	817	30,628	3,610	26,484	79	2,149
Pampamarca	539	79	460	1,430	957	9,238	245	852
Quehue	574	52	522	5,708	1,546	17,760	11	569
Túpac Amaru	710	157	553	2,376	1,066	8,640	380	866
Espinar	6,819	1,633	5,186	311,074	41,691	344,015	73	12,842
Yauri	2,120	472	1,648	77,547	11,663	83,209	25	4,533
Condoroma	210	8	202	30,336	285	10,839	8	224
Coporaque	2,055	726	1,329	50,821	9,329	72,001	7	3,400
Ocoruro	250	0	250	24,515	2,344	27,764	16	700
Pallpata	728	118	610	63,003	8,555	80,214	5	1,314
Pichigua	984	208	776	44,209	8,168	53,561	12	1,947
Stuyckutambo	472	101	371	20,643	1,347	16,427	0	724
Chumbivilcas	12,987	3,024	9,963	463,336	58,943	265,827	6,746	26,083
Santo Tomás	3,114	530	2,584	18,990	8,484	65,832	1,767	4,569
Capacmarca	1,084	359	725	38,777	3,979	11,049	406	1,602
Colquemarca	1,958	488	1,470	97,147	7,925	27,622	1,217	4,246
Chamaca	1,129	203	926	18,558	7,955	22,146	30	2,942
Livitaca	1,970	540	1,430	100,603	8,551	61,653	672	4,330
Llusco	1,396	524	872	2,936	3,602	16,835	1,546	2,649
Quiñota	718	107	611	2,789	2,552	9,690	1,044	1,686
Velille	1,618	273	1,345	183,536	15,895	51,000	64	4,059

TABLE 19

Distribution of Alpacas in South America, 1966

Nation	Department	Number of head	Estimated area devoted to grazing (hectares)
Peru		3,865,000	3,290,000
	Junín	5,000	5,000
	Lima	60,000	45,000
	Huancavelica	400,000	230,000
	Ayacucho	200,000	110,000
	Apurimac	300,000	155,000
	Cuzco	500,000[a]	280,000
	Areguipa	300,000	240,000
	Moquegua	50,000	35,000
	Puno	2,000,000	2,150,000
	Tacna	50,000	40,000
Bolivia		500,000	300,000
	La Paz	300,000	200,000
	Oruro	200,000	100,000
Chile		80,000[b]	50,000
Total		4,245,000	3,640,000

Source: FAO, 1971. Provisional report of the mission to Peru and Bolivia for the development of the industries derived from the South American camel species, p. 23.

[a] Between 60 and 80% of these are in the provinces of Canas, Canchis, Espinar, and Chumbivilcas.

[b] This figure is based on extrapolations from the figures for adjacent departments.

Bibliography

Abler, Ronald, John S. Adams, and Peter Gould
1971 *Spatial organization: The geographer's view of the world.* Englewood Cliffs, N. J.: Prentice-Hall.

Adams, Richard Newbold
1966 Power and power domains. *América Latina* 9(2):3–11. Rio de Janeiro.
1970 *Crucifixion by power: Essays on Guatemalan national social structure, 1944 1966.* Austin: Univ. of Texas Press.

Aguirre Beltrán, Gonzalo
1967 *Regiones de refugio: el desarrollo de la comunidad y el proceso dominical en Mestizo América.* Ediciones Especiales 46. México: Instituto Indigenista Interamericano.

Alberti, Giorgio, and Rodrigo Sánchez
1974 *Poder y conflicto social en el valle del Mantaro (1900–1974).* Perú-Problema 10. Instituto de Estudios Peruanos. Lima: IEP ediciones.

Amin, Samir
1970 *L'accumulation à l'échelle mondiale. Critique à la théorie du sous-développement.* Paris: Anthropos.

Anderson, James N.
1973 Ecological anthropology and anthropological ecology. In *A handbook of social and cultural anthropology,* edited by John J. Honigman. Chicago: Rand McNally.

Aparicio Vega, Manuel Jesús
1965 Apuntes para la historiografía de Canchis. Tesis para el Bachillerato en Humanidades, Facultad de Letras y Ciencias Humanas, Universidad Nacional de San Antonio Abad del Cuzco.
1971 *Cartografia histórica cuzqueña: Mapas del Cuzco existentes en el Archivo General de Indias.* Cuzco: Gráfico Rozas Luna.

Appleby, Gordon
 1976a The role of urban food needs in regional development, Puno, Peru. In *Regional analysis,* edited by Carol A. Smith. Vol. 1. *Economic systems.* New York: Academic Press. Pp. 147–181.
 1976b Export monoculture and regional social structure in Puno, Peru. In *Regional analysis,* edited by Carol A. Smith. Vol. 2. *Social systems.* New York: Academic Press. Pp. 291–307.
Aranguren Paz, Angélica
 1972 Pastores de altura: Economia y ritos. Tesis de Doctorado, Programa Académico de Antropología y Arqueología, Universidad Nacional Mayor de San Marcos, Lima.
Arguedas, José María
 1947 La feria. *La Verdad,* 16 octubre 1947. Sicuani.
Astiz, Carlos
 1969 *Pressure groups and power elites in Peruvian politics.* Ithaca, N.Y.: Cornell Univ. Press.
Baker, Paul T., and Michael A. Little (Eds.)
 1976 *Man in the Andes: A multidisciplinary study of high-altitude Quechua.* Stroudsburg, Pa.: Dowden Hutchinson and Ross.
Barker, Alfred F.
 1927 *The prospective development of Peru as a sheep-breeding and wool-growing country.* Leeds: Jowett & Sowry.
Barrionueva, Alfonsina
 1973 Cuidado con la alpaca. *Caretas,* 23 julio 1973, pp. 62–64. Lima.
 1976 Dependency analysis of Latin America. *Latin American Research Review* 11(3):3–54.
Beck, Brenda B. F.
 1976 Centers and boundaries of regional caste systems: Towards a general model. In *Regional analysis,* edited by Carol A. Smith. Vol. 2. *Social systems.* New York: Academic Press. Pp. 255–288.
Bendix, Reinhart
 1967 Tradition and modernity reconsidered. *Comparative Studies in Society and History* 9(2):292–346.
Benedict, Burton
 1968 Family firms and economic development. *Southwestern Journal of Anthropology* 24(1):1–19.
Bennett, John W.
 1969 *Northern plainsmen: Adaptive strategy and agrarian life.* Chicago: Aldine-Atherton.
Bergsten, C. Fred
 1974 The threat is real. *Foreign Policy* 14:84–90.
Bertram, I. Geoffrey
 1974 Development problems in an export economy: A study of domestic capitalists, foreign firms and government in Peru, 1919–1930. Unpublished Ph.D. thesis, Faculty of Social Sciences, Oxford University.
Blanco, José María
 1835 *Este diario lo trabajo el cura de Marcabal en el Obispado de Trujillo del Peru y provincia de Huamachuco.* (Original in Archivo Nacional del Ecuador, Quito.)
Blau, Gerda
 1946 Wool in the world economy. *Journal of the Royal Statistical Society* 109(3):179–235.

Bonilla, Frank, and Robert Girling (Eds.)
1973 *Structures of dependency.* Stanford: n. pub.
Bourricaud, François
1967 *Pouvoir et société dans le Pérou contemporain.* Cahiers de la Fondation Nationale des Sciences Politiques No. 149. Paris: Armand Colin.
Bowden, Peter J.
1962 *The wool trade in Tudor and Stuart England.* London: Macmillan.
Bowman, Isiah
1916 *The Andes of southern Peru: Geographical reconnaissance along the seventy-third meridian.* New York: Henry Holt.
Brearley, Alan
1963 *The woollen industry.* Metuchen, N. J.: Textile Book Service.
Brownrigg, Leslie Ann
1974 Boundary-maintaining mechanisms of a regional elite (Ecuador). Paper presented at the XLI Congreso Internacional de Americanistas, México.
Brush, Stephen B.
1976a Introduction to the Symposium on Cultural Adaptations to Mountain Ecosystems. *Human Ecology* 4(2):125–133.
1976b Man's use of an Andean ecosystem. *Human Ecology* 4(2):147–166.
1977 Mountain, field and family: The economy and human ecology of an Andean valley. Philadelphia: Univ. of Pennsylvania Press.
Burchard, Roderick R.
1972 Village exogamy and strategies of inter-zonal exchange in central Andean Peru: A case study. Paper presented at the 71st annual meeting of the American Anthropological Association, Toronto.
Cardoso, Fernando Henrique, and Enzo Faletto
1969 *Dependencia y desarrollo en América Latina.* México: Siglo Veintiuno Editores.
Carus-Wilson, Eleanora
1952 The woollen industry. In *The Cambridge economic history of Europe,* edited by M. Postan and E. E. Rich. Vol. 2. Cambridge: Cambridge Univ. Press. Pp. 355–429.
Centeno Zela, Antonio
1953 La arriería en Antabamba: Una contribución a la etnología peruana. Tesis para optar al grado de Bachiller en Letras, Facultad de Letras, Universidad Nacional del Cuzco.
Centro de Colaboración
1951 *Monografía de la Provinica de Parinacochas.* 2 vols. Lima: Centro de Colaboración Pedagógica Provincial del Magisterio Primario de la Provincia de Parinacochas.
Chaplin, David
1967 *The Peruvian industrial labor force.* Princeton, N.J.: Princeton Univ. Press.
Chaplin, David (Ed.)
1976 *Peruvian nationalism: A corporatist revolution.* New Brunswick, N.J.: Transaction Press.
Chayanov, A. V.
1966 *The theory of peasant economy* [1925]. Homewood, Ill.: Richard D. Urwin. (For the American Economic Association.)
Chevalier, François
1970 Official *Indigenismo* in Peru in 1920: Origins, significance, and socioeconomic scope. In *Race and class in Latin America,* edited by Magnus Mörner. Institute of Latin American Studies. New York: Columbia Univ. Press.

Chilcote, Ronald H.
   1974   A critical synthesis of the dependency literature. *Latin American Perspectives*
          1(1):4–29.
Chuquibambilla
   1939   Informe del Trabajo Efectuado Durante el Año 1939. Granja Modelo Puno. Un-
          published manuscript.
Clapham, J. H.
   1907   *The woollen and worsted industries.* London: Methuen.
Cockcroft, James D., André Gunder Frank, and Dale L. Johnson
   1972   *Dependence and underdevelopment: Latin America's political economy.* Garden City,
          N.Y.: Doubleday.
Cole, G. D. H.
   1952   *Introduction to economic history, 1750–1950.* London: Macmillan.
Cole, John W., and Eric R. Wolf
   1974   *The hidden frontier: Ecology and ethnicity in an alpine valley.* New York: Academic
          Press.
Collier, George A.
   1975   *Fields of the Tzotzil: The ecological bases of tradition in highland Chiapas.* Austin:
          Univ. of Texas Press.
Concha Contreras, Juan de Dios
   1971   *Los pueblos pastores del Sur del Perú y las relaciones económicas con los agricultores.*
          Tesis presentada para optar al grado de Bachiller en Letras, Programa Académico
          de Antropología, Universidad Nacional de San Antonio Abad del Cuzco.
Concolorcorvo
   1959   *El Lazarillo de Ciegos Caminantes desde Buenos Aires hasta Lima con sus itinerarios,*
          según la mas punctual observación, con algunas noticias, útiles a los Nuevos Comer-
          ciantes que traten en Mulas, y otras Historias Sacado de las memorias que hizo Don
          Antonio Carrión de la Vandera, en este dilatado viaje, y comisión que tuvo por la Corte
          para el arreglo de Correos, y Estafetas, Situación y Ajuste de Postes, desde Montevideo
          [1773]. Por Don Calixto Bustamante Carlos Inca, alias Concolorcorvo, natural del
          Cuzco, que acompañó al referido en dicho Viaje y escribio sus Extractos. Vol.
          122. Madrid: Biblioteca de Autores Españoles.
Conrad, Joseph
   1963   *Heart of darkness.* Robert Kimbrough (Ed.). A Norton critical edition. New York:
          W. W. Norton.
Cotler, Julio
   1970   Crisis política y popularismo militar en el Perú. *Revista Mexicana de Sociologia*
          32(3):737–784. México.
   1972   Bases del corporativismo en el Perú. *Sociedad y Política* **1**(2):3–12. Lima.
Custred, Glynn
   1973   Puna zones of the south central andes. Paper presented at the 72nd annual
          meeting of the American Anthropological Association, New Orleans.
   1974   Llameros y comercio interzonal. In *Reciprocidad e intercambio en los Andes*
          peruanos, edited by Enrique Mayer and Giorgio Alberti. Perú-Problema 12.
          Instituto de Estudios Peruanos. Lima: IEP ediciones. Pp. 252–289.
Custred, Glynn, and Benjamin Orlove
   1974   Sectorial fallowing and crop rotation systems in the Peruvian Andes. Paper
          presented at the XLI Congreso Internacional de Americanistas, México.
Davies, Thomas M., Jr.
   1974   *Indian integration in Peru: A half century of experience, 1900–1948.* Lincoln: Univ.
          of Nebraska Press.

Davis, William G.
 1973 *Social relations in a Philippine market: Self-interest and subjectivity.* Berkeley: Univ.
   of California Press.
Dew, Edward
 1969 *Politics in the altiplano: The dynamics of change in rural Peru.* Latin American
   Monographs No. 15. Institute of Latin American Studies. Austin: Univ. of Texas
   Press.
Dorado, Marta
 1973 Moda super-sport en el Cuzco. *Claudia,* junio 1973, pp. 135–144. Buenos Aires.
Eisenstadt, Shmuel N.
 1964 Breakdowns of modernization. *Economic Development and Cultural Change*
   12(4):345–367.
 1973 *Tradition, change, and modernity.* New York: John Wiley.
FAO
 1971 Provisional report of the mission to Peru and Bolivia for the development of
   industries derived from the South American camel species. United Nations,
   Food Agriculture Organization, New York.
Fernández Baca, Saul
 1971 *La alpaca: Reproducción y crianza.* Centro de Investigación Instituto Veterinario
   de Investigaciones Tropicales y de Altura. Dirección de Investigación Universidad Nacional Mayor de San Marcos. Contrato Universidad Nacional Mayor de
   San Marcos-Zona Agraria XII (Puno) del Ministerio de Agricultura. Boletín de
   Investigación No. 7. Lima.
Fernández, Raul A., and José F. Ocampo
 1974 The Latin American revolution. *Latin American Perspectives* **1**(1):30–61.
Fitzgerald, E. V. K.
 1977 Peru: The political economy of an intermediate regime. *Journal of Latin American
   Studies* **8**(1):53–71.
Flores, Jorge Aníbal
 1968 *Los pastores de Paratía: Una introducción a su estudio.* Antropología Social, 10.
   México: Instituto Interamerican Indigenista.
 1975 Sociedad y cultura en la puna alta de Los Andes. *América Indígena* **35**(2):297–319.
 1977 Pastores de alpacas [1975]. *Allpanchis Phuturinqa* **8**:5–23. Cuzco.
Flores Galindo, Alberto
 1976 *Arequipa y el sur peruano.* Programa académico de ciencias sociales. Lima: Pon-
   tificia Universidad Católica.
Fonseca Martel, César
 1976 Diferenciación campesina en los Andes peruanos. *Discusión Antropológica*
   2(2):1–20. Lima.
Forman, Shephard
 1970 *The raft fishermen: Tradition and change in the Brazilian peasant economy.*
   Bloomington: Univ. of Indiana Press.
Foster, Brian L.
 1974 Ethnicity and commerce. *American Ethnologist* **1**(3):437.
Frank, André Gunder
 1966 The development of underdevelopment. *Monthly Review* **17**(9):17–31.
 1967 *Capitalism and underdevelopment in Latin America: Historical studies of Chile and
   Brazil.* New York: Monthly Review Press.
Fuentes, Hildebrando
 1905 *El Cuzco y sus ruinas: Tahuantinsuyoc kapacllacta.* Lima: n. pub.

Fuenzalida, Fernando
  1970a La estructura de la comunidad de indígenas tradicionales. In Robert G. Keith *et al*.
       La hacienda, la comunidad y el campesino en el Perú. Perú-Problema 3. Instituto de
       Estudios Peruanos. Lima: Moncloa-Campodónico.
  1970b Poder, raza y etnía en el Perú comtemporáneo. In Fernando Fuenzalida *et al*. *El
       indio y el poder en el Perú*. Perú-Problema 4. Instituto de Estudios Peruanos. Lima:
       Moncloa-Campodónico.
Gade, Daniel
  1971 Grist milling with the horizontal waterwheel in the central Andes. *Technology and
       Culture* **12**(1):44–51.
  1975 *Plants, man and the land in the Vilcanota Valley of Peru*. The Hague: Junk.
Galloway, D. B.
  1961 Australian and New Zealand experience in problems of reproductive wastage in
       sheep. Fourth FAO-Swedish International Postgraduate Training Centre on Ani-
       mal Reproduction. Stockholm: Royal Veterinary College.
García Márquez, Gabriel
  1975 *El otoño del patriarca*. Barcelona: Esplugas de Llobregat.
Geertz, Clifford
  1962 Studies in peasant life: Community and society. In *Biennial review of anthropology
       1961*, edited by Bernard J. Siegel. Pp. 1–41. Palo Alto, Cal.: Annual Reviews, Inc.
  1963a The integrative revolution: Primordial sentiments and civil politics in the new
       states. In *Old societies and new states: The quest for modernity in Asia and Africa*,
       edited by Clifford Geertz. New York: Free Press.
  1963b *Agricultural involution: Processes of ecological change in Indonesia*. Berkeley: Univ. of
       California Press.
González Casanova, Pablo
  1965 *La democracia en México*. México: Era.
Grigg, David
  1965 The logic of regional systems. *Annals of the Association of American Geographers*
       55(3):465–491.
Hamilton, Nora Louise
  1975 Mexico: The limits of state autonomy. *Latin American Perspectives* **2**(2):81–108.
Handelman, Howard
  1975 *Struggle in the Andes: Peasant political mobilization in Peru*. Latin American Mono-
       graphs No. 25. Austin; Univ. of Texas Press.
Heaton, Herbert
  1965 *The Yorkshire woollen and worsted industries from the earliest times to the industrial
       revolution*. 2nd ed. Oxford: Clarendon Press.
Hein, Wolfgang, and Konrad Stenzel
  1973 The capitalist state and underdevelopment in Latin America—The case of Ven-
       ezuela. *Kapitalistate* **2**:31–48.
Hill, Christopher
  1967 *The Pelican economic history of Britain*. Vol. 2. *Reformation to Industrial Revolution*.
       London: Weidenfeld & Nicolson.
Hill, S. S.
  1860 *Travels in Peru and Mexico*. 2 Vols. London: Longman, Green.
Hobsbawn, Eric J.
  1959 *Primitive rebels: Studies in archaic forms of social movements in the nineteenth and
       twentieth centuries*. Manchester: Univ. of Manchester Press.
  1968 *The Pelican economic history of Britain*. Vol. 3. *Industry and empire*. London:
       Weidenfeld & Nicolson.

Hultz, Frederic S.
   1940   *Corriedale sheep: The dual-purpose breed*. Laramie, Wyo.: American Corriedale Association.
Hultz, Frederick S., and John A. Hill
   1931   *Range sheep and wool in the seventeen western states*. New York: John Wiley.
Hunt, Shane J.
   1973   Price and quantum estimates of Peruvian exports, 1830–1962. Discussion Paper No. 33. Research Program in Economic Development, Woodrow Wilson School, Princeton, N. J.
IBEAS
   1968   *Sicuani: Un estudio socio-religioso*. La Paz: Instituto Boliviano de Estudio y Acción Social.
INCOLANA EPS
   1976   *Boletín Informativo del Sistema de Industrialización y Comercialización de Lana de Ovino, "INCOLANA" EPS en formación*. Lima.
Kahl, Joseph A.
   1976   *Modernization, exploitation and dependency in Latin America*. New Brunswick, N. J.: Transaction Press.
Kapsoli, Wilfredo
   1972   *Los movimientos campesinos en Cerro de Pasco 1880–1963*. Lima: n. pub.
Kaufman, Robert R.
   1974   The patron–client concept and macro-politics: Prospects and problems. *Comparative Studies in Society and History* **16**(3):284–309.
Kershaw, S.
   1953   *Wool from the raw material to the finished product*. 7th ed. London: Sir Isaac Pitman & Sons.
Klarén, Peter
   1970   *La formación de las haciendas azucareras y los orígenes del APRA*. Perú-Problema 5. Instituto de Estudios Peruanos. Lima: Moncloa-Compodónico.
Koford, Carl B.
   1957   The vicuña and the puna. *Ecological Monographs* **27**(1):153–219.
Krasner, Stephen D.
   1974   Oil is the exception. *Foreign Policy* **14**:68–84.
Kula, Witold
   1970   *Théorie économique du système féodal: Pour un modèle de l'économie polonaise 16ᵉ–18ᵉ siècles*. Ecole Pratique des Hautes Etudes. VIᵉ section: Sciences Economiques. Centre de Recherches Historiques. Civilisations et Sociétés 15. Paris and the Hague: Mouton.
Kuznets, Simon
   1971   *Economic growth of nations, total output and production structure*. Cambridge, Mass.: Harvard Univ. Press, Belknap Press.
Landes, David S.
   1965   Technological change and development in Western Europe 1750–1914. In *The Cambridge economic history of Europe*, edited by H. J. Habakkuk. Vol. 6. Cambridge: Cambridge Univ. Press. Pp. 274–603.
Lanning, Edward P.
   1967   *Peru before the Incas*. Englewood Cliffs, N. J.: Prentice-Hall.
Leeds, Anthony
   1964a   Brazilian careers and social structure: An evolutionary model and case study. *American Anthropologist* **66**(6):1321–1347.

1964b Brazil and the myth of Francisco Julião. In *Politics of change in Latin America*, edited by Joseph Maier and Richard W. Wetherhead. New York: Praeger.

1965   Reindeer herding and Chukchi social institutions. In *Man, culture, and animals: The role of animals in human ecological adjustments*, edited by Anthony Leeds and Andrew P. Vayda. Based on a symposium presented at the Denver meeting of the American Association for the Advancement of Science. Publication No. 78. Washington, D. C.: American Association for the Advancement of Science.

1969   The significant variables determining the character of squatter settlements. *América Latina* **12**(3):44–86. Rio de Janeiro.

Lerner, Daniel

1958   *The passing of traditional society: Modernizing the Middle East.* Glencoe, Ill.: Free Press.

Levi-Strauss, Claude

1950   The use of wild plants in tropical South America. In *Handbook of South American Indians*, edited by Julian H. Steward. Vol. 6. Smithsonian Institution, Bureau of American Ethnology, Bulletin 143. Washington: United States Government Printing Office. Pp. 465–486.

Levy, Marion J., Jr.

1972   *Modernization: Latecomers and survivors.* New York: Basic Books.

Lewin, Boleslao

1967   *La rebelión de Túpac Amaru y los orígenes de la independencia de Hispanoamérica* [1943]. Tercera edición ampliada. Buenos Aires: Sociedad Editoria Latino Americana.

Lewis, I. M.

1961   *A pastoral democracy.* London: Oxford Univ. Press.

Lipson, E.

1953   *A short history of wool and its manufacture (mainly in England).* Cambridge, Mass.: Harvard Univ. Press.

Love, Thomas F.

1977   Ecological niche theory in sociocultural anthropology: A conceptual framework and an application. *American Ethnologist* **4**(1):27–41.

Lowenthal, Abraham F. (Ed.)

1975   *The Peruvian experiment: Continuity and change under military rule.* Princeton, N. J.: Princeton Univ. Press.

Macera, Pablo

1966   *Instrucciones para el manejo de las haciendas jesuitas del Perú (ss. XVII–XVIII).* Departmento de Historia, Facultad de Letras y Ciencias Humanas, Universidad Nacional Mayor de San Marcos. Lima: Imprenta de la Universidad Nacional Mayor de San Marcos.

1968   *Mapas coloniales de haciendas cuzqueñas.* Seminario de Historia Rural Andina, Universidad Nacional Mayor de San Marcos. Lima: n. pub.

Mantoux, Paul

1965   *The Industrial Revolution in the eighteenth century: An outline of the beginnings of the modern factory system in England* [1927]. New York: Harper & Row.

Marshall, John Urquhart

1969   *The location of service towns: An approach to the analysis of central place systems.* Univ. of Toronto Department of Geography Research Publications No. 3. Toronto: Univ. of Toronto Press.

Martínez-Alier, Juan

1973   *Los huacchilleros del Perú: Dos estudios de formaciones sociales agrarias.* Paris: Ediciones Ruedo Ibérico.

Mayer, Enrique
    1971 Un carnero por un saco de papas: Aspectos del trueque en la zona Chaupiwaranga, Pasco. *Revista del Museo Nacional del Perú* **37**:184–196.
    1974 Las reglas del juego en la reciprocidad andina. In *Reciprocidad e intercambio en los Andes peruanos*, edited by Giorgio Alberti and Enrique Mayer. Perú-Problema 12. Lima: Instituto de Estudios Peruanos. Pp. 37–65.

Medina Díaz, Lucio
    1965 *Historia del periodismo canchino*. Lima: La Confianza.

Meyer, J. R.
    1963 Regional economics: A survey. *American Economics Review* **53**(1):19–54.

Mörner, Magnus
    In press Continuidad y cambio en una provincia del Cuzco: Calca y Lares desde los años 1680 hasta los 1790. *Historia y Cultura*. Lima.

Moro, Manuel, and Carlos Guerrero
    1971 *La alpaca*. Enfermedades infecciosas y parasitarias. Centro de Investigaciones Instituto Veterinario de Investigaciones Tropicales y de Altura. Dirección de Investigaciones Universidad Nacional Mayor de San Marcos. Contrato Universidad Nacional Mayor de San Marcos-Zona Agraria XII (Puno). Boletín de Divulgación No. 8. Lima.

Munz, H.
    1950 *The Australian wool industry*. Sydney: Angus and Robertson.

Murra, John V.
    1964 Una apreciación etnológica de la visita. In *Visita hecha a la provincia de Chucuito por Garci Diez de San Miguel en el ano 1567*. Documentos Regionales para la Etnología y Etnohistoria Andinas, Vol. 1. Lima: Ediciones de la Casa de la Cultura del Perú. Pp. 419–442.
    1965 Herds and herders in the Inca state. In *Man, culture and animals: The role of animals in human ecological adjustments*, edited by Anthony Leeds and Andrew P. Vayda. Based on a symposium presented at the Denver meeting of the American Association for the Advancement of Science. Publication No. 78. Washington, D. C.: American Association for the Advancement of Science.
    1967 La visita de los Chupachu como fuente etnológica. In *Visita de la Provincia de León de Huánuco en 1562*, edited by John V. Murra. Huánuco, Perú: Universidad Nacional Hermilio Valdizán, Facultad de Letras y Educacion. Pp. 383–417.
    1968 An Aymara kingdom in 1567. *Ethnohistory* **15**:115–151.
    1970 Current research and prospects in Andean ethnohistory. *Latin American Research Review* **5**(1):3–36.
    1972 El "control vertical" de un máximo de pisos ecológicos en la economía de las sociedades andinas. In *Visita de la Provincia de León de Huánuco en 1562*, edited by John V. Murra, Vol. 2. Huánuco, Perú: Universidad Nacional Hermilio Valdizán, Facultad de Letras y Ciencias. Pp. 427–468.

Nash, Manning
    1966 *Primitive and peasant economic systems*. San Francisco: Chandler Publishing.

Neira, Hugo
    1964 *Cuzco: tierra y muerte. Reportaje al sur*. Lima: Problemas de Hoy.

Nieto, Luis
    1943 *Charango (Romancero Cholo)*. Cuzco: Editorial H. G. Rozas Sucs.

Novoa, C.
    1970 Reproduction in Camelidae. *Journal of Reproduction and Fertility* **22**(1):3–20.

Odum, Eugene P.
    1959 *Fundamentals of ecology*. Philadelphia: Saunders.

Olsen, Stephen M.
  1976   Regional social systems: Linking quantitative analysis and field work. In *Regional analysis*, edited by Carol A. Smith. Vol. 2. *Social systems*. New York: Academic Press. Pp. 21–61.
ONERN
  1969   *Inventario de estudios del suelo del Perú*. Segunda aproximación. Departamento de Suelos. Lima: Oficina Nacional de Evaluación de Recursos Naturales.
Orlove, Benjamin
  1973   Abigeato: La organización social de una actividad ilegal. *Allpanchis Phuturinqa* 5:65–81.
  1974a Urban and rural artisans in southern Peru. *International Journal of Comparative Sociology* 15(3–4):193–211.
  1974b Reciprocidad, desigualdad y dominación. In *Reciprocidad e intercambio en los Andes peruanos*, edited by Enrique Mayer and Giorgio Alberti. Perú-Problema 12. Instituto de Estudios Peruanos. Lima: IEP ediciones. Pp. 290–321.
  1974c Molloccahua 1931: A peasant uprising in southern Peru. Paper presented at the XLI Congreso Internacional de Americanistas, Mexico.
  1974d Land and power: Aspects of elite–peasant relations in Surimana and Quehue. Paper presented at the 73rd annual meeting of the American Anthropological Association, Mexico.
  1975   Surimana: Decaimiento de una zona, decadencia de un pueblo. *Antropología Andina* 1–2:75–110.
  1976   *Tomar la bandera*: Politics and punch in southern Peru. Paper presented at the XLII Congrès International des Américanistes, Paris. In press.
  1977a Against a definition of peasantries: Agrarian production in Andean Peru. In *Studies in Peasant Livelihood*, edited by Rhoda Halperin and James Dow. New York: St. Martin's Press. Pp. 22–35.
  1977b Inequality among peasants: The forms and uses of reciprocal exchange in Andean Peru. In *Studies in Peasant Livelihood*, edited by Rhoda Halperin and James Dow. New York: St. Martin's Press. Pp. 201–214.
  1977c Integration through production: The use of zonation in Espinar. *American Ethnologist* 4(1): 84–101.
  1977d The decline of local elites: Canchis in southern Peru. In *The anthropology of power: Ethnographic studies from Asia, Oceania and the New World*, edited by Raymond D. Fogelson and Richard N. Adams. New York: Academic Press. Pp. 337–348.
  1977e The tragedy of the commons revisited: Land use and environmental quality in high-altitude Andean grasslands. *Proceedings of the International Hill Lands Symposium*. Morgantown, W. Va.: West Virginia Univ. Press. In press.
  1977f *Culturalecology: A critical essay and a bibliography*. Institute of Ecology Publication No. 14. Davis, Calif.: Institute of Ecology.
Orlove, Benjamin, and Glynn Custred
  1974   The hacienda and the community reconsidered: The Andean case. Paper presented at the 73rd annual meeting of the American Anthropological Association, Mexico.
Ortiz, Sutti
  1967   Colombian rural market organisation: An exploratory model. *Man (n.s.)* 2(3):393–414.
  1973   *Uncertainties in peasant farming: A Colombian case*. London School of Economics Monographs on Social Anthropology No. 46. New York: Humanities Press.

Parsons, Talcott
  1966 *Societies: Evolutionary and comparative perspectives.* Englewood Cliffs, N. J.: Prentice-Hall.
Pastner, Stephen
  1971 Camels, sheep and nomad social organisation: A comment on Rubel's model. *Man (n.s.)* 6(2):285–288.
Payne, Ruth
  1968 *La misión educativa de la iglesia en Sicuani.* La Paz: Instituto Boliviano de Estudio y Acción Social.
Peattie, Roderick
  1936 *Mountain geography. A critique and field study.* Cambridge, Mass.: Harvard Univ. Press.
PEIFEDER
  1971 *Estudio socio-económico cultural y pedagógico de las provincias de Canas y Canchis (Cuzco).* Sicuani: Proyecto Especial Integrado Sobre la Función de la Educación en el Desarrollo Rural.
Peruvian Corporation, Ltd.
  1956/57–1970/71
          Annual reports of the traffic department. Southern Peruvian Railway, Arequipa.
Piel, Jean
  1967 A propos d'un soulèvement rural péruvien au début du vingtième siècle: Tocroyoc (1921). *Revue d'Histoire Moderne et Contemporaine* 14:375–405.

  1970 The place of the peasantry in the national life of Peru in the nineteenth century. *Past and Present* 46:108–133.
Poggie, John J., Jr., and Robert W. Lynch (Eds.)
  1974 *Rethinking modernization: Anthropological perspectives.* Westport, Conn.: Grenwood Press.
Ponting, K. G.
  1961 *The wool trade: Past and present.* Manchester: Columbine Press.
Quijano, Aníbal
  1971 *Nationalism and capitalism in Peru: A study in neo-imperialism.* New York: Monthly Review Press.

  1972 Imperialismo y capitalismo del estado. *Sociedad y Política* 1(1):5–18. Lima.
Quino
  1972 *Mafalda 1.* Buenos Aires: Ediciones de la Flor.
Rafez, E. S. E., E. B. Cairne, C. V. Hulet, and J. P. Scott
  1969 The behaviour of sheep and goats. In *The behaviour of domesticated animals*, edited by E. S. E. Rafez. 2nd ed. London: Baillière, Tindell and Cassell.
Reiter, Rayna
  1972 Modernization in the south of France: The village and beyond. *Anthropological Quarterly* 45(1):35–53.
Rhoades, Robert E. and Stephen I. Thompson
  1975 Adaptive strategies in alpine environments: Beyond ecological particularism. *American Ethnologist* 2(3):535–551.
Richerson, Peter J.
  1977 Ecology and human ecology: A comparison of theories in the biological and social sciences. *American Ethnologist* 4(1):1–26.
Ross, F. E.
  1912 Peruvian wools. *Peru To-day* 3(10):25–31. Lima.

Rostow, Walter
   1961 *The stages of economic growth: A non-communist manifesto.* Cambridge: Cambridge
         Univ. Press.
Rowe, John Howland
   1946 Inca culture at the time of the Spanish conquest. In *Handbook of South American
         Indians,* edited by Julian H. Steward. Vol. 2. Smithsonian Institution, Bureau of
         American Ethnology, Bulletin 143. Washington: United States Government Print-
         ing Office. Pp. 183–330.
   1957 The Incas under Spanish colonial institutions. *Hispanic American Historical Review*
         37(2):155–199.
Rubel, P. G.
   1969 Herd composition and social structure: On building models of nomadic pastoral
         societies. *Man (n.s.)* **4**(2):268–273.
Runciman, W. G.
   1972 *A critique of Max Weber's philosophy of social science.* Cambridge: Cambridge Univ.
         Press.
Sahlins, Marshall
   1972 *Stone Age economics.* Chicago: Aldine-Atherton.
Schaedel, Richard P.
   1967 *La demografía y los recursos humanos del Sur del Perú.* Antropología Social, 8.
         México: Instituto Interamericano Indigenista.
Schultze, Charles L.
   1964 *National income analysis.* Foundations of Modern Economics Series. Englewood
         Cliffs, N. J.: Prentice-Hall.
Scott, James C.
   1972 The erosion of patron–client bonds and social change in rural Southeast Asia.
         Journal of Asian Studies **32**(1):5–37.
Shiner, L. E.
   1975 Tradition and modernity: An ideal type gone astray. *Comparative Studies in Society
         and History* **17**(2):245–252.
Sigsworth, Eric N.
   1958 *Black Dyke mills, with introductory chapters on the development of the worsted
         industry in the nineteenth century.* Liverpool: Liverpool Univ. Press.
Silva Santisteban, Fernando
   1964 *Los obrajes en el virreinato del Perú.* Lima: Publicaciones del Museo Nacional de
         Historia.
Skinner, G. William
   1964 Marketing and social structure in rural China. Part I. *Journal of Asian Studies*
         24:3–43.
   1965 Marketing and social structure in rural China. Part II. *Journal of Asian Studies*
         24:195–228.
Smith, Carol A. (Ed.)
   1976a *Regional analysis.* Vol. 1. *Economic systems.* New York: Academic Press.
   1976b *Regional analysis.* Vol. 2. *Social systems.* New York: Academic Press.
Smith, Carol A.
   1976c Regional economic systems: Linking geographical models and socioeconomic
         problems. In *Regional analysis,* edited by Carol A. Smith. Vol. 1. *Economic systems.*
         New York: Academic Press. Pp. 3–63.
   1976d Analyzing regional social systems. In *Regional analysis,* edited by Carol A. Smith.
         Vol. 2. *Social systems.* New York: Academic Press. Pp. 3–20.

Smith, Henry B., and Harold Haile
   1929   *The sheep and wool industry of Australia and New Zealand, a practical handbook for sheep-farmers and wool-classifiers, with chapters on wool-buying and selling sheepskins and kindred products.* Melbourne and Auckland: Whitcombe and Tombs.
Sociedad Nacional de Industrias
   1969   Informe de Comité Textil. Mimeo, unpaginated. Lima.
Sotillo Humire, Héctor
   1962   *Los auquénidos y su importancia en la economía del sur.* Tesis de Bachillerato, Facultad de Ciencias Económicas y Comerciales, Universidad Nacional de San Agustín de Arequipa.
South African Wool Board
   1970   *An illustrated world history of the sheep and wool industry.* Pretoria: South African Wool Board.
Stavenhagen, Rodolfo
   1969   *Las clases sociales en las sociedades agrarias.* México: Siglo Veintiuno Editores.
Steward, Julian H.
   1951   Levels of sociocultural integration: An operational concept. *Southwestern Journal of Anthropology* **7**(3):374–390.
   1955   *Theory of culture change.* Urbana: Univ. of Illinois Press.
Steward, Julian H. (Ed.)
   1956   *The peoples of Puerto Rico.* Urbana: Univ. of Illinois Press.
Superintendencia General de Aduanas
   1904   *Comercio especial del Perú: Año 1902.* Sección de Estadística General de Aduanas, Callao-Perú. Leyenda de la nomenclatura commercial de la estadística. Lima: Imprenta del Estado.
Sweet, Louise
   1965   Camel raiding of North Arabian Bedouin: A mechanism of ecological adaptation. *American Anthropologist* **67**(5):1132–1150.
Symington, R. B., and J. Oliver
   1966   Observations of the reproductive activity of tropical sheep in relation to the photoperiod. *Journal of Agricultural Sciences* **67**(1):7–12.
Thompson, E. P.
   1963   *The making of the English working class.* New York: Random House.
Tipps, Dean C.
   1973   Modernization theory and the comparative study of societies: A critical perspective. *Comparative Studies in Society and History* **15**(2):199–226.
Tristán, Flora
   1971   *Peregrinaciones de una paria* [1838]. Collección Tiempo. Lima: Moncloa-Campodónico.
Troll, Carl
   1958   *Las culturas superiores andinas y el medio geográfico* [1931]. Publicaciones del Instituto de Geografía, Facultad de Letras, Universidad Nacional Mayor de San Marcos. Serie I. Monografías y Ensayos Geográficos No. 1. Lima: Editorial San Marcos.
Valencia, Abraham
   1970   Cultura i platería en San Pablo. Tesis de Doctorado, Programa Académico de Antropología. Universidad Nacional San Antonio Abad del Cuzco.
van den Berghe, Pierre L., and George P. Primov
   1977   *Inequality in the Peruvian Andes: Class and ethnicity in Cuzco.* Columbia, Mo.: Univ. of Missouri Press.

Vargas Llosa, Mario
    1973   *Pantaleón y las visitadoras*. Barcelona: Editorial Seix Barral.
Verástegui Serpa, Samuel
    1972   *Algunos aspectos artesanales de la provincia Canchis, Cuzco*. Estudio No. 3. Lima:
           Ministerio de Trabajo.
Wallerstein, Immanuel
    1974   *The modern world-system: Capitalist agriculture and the origins of the European
           world-economy in the sixteenth century*. New York: Academic Press.
Webb, Richard, and Adolfo Figueroa
    1975   *Distribución del ingreso en el Perú*. Perú-Problema 14. Lima: IEP ediciones.
Weingrod, Alex, and Emma Morin
    1971   Post peasants: The character of contemporary Sardinian society. *Comparative
           Studies in Society and History* **13**(3):301–324.
Williams, Tennessee
    1947   *A streetcar named desire*. New York: New Directions.
Whyte, William Foote
    1975   Conflict and cooperation in Andean communities. *American Ethnologist* **2**(2):373–
           392.
Whyte, William Foote, and Giorgio Alberti
    1976   *Power, politics and progress: Social change in rural Peru*. New York: Elsevier Scien-
           tific Publishing.
Wolf, Eric R.
    1956   Aspects of group relations in a complex society: Mexico. *American Anthropologist*
           58(6):1065–1078.
    1966   Kinship, friendship and patron–client relations in complex society. In *Social
           anthropology of complex society*, edited by Michael Banton. Association of Social
           Anthropologists Monograph No. 4. New York: Prager.
    1967   Levels of communal relations. In *Handbook of Middle American Indians*, edited by
           Robert Wauchope. Vol. 6, edited by Manning Nash. New Orleans: Tulane
           Univ. Press. Pp. 299–316.
    1969   *Peasant wars of the twentieth century*. New York: Harper & Row.
    1972   *The human condition in Latin America*. New York: Oxford Univ. Press.
Yambert, Karl A.
    1974   Alien traders: The Chinese of Southeast Asia and the Asians of East Africa.
           Unpublished manuscript.
    1976   Cultivator politics and export agriculture in Peru. Unpublished manuscript.
Yépes del Castillo, Ernesto
    1972   *Perú 1820-1920: Un siglo de desarrollo capitalista*. Instituto de Estudios Peruanos.
           Lima: Campodónico Ediciones.

Glossary

Aguardiente	Distilled cane alcohol
Altiplano	High, flat interior-drainage basin around Lake Titicaca
Añu	Andean tuber, *Tropaeolum tuberosum*
Astana	Temporary residence of transhumant herders
Ayni	A form of reciprocal labor exchange, in which one day's labor is traded for a day's labor in a similar form of activity
Bayeta	Rough cloth of homespun wool made by local weavers
Bofedal	An area where water seeps from the ground and permits pasture to grow throughout the year
Cabaña	Permanent residence of transhumant herders
Cañihua	Andean grain, *Chenopodium pallidicaule*
Caserío	Central complex of buildings on an *hacienda*
Charki	Freeze-dried meat (cognate with English 'jerky')
Chicha	Home-brewed beer, usually made of maize or barley
Chuño	Freeze-dried potatoes
Comunero	An adult member of a *comunidad*
Comunidad	A community or a set of peasant households possessing rights to specific territories, with official recognition of these rights in certain cases
Guardia Civil	The national police force
Habas	Broad beans, *Vicia faba*
Hacendado	The owner of an *hacienda*
Hacienda	A privately owned estate
Huarizo	A llama–alpaca hybrid
Ichu	Native Andean bunch grass

Kemp	The stiff hairy fibers of the outer coat of wool-bearing animals, often found mixed with wool
Laymi	Collective system of crop rotation and fallowing found in lower portions of the *puna*
Maestro	Full-time urban artisan
Mink'a	A form of reciprocal labor exchange, in which one day's labor is traded for a large meal and *aguardiente* or for other goods
Oca	Andean tuber, *Oxalis crenata*
Olluco	Andean tuber, *Ullucus tuberosa*
Oqho	See *Bofedal*
Partido	Spanish colonial administrative unit, roughly corresponding to present-day province
Peleteros	Furriers, especially those who sew items from skins of infant alpacas
Peon	A permanent resident worker on an *hacienda*
Pulled wool	Wool shorn from hides rather than from living animals
Puna	Rolling Andean grasslands, usually at elevations between 3600 and 5200 meters above sea level
Quinua	Andean grain, *Chenopodium quinoa*
Quebradas	Intermontane valleys, generally below 3600 meters above sea level
Rancho	Small nucleated settlements, generally of three to seven agnatically related households
Round lots	Shipments of alpaca wool consisting of 12% white wool, 18% light fawn, and 70% darker shades
Saca	The annual slaughter of animals at the beginning of the dry season
Tablada	Livestock market
Tarwi	Andean legume, *Lupinus mutabilis*
Tops	Wool that has been scoured and combed but not yet spun into yarn
Waqcho	The livestock which belongs to a *peon* and is grazed on the *hacienda* in which he lives
Yapa	Overweight; additional goods given to a customer with a purchase

Name Index

258

Subject Index

Tribute, 159, 161
Triciclos, 151
Trucks, 143
Tungasuca, 69, 75, 118, 147, 152, 220
Túpac Amaru (district), *see* Tungasuca

U
Unions, 101, 184, *see also* Strikes
United States, 211
  English wool trade, 24
  Peruvian wools, 28, 62
  wool purchases, 26
Universidad Nacional Mayor de San Marcos,
  45
Urban sectors, 159, 188–189, 197–201
Urbanization, 71
Urinsaya, 76
Urubamba, 34, 76

V
Velille (district), 69, 76, 176n
Velille, Río, 68, 75
Venta a firma, 62
Verticality, 66–70, 122, *see also* Zonation
Vicuña, 205, 207–208
Vilcanota campaign, 77, 174–176, 198, 202
Vilcanota, Río, 65, 67, 68, 71, 75, 114, 116,
  117, 122, 126, 143
Virginiyoc, 69, 76, 220
Volcanic activity, 81

W
Wages, 129, 133
Waqcho, 43, 49, 89, 120, 192
  reductions of, 45
War of the Pacific, 159
Wheat, 66, 126, 139
Wholesale traders, 75, 140, 146
  education and, 172–173
Women, 108, 142, 152, 174
Wool, *see also* Alpaca(s), wool, Llama(s), wool
  artisans, 38–39
  artisans and, 108–110
  auctions, 26, 36
    alpaca, 28
  brokers, 26
  classification, 47
  color, 49, 58–59, 98
  export firms, 28, 36
    activities of, 47
    Arequipa, 49

  history of, 46
  international ties, 46
exports
  artisans, and, 133
  Peruvian, 211–215
  Sicuani region, and, 165, 166–167,
    190–199
grades, 97–98
manufacturing, *see also* Textile factories
  Flemish, 22
  Italian, 22
  medieval, 21
marketing, 45–49, 51–62, *see also* English
    wool trade, Peruvian wool economy,
    World wool trade
  activity, 52–54
  constraints, 52
  credit relations in, 53
  decisions in, 124
  personal ties, in, 54–57
  producers, and, 51–52
  sale by consignment, 61
  transportation, 48
prices, 47, 51–62, 123
  bargaining over, 56
  fluctuations, 98, 108
  information about, 51
  local variation in, 53
  rises in, 191
  support of, 98
production,
  bottlenecks in, 93–95
  economic limitations of, 93
  elasticity of, 47
  political limitations of, 93
properties of, 205–210
retention of stocks, 59
sales
  local marketing, and, 137
  Sicuani region, 229–234
trade,
  credit, 175
  English, 22–29
  traders, 52–57
    competition among, 56
    goals, 52
  transportation of, 150–151
World-system, 1
World wool trade, 21–29
  European wools in, 26
  futures market, 27